ISLANDS OF THE MIND

ISLANDS OF THE MIND

How the Human Imagination Created the Atlantic World

JOHN GILLIS

palgrave
macmillan

ISLANDS OF THE MIND
Copyright © John Gillis, 2004.
All rights reserved.

First published in hardcover in 2004 by PALGRAVE MACMILLAN® in the United States–a division of St. Martin's Press LLC, 175 Fifth Avenue, New York, NY 10010.

Where this book is distributed in the UK, Europe and the rest of the world, this is by Palgrave Macmillan, a division of Macmillan Publishers Limited, registered in England, company number 785998, of Houndmills, Basingstoke, Hampshire RG21 6XS.

Palgrave Macmillan is the global academic imprint of the above companies and has companies and representatives throughout the world.

Palgrave® and Macmillan® are registered trademarks in the United States, the United Kingdom, Europe and other countries.

ISBN: 978-0-230-62086-5 paperback

Library of Congress Cataloging-in-Publication Data is available from the Library of Congress.

A catalogue record of the book is available from the British Library.

Design by Letra Libre, Inc.

First PALGRAVE MACMILLAN paperback edition: January 2010
10 9 8 7 6 5 4 3 2 1
Printed in the United States of America.

Transferred to Digital Printing 2009

*To Great Gott Island
and Gotts Islanders*

CONTENTS

LIST OF ILLUSTRATIONS

Acknowledgments

I HAVE DEDICATED THIS BOOK TO GREAT GOTT ISLAND and those who treasure it. In writing it I have become intensely aware of how much the islands in my mind have been shaped by the thoughts and feelings of others. The person I have shared Gotts with longest is Christina Marsden Gillis, whose conversations and writings have affected me deeply, often in ways I am not even aware of. Our sons, Christopher and Benjamin, spent their childhoods on the island, and memories of those days are very powerful. Chris was married to Kathy Armstrong in an island ceremony and now we are seeing the island from an entirely fresh perspective through the eyes of our grandchildren, Peter and Astrid.

My desire to write about islands began years ago as I listened to the fascinating stories of Russell Gott, who until his death in 1991 was a living link to the island's first settlers. I have learned from Rita Kenway, the island's historian, and from Northwood Kenway, its chief conservationist. This book reflects an ongoing conversation with other Gotts Island summer residents—the Beamans, the Archibalds, the Holmes, the Silvers, the Weinbergs, the Taplins—as well as knowledge shared by descendants of the island's original population. I owe no less a debt to our many visitors, whose reactions to the island are a never-ending source of insight and pleasure. I am thinking foremost of the late Majorie Farrar and Lance Farrar, but there are also Rhys and Colleen Isaac, Joan and David Hollinger, Candace Falk and Lowell Finlay, Lige Gould and Nicky Gullace, Jim and Elizabeth MacLachlan, and Scott and Kay Armstrong, to name only a few.

I am no less indebted to those who have read all or substantial parts of this book, namely Phil Steinberg, Eric Leed, David Lowenthal, Jackson Lears, Eviatar and Yael Zerubavel, Herman Bennett, and Lance Farrar. I also owe much to those who have taken the time to discuss parts of it with me. I am thinking particularly of Matt Matsuda, Al Howard, Bernhard Klein, and Arno Mayer, but also wish to acknowledge Ian Watson, Susan Stewart, Rhys Isaac, Eric Clark, Peter Fritzsche, Grey Brechin, Steve Mintz, Randy Starn, Shelly Erington, Karen Lears, Joseph Dunn, David Burns, Victoria de Grazia, Bob Scally, Susanna Barrows, Gesa MacKenthun and Michael Zuckerman. Particular thanks go to

Vanessa Smith and Rod Edmond for their thoughtful editorship of the volume on islands I contributed to.

The book's research and writing have taken me on an odyssey with many ports of call including the Swedish Collegium for Advanced Study in the Social Sciences in the spring of 2001, which supported this project so generously and where I was fortunate to have the stimulating company of Gerd Carling, Arne Jarrick, Lars Johanson, Ella Johansson, Thomas Lindkvist, Jan Retso, and Bo Utas. I also want to recognize the gracious hospitality of the Collegium's three directors, Bjorn Wittrock, Barbro Klein, and Göran Therborn, and the friendship of Stefan Brink and Tore Frangsmyr. Owe Ronstrom was a wonderful host during my visit to the island of Gotland, and Jonas Frykman, Eric Clark, and Orvar Löfgren were no less generous during my time in Lund. I also wish to thank the members of the Tromso History Department for introducing me to the Norwegian islands. Last but not least, there are my Danish friends, Kirsten Drotner and Ning Connick-Smith.

No less important are the great libraries that have made its research such a pleasure: Firestone Library of Princeton University, Library of the University of California at Berkeley, and Carolina Redivica, the University Library at Uppsala. But I would be remiss if I did not mention the Southwest Harbor Library, a treasury of materials on Maine islands.

Also helpful to me were the various seminars and conferences where I have presented my work, including the "Seascapes, Littoral Cultures, and Trans-Oceanic Exchanges" meeting at the Library of Congress in February 2003. Organized by Renate Bridenthal and Jerry Bentley, this gave me the opportunity to benefit from the wisdom of Laurie Benton, Harry Liebersohn, Lige Gould, Alan Karras, Carla and William Philips, Marcus Rediker, Hans Konrad van Tilberg, Kären Wigen, and Michael Pearson. Closer to home, the seminar "Beginnings and Endings" at the Center for Critical Analysis of Contemporary Culture at Rutgers was a wonderfully stimulating forum. I owe much to Finas Dunaway, Mike Aronoff, Jennifer Milligan, Dan Rosenberg, Dorothy Ko, Carolyn Williams, Michael Warner, and Ruth Simpson, but perhaps most to my co-director, Eviatar Zerubavel. No less valuable was the salon organized by Michael Zuckerman at the University of Pennsylvania in October 2003.

Rutgers University's generous leave and research support programs have benefited this project enormously, but so too has the extraordinary collegiality that exists in its great history department. I thank my dear colleagues and good friends Bonnie Smith, Ginny Yans, Don Kelley, Rudy Bell, Dee Garrison, Paul Clemens, Ziva Galili, Ann Gordon, Jim Reed, Paul Israel, Norman Markowitz. Mention must also be made of the undergraduates who have participated in senior seminars on the island theme, including Brian Baum, Ezra Fischer, Cait Lange, and Robert Starkins.

Special mention must be made of meetings in Berkeley and at Rutgers in the spring of 2004. The first gathered together a remarkable group of geographers, naturalists, and anthropologists, including Rebecca Solnit, David Hooson, Edwin Bernbaum, Ian Boal, and Burton Benedict. The second cast an even wider net to include writers, artists, and environmentalists. I like to think that this gathering, which brought together Godfrey Baldacchino, Philip Conkling, Greg Dening, Christina Gillis, Eric Hopkins, Orvar Löfgren, Adam Nicolson, Karen Fog Olwig, Kenneth Olwig, Owe Ronstrom, and Matt Matsuda, moved island studies in a new direction. Both meetings owed their success to that man of many parts and many islands, David Lowenthal.

Many people have contributed materially to the production of this book. I want to thank Christopher DeRosa for his translations, Northwood Kenway and Annmarie Adams for their photos, and Eric Hopkins for his inspiring paintings. Joyce Seltzer helped me more than she can ever know at an early stage of the manuscript. Loretta Barrett's confidence in this book is deeply appreciated, as is the enthusiasm of my first editor at Palgrave, Michael Flamini, who acquired the book. I am grateful to Brendan O'Malley for seeing the book through to publication. Matthew Ashford's editorial assistance was both caring and efficient; and I owe an enormous debt to Norma McLemore's superb copyediting.

ISLANDS OF THE MIND

INTRODUCTION

ISLOMANIA

As Lawrence Durrell tells it, *ISLOMANIA* was a word coined during late night drinking sessions at the Villa Cleobolus on the isle of Rhodes just after the Second World War. It first appears in his *Reflections on a Marine Venus,* published in 1953, attributed to a fictional character named Gideon who used it to describe the mental state of the expatriots gathered there. "There are people, Gideon used to say, . . . who find islands somehow irresistible."[1] The word caught on and by the 1970s was used by some psychologists, though it never found way into mainstream medical literature. We should be thankful for that because the fascination with islands is no mere pathology confined to a few eccentric individuals. Islomania in its many different guises is a central feature of Western culture, a core idea that has been a driving force from ancient times to the present. "The island seems to have a tenacious hold on the human imagination," notes Yi-Fu Tuan, "but it is in the imagination of the Western world that the island has taken the strongest hold."[2] The island of the mind is not just an object of passive contemplation. It has been an incentive to action, an agent of history.

Why should this be so? Western culture did not originate on islands and was slow to populate its own offshore archipelagos. Its relationships with islands have been ambivalent, a combination of attraction and repulsion that suggests that there is a deeper, less obvious story to be explored. Islomania is most common among those who seldom, if ever, reside on islands. It is one of those things generated by absence rather than by presence. It is not real islands that are irresistible, but the idea of the island that is the true source of Western islomania.

Islands are among the features of the landscape that are indispensable to Western thought processes. Along with mountains, seas, and rivers, islands provide metaphors that allow us to give shape to a world that would otherwise be formless and meaningless. Western culture not only thinks about islands, but thinks *with* them. We see islands everywhere, whether it be desert oases or city ghettos, kitchen workspaces, highway dividers, groups of cells (the islets of

Langerhans), parts of the brain (Island of Reil), and patterns found in finger-prints. For centuries Europeans have been seeing islands in forests and on mountaintops. Now we imagine cyberspace archipelagically—we speak of "surf-ing" the Net and describe our web browsers as "navigators."[3]

It has been said that "islands are good to think on if man would express him-self neatly"; and Gretel Ehrlich has written: "To separate our thoughts into is-lands is a peculiar way we humans have of knowing something."[4] However, thinking with islands is not universal among humankind. Dividing the world into discrete things, islanding it as a means of understanding, is a peculiarly Western way of navigating a world that seems otherwise without shape and di-rection. Western thought has always preferred to assign meaning to neatly bounded, insulated things, regarding that which lies between as a void. We not only think of our individual selves as islands, but conceive of nations, commu-nities, and families in the same insular fashion, ignoring that which connects in favor of stressing that which separates and isolates. When boundaries become blurred we say we are "at sea," for the ocean is the favorite Western metaphor for chaos and confusion.[5]

If in the West there has been a tendency to think archipelagically, to focus on the parts and ignore the whole, other cultures pay much more attention to that which connects than that which divides. The islanders of Polynesia, for exam-ple, have traditionally thought of themselves as belonging to a "sea of islands" rather than to any one particular territory. It was Europeans and Americans who, when they entered the Pacific, introduced the concept of insularity, creat-ing boundaries and isolating one island from another, turning the sea into empty space.[6] A similar thing happened in the Caribbean when colonialism di-vided up its archipelagos, severing the islands from one another and from their prior history. The empires are now gone, but Western tourists still come look-ing for the kind of splendid isolation and aura of timelessness that the islanders themselves struggle to escape.

It is important to recognize that islands and continents are but names we give to different parts of one interconnected world. Islands and mainlands de-rive their meaning from their relationship to one another, a relationship that has changed dramatically over time. Ian Watson writes that "most typical is-lands have a *mainland* from which one can look across at the island and think of it as 'off' the mainland, subordinate to the mainland, an outpost of the mainland, and more remote and isolated than the mainland."[7] But this is only the most recent rendering of the relationship. There have been times when it was continents that were remote and isolated, the outposts of islands. Up to the end of the eighteenth century insularity was associated with mainlands, not is-lands. We must therefore heed Eric Wolf's admonition not to be too quick to turn "names into things," to naturalize or essentialize either islands or continents.[8] Above all, we must guard against the temptation to project contemporary understandings of geography onto a past in which a very different set of relationships was operative.

Geographers have already begun to question categorical differences ascribed to islands and continents, and it seems time for the rest of us also to explore the ways that islands and continents are cultural constructions, a product of history rather than nature.[9] In reality Atlantic islands and mainlands are not internally coherent, clearly bounded things, but interdependent parts of a larger world that includes coasts and hinterlands as well as all that lies between the shores of western Europe, west Africa, and the Americas. Only by taking the broadest possible geographical and historical frameworks can we avoid essentializing the distinction between islands and continents, thereby illuminating their dynamic historical interaction, revealing how mainlands have shaped islands and how islands have affected the course of continental history. To be sure, islands and islanders have rarely had the power or influence of continents, but they have had a large and generally underappreciated impact on the destiny of larger landmasses. As we shall see, much of mainland history has been shaped offshore. Islands have played a crucial role in the course of European, African, and American onshore political, social, cultural, and economic developments.

The legacy of Western islomania should not be underestimated. Islands may no longer be the material prizes they once were, but islands of the mind continue to be extraordinarily valuable symbolic resources, a treasure trove of images through which the West understands itself and its relations with the larger world. Like all master metaphors, the island is capable of representing a multitude of things. It can symbolize fragmentation and vulnerability but also wholeness and safety. Islands stand for loss but also recovery. They are figures for paradise and for hell. Islands are where we quarantine the pestilential and exile the subversive, but they are also where we welcome the immigrant and the asylum seeker. They can represent both separation and continuity, isolation and connection. Over time the island has been the West's favorite location for visions of both the past and future. It is also there that we most readily imagine origins and extinctions.

Islands evoke a greater range of emotions than any other land form. We project onto them our most intense desires, but they are also the locus of our greatest fears. We feel extraordinarily free there, but also trapped. Associated with pleasure, islands also harbor pain, for they are prisons as frequently as escapes or refuges. Isles remind us of our individuality while sustaining our sense of family and community; and though they are unparalleled as places of solitude, they are also among the few places we feel cosmically connected. Islands bring out our possessive instincts, but also our most generous impulses. They are objects of our will to mastery and reminders of our powerlessness. Long the objects of human curiosity, they remain shrouded in mystery. It is on islands that one feels closest to the secrets of both origins and the world that lies beyond life itself.

Islands are also the location of a set of social practices—pilgrimages, voyages of exploration, scientific expeditions, and summer sojourns—that, if not uniquely Western, have an important place in European and American culture. In Western cosmogony water stands for chaos, land for order. Islands are a third kind of place, partaking of both earth and water, something betwixt and between. As liminal places, islands are frequently the location of rites of passage. We do not just think with islands, we use them as thresholds to other worlds and new lives. Mainlanders have often found insularity liberating and transformative. Greek heroes turned to islands as a place to shed the mortal self; medieval Christians also expected to find transcendence there. During the Renaissance, insularity provided space to imagine new worlds and to rethink the social order. In the Age of Enlightenment, science turned islands into nature's laboratory, while anthropology found them ideal for fieldwork, its professional rite of initiation. Today, islands are the places we go as tourists and vacationers to find out who we really are. But as in the past, the island journey is always a sojourn undertaken with the ultimate intention of returning to the mainland somehow changed.

Islands deserve a much larger place in our understanding of the past than they have been given, and this book attempts to correct history's continental bias. Islands and islanders themselves have both benefited and suffered from mainlanders' islomania. Because they have occupied such a central place in the Western imagination, they have rarely been understood on their own terms. As master symbols and metaphors for powerful mainland cultures, their own realities and consciousnesses have been more obscured than illuminated. This book is devoted to correcting this imbalance. The author is a mainlander whose experience of islands has been largely confined to sojourns, especially to one small place off the coast of Maine. I cannot claim to represent the resident islander's point of view, but I have made every effort to take offshore realities into account. We cannot ignore the fact that mainlanders have been the predominant players in the making of the Atlantic world. However, they have not had it all their own way. The relationship of islands and continents, however asymmetrical, has been dialectical, producing a history full of fascinating twists and turns that have had fateful consequences for those living onshore as well.

CHAPTER 1

ANCIENT MARINERS OF THE MIND

"mythical geography" [is] the only geography man could never do without.

—Mircea Eliade, *Patterns in Contemporary Religion*

ANY HISTORY OF ISLOMANIA MUST BEGIN WITH THE *ODYSSEY.* We know little about Homer or the world he inhabited, but we can be reasonably sure he was not a man of the sea or of the islands. Had he been more familiar with the offshore world we might never have had this work of genius, for it was the unknown sea and its equally unknown islands that gave latitude to Homer's unsurpassed imagination. The Greeks of his time were just beginning to explore the western Mediterranean, and detailed knowledge of its coasts and islands was still scarce. We can be thankful for the ignorance that provided us with an epic hero and a mythical geography that still resonates throughout Western culture.

The Greeks were thinking *with* islands long before they settled them. The occupants of the Grecian mainlands were not the first to occupy the Aegean Islands. Neolithic people from Asia Minor were the first settlers. The Minoans developed a great civilization on Crete, but unfortunately we have no record of their thoughts. What must have been their extensive knowledge of the Mediterranean was long forgotten by the ninth or eighth century B.C. when Homer composed the *Odyssey.* His understanding of the seas to the west and south of Greece is confused, but it was precisely this lack of knowledge of physical geography that allowed him to create a magnificent mythical geography.[1]

Still today islands provide more scope to the Western imagination than any other land form. Half the entries in *The Dictionary of Imaginary Places* are islands.[2] In addition to being our favorite fictions, islands are the master metaphors that permit us to navigate a world to which we apply another of our favorite tropes, the vast and unpredictable sea. From beginning, water has constituted Western culture's most formidable and telling boundary. For the Greeks the distinction between earth and water was elemental. They saw themselves as inhabiting an earth island completely surrounded by watery chaos. As mainlanders, they regarded land as familiar and comforting, the sea as strange and corrupting. Strabo attributed to Plato the view that "those who want a well governed city ought to shun the sea as a teacher of vice."[3] The existence of encircling waters gave the earth its definition, for the ocean's chaos (*aperion*) reinforced earth's apparent order (*cosmos*). At a later stage the walls of the city (*polis*) would form for the Greeks a new kind of boundary between order and chaos, between civilization and barbarism, but they never gave up the idea that the earth was itself an island, surrounded by a great impassable river. In Greek geography "the terrifying *aperion* of primal chaos was banished to the outmost edge of the globe, where flowed the stream of Ocean."[4]

It is said of the mainland Greeks of Homer's time that they believed that if they walked far enough in any direction they would come to water. The notion of an earth island surrounded entirely by water is common to many civilizations, but it has been foundational to the West's way of thinking about itself as being at the center of things. Classical Greeks of the fifth century B.C. held a concentric view of the world, which placed order at the center and projected all that was strange, supernatural, and mysterious on the periphery. This geocentrism was passed on to the Romans and ultimately to medieval Europe, where it would prevail until the Age of Discovery and beyond.[5]

Mythical Geographies of the Ancient Mariners

There are places we live *in* and places we live *by*. The first is what might be called our material geography, the second what Mircea Eliade calls our mythical geography. The one allows us to live our lives, the other gives meaning to our existence. As humans we require both. Material and mythical geographies may sometimes overlap, but usually we keep them separate so that they complement rather than interfere with one another. For example, we commonly distinguish the place we live *in* (house) from the place we live *by* (home). The first meets our material needs, the second our desire for a meaningful place in the world.[6]

Mythical geographies always exist beyond the edge of everyday existence. They are frequently located in remote and isolated places about which we have little practical information.[7] In the Western world, the sea has been a favored location because Europeans were late in mastering it. Had the Mediterranean already been mapped by his contemporaries, Odysseus would have had to have sailed on more distant seas. It took a very long time for the Atlantic to give up its secrets. That did not happen until the eighteenth and nineteenth centuries, and it was only then that the frontiers of mythical geography moved inland. In

Illustration 1   The World as pictured by Hecataeus, 500 B.C.

our own day, when the continents have been fully explored, mythical geographies have shifted again, this time to outer space. But wherever they may be located, mythical geographies serve us in the same ways they have always done, providing meaning and direction. Like the cardinal points of a compass, they tell us not only where we are but who we are—westerners or easterners, northerners or southerners, earthlings as opposed to space aliens.

We also place our temporal myths at a distance, locating origins at some remote point in prehistory about which little verifiable information exists. Endings are similarly projected to some vague, distant future. The modern world finds safe storage for its origin myths in the millions of years of evolution. The ancients also placed beginnings in deep time, which they imagined to have been a watery chaos.[8] In many Middle Eastern myths, the world begins with water. The Hebrew book of Genesis also tells us that in the beginning there was only water. This is a foundational idea in many ancient religions, but also in the earliest forms of science. When Thales created the first nonreligious cosmogony in the sixth century B.C. he made water the original element.[9] But, while water was the source of life, it was also the cause of the great destruction. Floods were central to all the ancient Near East cultures from which the West inherited its most compelling mythologies. Today, rising waters produced by global warming still evoke the image of the end of the world.

The sea has always been a great mystery to land-based mankind. It took a very long time for humans to reach its shores from the African interior, and it must have seemed to them an extraordinary place of opportunity but also of extreme danger. It is little wonder that they offered sacrifices to its gods and goddesses before venturing into the waters to travel or harvest its resources.[10] Even today's shores are the site of rites of propitiation that date back centuries. Some ancient cultures, such as the Phoenicians, established a certain rapport with their sea gods, but others, including the Egyptians, who worshiped water when it took the form of a river, had an intense antipathy toward the sea.

The classical Greeks were too dependent on the sea to share this loathing, but they were never comfortable with it either. Even in the waters they knew best, the eastern Mediterranean, they always tried to stay within sight of land, coasting or island hopping. They were more comfortable onshore than off, and did not sleep or take meals on ships if they could help it.[11] It was always with the intention of returning to *terra firma* that Greek heroes began their voyages. As Alain Corbin notes, "In ancient epics, shore keeps alive the dream of fixed abode prescribed by the gods or provides a focus for hope of return."[12]

The Greeks were homebodies who did not voluntarily go in search of new worlds. Travel in the ancient world was almost exclusively a masculine endeavor. Good women waited at home on the mainlands, while seductresses lurked on every island, delaying the hero's triumphant return.[13] Odysseus had no other intention but to return at war's end to Ithaca as quickly and directly as possible, but it was his fate, Homer writes, to be "the man of twists and turns, driven time and again off course," delayed in his homecoming for so many years.[14] It was fate, not choice, that precipitated his encounters with the sea and its islands. The heroic male journey was anything but the deeply personal experience that modern travel is supposed to be. The ancients had no notion of exploration in our sense. They did not leave home to discover new truths about themselves or others. The modern idea of the island journey as self-discovery had no meaning then. The hardships that Odysseus endured tested his ability to transcend the merely mortal and attain the status of hero.[15]

For the Greeks the sea was a non-place, a void, "as worrying metaphysically as it was physically."[16] For them it was boundless space (*aperion*), representing everything they feared: "vast extent, impassability, atavism, and monstrous disorder."[17] Earth, by contrast, represented order (*cosmos*). By constructing their mythical geography in this dichotomous way, the Greeks managed to project all they found disturbing beyond their shores, thus reinforcing their own unshakable sense of earthly order. Greek city-states have been described as "islands on dry land," and Greece itself as a "pattern of islands."[18] This preference for insularity would be one of Greece's legacies to Western civilization.

Water frightened the Greeks, rivers as much as the sea. They located their cities back from the shores and built few bridges out of fear of invasion. Unlike those seafaring peoples of the Pacific who learned to understand the sea as having its own topography, neither the Greeks nor the Romans were ever able to see it as anything but a mirror reflecting back their own land-based perceptions. It was this notion of the sea as a kind of blank slate, as a space to inscribe all kinds of landlubberly fantasies of monsters and mermaids, that was to be the inheritance of later European civilizations.[19]

There are peoples, perhaps the Phoenicians but most notably the Polynesians, for whom the sea was very much a place with its own landscapes, complete with known features providing orientation as well as direction. But this was not the view that has been handed down to mainstream Western culture. Though some Western peoples, such as the Norse, developed a much greater familiarity with the sea, their understandings have either not survived or have been marginalized. As Jonathan Raban has pointed out, the perceived emptiness of the sea, the fact that is not a "verifiable object," has allowed it to serve as the West's most protean symbol, "the supremely liquid and volatile element, shaping itself newly for every writer and every generation."[20]

For the ancient Greeks and Romans the sea was not only geographically but temporally empty. They imagined the sea to be closely associated with origins and endings, but without a history to call its own.[21] Their notion of time was essentially cyclical, a matter of eternal return. Aristotle believed the universe to be eternal, without a beginning or an end. And if time was cyclical, space was concentric. The Greek polis constituted a center from which every other place appeared peripheral. Rome also saw itself at the very center of the world, and although its imperial ambitions set its frontiers at a great distance, this did not disturb either the sense of centrality or eternity that constituted the Roman worldview. It was only when the empire faltered that a very different sense of time and space, one generated by Judeo-Christian tradition, entered into European consciousness.

Biblical Geography

The mythical geography of the West is a legacy not only of the Greeks and Romans. It also owes much to Jewish cosmologies, which were given universal significance by Christianity when it became the official religion of the Roman Empire in the fourth century. The gods of the Greeks were rooted in place and were eternal, but the God of the Jews and Christians made himself known through events and endowed the world with a dynamism it had not had before. The Judeo-Christian tradition provided the sea and the earth with a history as well as a location, a history that was linear rather than cyclical. For the next fourteen hundred years biblical geography would gain ever greater influence, first in Europe and then worldwide.

Like other Near Eastern peoples, the ancient Hebrews subscribed to the idea that the sea was the primordial chaos from which God in his wisdom had brought forth the earth, and from that earth had made man and then woman. According to biblical geography the original earth had been a garden of delights, a place of peace, abundance, and good order. In this mythic place there was no toil, disease, or death, and no sea.[22] But the first earthlings, Adam and Eve, had forfeited everlasting life through their willful disobedience. They were cast out of the garden and compelled to wander on a earth that was also made to suffer for their original sin. These fallen humans were exiles in an equally fallen sublunar world, which was no longer fruitful or eternal, but was to experience the same decay and death to which humans were now susceptible. Unlike heroic pagan travelers, Adam, Eve, and their progeny were permanent exiles with no hope of returning home.[23]

In the mythical geography of both Jews and Christians the Garden of Eden continued to exist, but only as an island to itself, surrounded by physical barriers that made it forever inaccessible to fallen mankind. While the heavens, the abode of God and his angels, remained a model of perfection, the sublunar world was ceded to the devil. In contrast to the mythical geography of the Greeks, which made no strong distinction between the heavens and the earth, the Bible assigned to the celestial world a permanence and perfection that it denied to the earth, rendered mutable and corruptible by the sins of Adam and Eve. The pagans had assigned order to the center and chaos to the periphery; Jews and Christians constructed their cosmos vertically, projecting all that was desirable to the heavens above and locating hell in the depths of the earth. Christian tradition remained deeply distrustful of all earthly things. It was a restless, essentially homeless religion with a dynamism that would ultimately disperse its missionaries throughout the entire world.[24]

According to biblical geography, conditions became even worse when Adam and Eve's progeny proved disobedient and God decided to punish them with a catastrophic flood. Noah managed to save his family and representatives of other species, but when land appeared from the waters for a second time it was no longer a smooth, habitable whole earth but a shrunken, distorted terrain of monstrous mountains, yawning chasms, and raging rivers that divided mankind and made life more difficult than before. This biblical geography was still predominant in the seventeenth century, when George Owen wrote in 1603 that the biblical flood had torn "the erthe in peeces and separated the Illands from the Contynent, and made the hilles and vallies as we now finde theme."[25]

The irregularity of coasts and the perceived ugliness of islands scattered like flotsam and jetsam offshore contrasted with the perfect symmetry and tranquility of the antediluvian world. As an instrument of God's will, the earth had become violently dynamic, earthquakes "vomited up Islands in some places, and swallowed them in others."[26] The sea was also a menacing dynamo, confining Noah's descendants to what amounted to an earth island divided into three parts. Noah's three sons colonized this new world, Sem in the part known as Asia, Cham in Africa, Japhet in Europe, but the earth was now forever fragmented.

Judeo-Christian mythical geography paralleled the Greek and Roman understandings of the dichotomy between land and sea to some extent, but added a novel temporal dimension. The earth was now seen, like man, as being in a fallen state, perpetually degenerating toward its own death and destruction. Its rough surfaces were likened to the warts and wrinkles of elderly persons. Just as each generation of fallen mankind brought forth a race of ever more dwarfish, less creative, and less intelligent men and women, so the earth itself was losing its fertility, becoming less hospitable as earthquakes and other catastrophic events became more frequent. As late as the eighteenth century, Thomas Burnet would describe the earth as a "broken and confus'd heap of bodies, plac'd in no order to one another," leaving no place for progress, only further ruination.[27]

Although God had promised Noah that there would be no more floods, the sea was viewed as a reminder of God's wrath. Its shores were associated with danger, death, and destruction, held back only by divine will. Floods were central to all Near Eastern mythologies and fit neatly into the Greek preoccupation with cycles of destruction and reconstruction, which Plato modified for his own purposes when he created the political allegory of the destruction of Atlantis by water.[28] In Christianity's mythical geography humans would never be truly at home, for the world, as Edmundo O'Gorman put it, "really belongs to God and exists for his sake. Man is not only a prisoner, he is not even master in the house in which he is confined."[29] Homeless mankind was doomed to be a traveler (*homo viator*) on a constantly changing earth until the end of time; to be in this world but not in possession of it. After the Fall, true home awaited either in heaven above or at the end of time, when both mankind and the earth itself would be redeemed by divine will. Home for the Christian was no longer, as it was for the pagan traveler, a sure destination.

Unlike the pagans, who occupied an essentially static world, Christians were time travelers on a journey that led from Genesis to the Second Coming of Christ, reckoned to be a span of little more than six thousand years. The earth itself was on a similar timetable. Biblical geography divided the earth's history into three periods. The first had lasted from Creation to the Fall; this was followed by a long period of degeneration ending in utter destruction, followed by a period of regeneration, coinciding with the Second Coming of a Messiah. For the Jews the coming of the Messiah was associated with a return to their homeland in Israel, but for Christians this event was a homecoming not just for a chosen people to a chosen land, but a universal event that involved the reoccupation by all of mankind of an earth made whole again.[30] As prophesied in Revelations this would be the moment when the earth would return to a more perfect condition, when islands and mainlands would be reunited and there would be "no more sea." But all this lay in a far distant future and depended ultimately on the will of the inscrutable God.

In the meantime, the Christian *viator* was fated to journey with no certainty of returning home, for the true destination was with God in a world above or a time yet to come. Unlike the Greek and Roman worldviews, which assumed to existence of an earthly center to return to, biblical geography described a dispersed mankind, divided in three parts and subdivided still further by mountains, rivers, and the sea. Mankind was isolated, imprisoned by the sea on a ruined earth. No amount of effort would unite what God had put asunder. All depended on the will of a God whose intentions were not only absolute but indecipherable.

Earth Island and River Ocean

The ancient world bequeathed to the medieval era a mythical geography that centered on an earth island, *Orbis Terrarum,* surrounded by the river *Oceanus.* The Greeks and Romans ultimately managed to tame to the Mediterranean, but fear was now projected beyond the Pillars of Hercules to what they called the Western Sea. It is doubtful that the ancients ever entertained the notion of another land to the west, and it is certain that they had no concept of another continent located there, because they believed the earth to be a single undivided island. There could be no continents as such.[31] It was noted at the time that "geographers crowd unto the edges of their maps parts of the world which they do not know about, adding notes in the margins to the effect that beyond this lies but sandy deserts full of wild beasts, unapproachable bogs, Scythians, or a frozen sea."[32] These constituted the mythical geographies of the ancients, reinforcing their sense that anything far away must be different, inaccessible, and ultimately unknowable. By and large, the ancients were not much interested in finding out what lay beyond the horizon, for they had no notion of discovery.

Envious, vengeful sea gods and goddesses populated the waters of the pagan world. These water spirits persisted in medieval Europe, but took form of devils "every bit as hungry for human victims as were their pagan counterparts."[33] Bridges over waters therefore constituted a danger and were placed in the custody of clergy, who were expected to exorcise the threat to travelers. As for the sea, it remained the great void, populated no longer by the old sea gods and goddesses but by demons commanded by none other than Satan himself.[34] The Church substituted its own rites of propitiation for pagan practices, but these only confirmed the dangers that lay offshore. Enclosed seas like the Mediterranean did not pose so great a problem, but a great river encircling earth island was quite another matter. Known to most Europeans as *Oceanus* and to the Norse as *Uthaf,* it constituted the edge of the known world. When they ventured on its waters, Europeans continued the practices of coasting and island hopping developed in the Mediterranean.[35] But, even then, the shores of the Atlantic were associated with extreme dangers, repellant to all but saints and heroes.

Crossing water was associated with crossing into other worlds. Things offshore were not just quantitatively distant, but qualitatively different. On the distant horizon where the sky met the sea, heaven and earth were thought to be connected.[36] There the meaning of time and space changed. The natural and the everyday gave way to the supernatural and the magical. The Greeks and Romans held the view that somewhere to the west lay places of plenty and tranquility, reserved for dead heroes. They called these Elysium or the Garden of Hesperides, and they located them in the near Atlantic on what were known as the Isles of the Blest or the Fortunate Isles. As described Hesiod in the eighth century B.C.: "Father Zeus, at the ends of the earth, presented a dwelling place, apart from man and far from the deathless gods. In the Islands of the Blest, founded by deep-swirling ocean, they live untouched by toil or sorrow. For them the grain-giving earth thrice yearly bears fruit as sweet as honey."[37]

The west beyond the horizon had become the place where immortals resided.[38] The idea of the land of the dead was vital to the land of the living, and according to Barry Cunliffe these islands were "comforting metaphors to help people come to terms with the inevitability of death, much in the way that many current religions have created their own concepts of 'heaven.'"[39] But the power of this mythical geography depended on keeping it in the realm of the unfamiliar, out of reach of mortals. As Pindar cautioned, this world must be kept off limits to mortals: "All beyond that bourne cannot be approached; Beyond Gadeira toward the gloom we must not pass."[40] The pagan Celts had also "placed the dead in the west, beneath the waves, beyond the mist, or on some remote island."[41] Their shamans and seers might make spirit journeys to these places for the purpose of reporting back to the world of the living, but ordinary people were not encouraged to venture into the unknown.[42]

Islanded Europe

"Space, to become a world and a home for self, must be defined," notes Yi-Fu Tuan. In Western culture this was done by islanding reality, dividing it into discrete objects to which meanings were attached. Europeans had been islanding themselves since the beginnings of neolithic settlement.[43] The first houses were round and grouped together in circles that constituted insular compounds or villages. The ideal form of the city was also a closed circle, and though the actual shape of settlement may not always have been regular, the representations of ancient and medieval cities invariably rounded off the rough edges. The circle was the symbol of wholeness, cohesion, and good order. Its bounds kept at bay the chaos that was believed to lurk beyond the circumference. In ordinary times people might tolerate a certain openness and irregularity, but in moments of disorder and conflict they turned to insularity and concentricity to assuage their anxieties.[44]

Insular metaphors were used frequently in the ancient world. Plato's notion of the polis was insular, and he argued in the *Laws* that the best place for a new city is "of course, an island." Rome saw itself as an island, and it built its empire archipelagically as a series of islandlike garrison towns, not bothering to connect these except by its famous road systems. All power radiated from the center outward, but, in contrast to modern nation-states, no attempt was made to control all the space in between. The Romans applied the term *territorium* to the town but not to the space between towns.[45]

The collapse of the Roman Empire left Europe without an imperial center. Its subsequent settling could not proceed from a single central place, but continued to proceed on the same islanding principle. Feudal settlement was carried out by independent groups of nobles, merchants, and clergy who carved out islandlike enclaves in a process that Robert Bartlett has likened to cellular replication, each enclave separate from others but sufficiently alike to create a sense of cultural if not territorial continuity by the thirteenth century.[46] Before these settlements became places, they were islands in the minds of the settlers. Europe's internal colonizers brought with them notions of shape and scale that no natural feature, whether it be a dense forest or swamp, was allowed to interfere with. In a manner that was to be repeated in overseas colonization in later centuries, the first acts of the settlers was to mark out an island of space with clearly defined boundaries. Only then could the business of settling begin in earnest.[47]

The result was that by the thirteenth century Europe comprised thousands of discrete insular territories, all bearing a resemblance to one another but in no way contiguous. The Roman term *insula,* which meant a jurisdiction as well as a physical place, was commonly used to describe all kinds of medieval tenancies.[48] In late medieval Marseille, the city was divided into *insula* for tax and administrative purposes, and an official called an *insularius* was responsible for collecting taxes in his part of town.[49] Medieval parishes were pictured as islands of Christian faith in a sea of paganism. When the crusades extended European frontiers to the eastern Mediterranean, the Christian states of the Holy Land were perceived as islands in a Muslim sea, autonomous enclaves held as fiefs or trade concessions. Within towns like Acre, Genoese merchants constituted themselves as self-governing islands. This kind of cellular replication was to provide a model for later colonization of the western Mediterranean and the near Atlantic.[50] Carried to the New World it would remain the dominant mode of European settlement until the eighteenth century, when monarchies finally replaced settler archipelagos with territorial states.[51]

Medieval people occupied a world that was substantially more geocentric and anthropocentric than our own. They regarded themselves as microcosms of the earth itself, their bones corresponding to its stones, their blood to its streams, their hair to its grasses.[52] Distance was measured anthropocentrically, by the foot or hand, or by the number of days it took someone to travel from one place to another. Distance was not a matter of numbers of miles, but of perceived qualitative differences between places. A place could be quite near but seem very far away if marked off, like a monastery, as sacred territory.[53] Though medieval settlements seem small to us, they were large in the eyes of their inhabitants because they were their own complete worlds, not just parts of some larger thing. Like islands, they seemed complete to those who resided there. During the Middle Ages most Europeans lived in miniature islanded worlds carved out of dense forests. Roads were few, bridges even rarer.[54] Though horizons were limited and the scale small, these worlds were extremely full and were not felt to be confining. "There were no empty places, no gaps, nothing was superfluous or unnecessary," notes historian P. N. Bitsilli, "In this world there were no unknown places, heaven was as familiar as earth and there was no reason why anyone should go astray. The traveler who wandered from the path fell into the nether regions or rose to heaven, where he could find familiar places and people he knew."[55]

The spatial world of medieval people was constituted less by distance than by difference. Even a short journey, such as into the sacred spaces of a cathedral, brought them into a wholly other world. The prime medieval orientation was vertical rather than horizontal; and the crucial dimension was up and down rather than near and far. In Christianity's dualistic understanding of heaven and earth, the two were not so much distant as different. In a cosmos that was hierarchical and centripetal, the heavens were high but not far. Hell was deep but near. No-trespassing signs were posted at both the lower and upper limits of earthly existence as well as at watery edges of the world itself, obligating those who ventured into the earth to mine its riches to look to propitiary rites similar to those practiced by those who ventured to sea. Going down involved rites of passage similar to those of going out, for the surface of the earth was, like the edge of the sea, a threshold fraught with both possibilities and dangers that required ritual treatment. As long as they stayed within their insular boundaries, however, medieval people felt quite safe and complete, for their worlds were full of meaning.

Like space, time was finite. Though limited to six thousand years, history was very full to those who lived by God's time. "Think not thy time short in this world, since the world itself is not long," wrote Sir Thomas Browne. "The created world is but a small parenthesis in eternity; and a short imposition, for a time, between such a state of duration was before it and may be after it."[56] A human life rarely extended more than forty or fifty years, but, lacking our notion of longevity, it did not seem particularly short.[57] As in the case of space, a lifetime did not seem brief when framed as an island in a sea of time, as a thing complete in itself.

The modern era has extended time in the same way it has extended space, beyond the boundaries of human and even earthly existence. It has differentiated it into a series of discrete moments known as the past, present, and future, drawing ever finer temporal distinctions that split seasons into years, years into months, days, hours, minutes, seconds, and, now, nanoseconds. Such distinctions had no meaning in a medieval world; rather, time was perceived as a closed system with very clear beginnings and endings, but only vaguely defined intervals of seasons or ages. There was no deep past or extended future, and the present appeared to contain everything that had ever happened or would happen in this world. In an era when the living shared time with both the dead and those yet to be born, there was no room for our sense of anachronism or the kind of nostalgia for lost places and vanished pasts that so affects us today.[58] Medieval time, like medieval space, was very full. In the words of Aaron Gurevich, it was "protracted, slow, and epic."[59]

Medieval people lived by divine rather than natural law. Nature set limits, but medieval people showed no reverence for nature in their settlement practices. They ignored what we would regard as natural boundaries, preferring cosmic archetypes to the irregularities of the physical world. In medieval culture nature was regarded as a veil of appearances, hiding deeper truths. Mountains, rivers, and islands were esteemed for their symbolic, not their scenic, value. As historian Wilcomb Washburn has pointed out, medieval thinkers were "blessedly free" of geographical categories, tending "merely to contrast land with sea, zone with zone, part with part, West with East, the known world to the unknown,"[60] Names for different kinds of land were used loosely and interchangeably. African, Europe, and Asia were simply parts of the great earth island. Nor was the definition of lands any more precise. Medieval cosmographers used *iland, ysland,* and *insula* to describe any remote and mysterious place, whether landlocked or surrounded by water. Marco Polo called any distant place about which he had no firsthand knowledge an "island" whether it was offshore or onshore. It was not until the sixteenth century that only places surrounded by water were called islands and clear distinction was made between them and continents.[61] Sir John Mandeville referred to Tibet is an "isle," and place names like the Isle of Avalon were applied to inland areas.[62]

In the Christian worldview, space was no more quantitatively differentiated than was time. Notions of near and far were used with as little precision as early and late.[63] Just as contemporaries lumped together quite different periods in what seems to us to be anachronistic confusion, they also conflated quite different places. Geographical terms that have come to have quite precise meanings in modern geography—islands, seas, deserts—were applied equally to very different landscapes. When medieval people thought of the sea they described it in terms of land—"land of fish"—and vice versa, describing forests as "sea of deer" or "lakes of spruce."[64] The sea was just as often described as wilderness, as a desert.

Each feature of the earth had its divinely ordained purpose, with a hidden meaning that could not be read off its surfaces, but understood only at some deeper, teleological level. The visual dimension was subordinated to the metaphysical, for the Middle Ages had no concept of landscape or seascape as we have come to understand it. Land and sea were merely backdrops for divine and human activity, and therefore of no scenic interest. Painters did not focus on nature as such, and writers largely left it out of their descriptions. Medieval people did not approach nature as objective observers because they did not separate themselves from the world in which they lived and worked.[65]

Before Geography

The geographer John Kirtland Wright has called medieval Europe's understanding of the world "geosophy" to distinguish it from the physical geography of later times.[66] Geosophy conceived of all land forms as serving God's purposes.

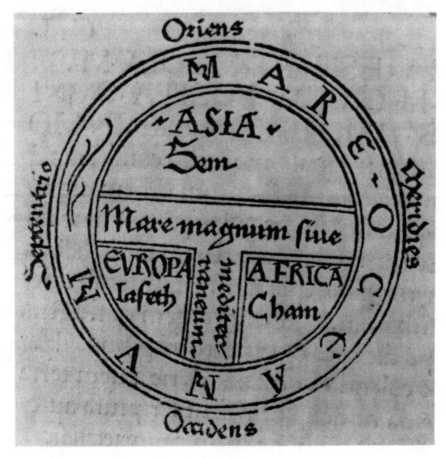

Illustration 2   T-O Map of the World, attributed to Saint Isidore of Seville, first printed 1472

"God made the Earth quite round, in the middle of the firmament," wrote Sir John Mandeville. But, in contrast to the heavens, earth was far from perfect, having been cursed, like mankind itself, first by the Fall and then by the Flood. According to Mandeville, "The hills and valleys that are now on earth are the result only of Noah's flood, by which soft earth moved form its place leaving a valley, and the hard ground stayed still and become a hill."[67] Natural phenomena continued to be attributed to divine will until the eighteenth century. To people who believed that earthquakes were caused by God and that rocks grew like plants, there could be no clear distinction between history and nature.[68] Before there was geography there was only cosmography. Much of the practical knowledge of the world that had been accumulated by the Greeks and the Romans was forgotten or lost during the Middle Ages. Ptolemaic maps were not rediscovered

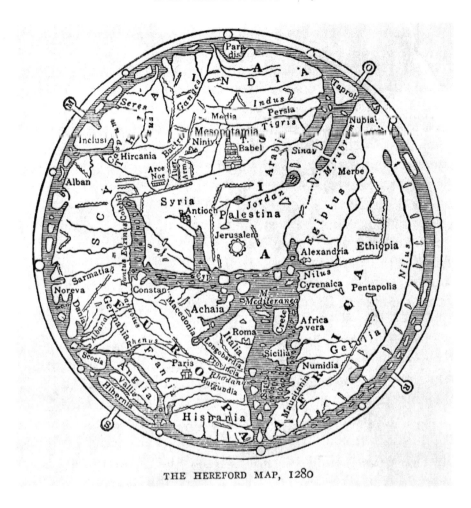

THE HEREFORD MAP, 1280

Illustration 3   Terrestrial Eden portrayed as island at the very top of the Hereford Mappaemundi

until the fourteenth century. From the sixth through the sixteenth centuries, the West had to do with the so-called T-O maps, which were highly schematic and provided no precise information about location.

Local maps and coastal sea charts called *portolan* served the medieval wayfarers and seafarers well enough. As long as they did not go great distances or stray far from land, maps of larger scale were not required. And when so-called world maps—*mappaemundi*—appeared in the thirteenth century, these replicated the form of the T-O maps, showing a river ocean surrounding an earth island.[69] Anything that lay beyond that edge of earth island belonged to another world, more supernatural than natural, not so much distant as different. The sea was represented as it had been since the Greeks, largely as a void. Earth island was divided into three parts, but the notion of separate continents was absent. On the edges of *mappaemundi* were located biblical places like Eden, invariably represented as remote, isolated, and islanded.

The *mappaemundi* are excellent guides to the mythical geography of the Middle Ages, but poor references to actual locations. They were full of meaning, but short on utility. David Woodward tells us that their chief purpose "was to instruct the faithful about the significant events in Christian history rather than to record their precise location."[70] To the medieval mind, space and time were joined in such a way that made biblical events and places seem contemporaneous. Medieval people believed that both the past and the future were always present, but located beyond the edge of the known world, in inaccessible regions or offshore in the timeless ocean.[71] The Garden of Eden was present, usually far to the east in some inaccessible islanded place. It shared that mythical terrain with Gog and Magog, monsters who would be loosed on the world as a prelude to the Second Coming.[72]

What medieval maps lacked in precision they made up for in their ability to bring alive that sense of place that is so noticeably absent in modern cartography. When space is inseparable from time, place is defined by where things happen or were remembered to have happened. History was then, as it is now, the record of events that have taken place, but because they had no abstract concept of time, medieval chroniclers paid little attention to precise dates, just as medieval geographers were inattentive to exact locations. To the modern mind, medieval histories are incomplete in the same way that their maps are unsatisfactory. Whereas the modern map plots everything on a prescribed (though invisible) Euclidean grid, careful to quantify distance and maintain scale, medieval cartography assigned location and scale on the basis of religious significance. Maps were entirely useless for calculating distance, but they were brilliant when it came to assigning significance. In *mappaemundi* it was not the size but the religious importance of towns that determined their location and prominence. Jerusalem was always to be found at the center of the world, always larger than any other city.

It should now be clear why medieval Europeans could live so comfortably with insularity, a condition which the modern age conflates with narrowness and incompleteness. In part it was a consequence of the acceptance of their lot as transient tenants—*insulari*—of a world they could not hope to possess or control. The finitude we find so confining, they experienced as comforting, even liberating, because, living in scattered settlements and valuing community over individuality, they felt anxious in the presence of precisely that openness and emptiness that invariably excites the modern imagination. Projecting chaos beyond the edges of earth island, medieval people felt, as had the ancients, safe in their imagined insularity.

The Ultimate Island

The ancients and the medievals found all they needed in their own small worlds, but this did not prevent them from making mental voyages into the unknown. Once colonized, the Mediterranean could no longer entertain a Homeric imagination, but now the Western Sea became Europe's mythical geography. The Greeks and the Romans knew its islands only secondhand. It is probable that the secretive Phoenicians explored the near Atlantic, including the Canaries, but their knowledge had long since melted into legend. *Oceanus* and its mythical islands "hovered on the boundaries of the actual and the credible."[73]

Off limits to mortals, the islands of the Western Sea remained for poets and philosophers wonderful figures to play with and speculate about. Plato invented a large island, Atlantis, to make his political point about the superiority of the small, well-governed city-state to the large empire. He used it as an allegory of what happens when polity becomes too large and commercial for its own good. Atlantis was envisioned as huge, "larger than Libya and Asia combined," which according to Plato's very seductive fiction disappeared when hit by a devastating flood sometime in the far distant past. Atlantis had been a thriving commercial empire, just the kind of expansive polity that Plato detested, and its destruction was to be a lesson to contemporaries to maintain the noncommercial virtues of the small landlocked polis. Few of those contemporaries gave his allegory any credence, and the legend of Atlantis virtually disappeared during the Middle Ages.[74]

Even when the Greeks and Romans made their first timid voyages into the waters of the Atlantic, legendary places were always just beyond the horizon. Instead of erasing these apparitions, the forays offshore only multiplied them, adding to the mystery and the lure of the unknown islands. A Greek named Pytheas, a resident of Massalia (now Marseille) voyaged north in the fourth century B.C. through the Pillars of Hercules scouting the sources of tin associated with the British Isles and amber known to come from the Baltic region. Following well-defined Atlantic coasting routes used for thousands of years by the neolithic peoples who settled along the shores and on the islands of the Atlantic littoral, Pytheus provided a remarkably accurate account of the coasts of France and of Britain, including the Orkney and Shetland isles. He may have sailed as far as Iceland, to which he gave the name Ultima Thule, the "furthest island," but his book of travels, *On the Ocean,* was subsequently lost and no one was able to confirm its existence.[75]

For the next three centuries Europeans showed little interest in the islands of the northern Atlantic. Julius Caesar was the next person to write about the British isles; and it was even longer before there were fresh accounts of the

Orkneys. The next sightings of Iceland were even further in the future. But the image of Ultima Thule never faded and became even more powerful in the absence of further exploration. "Like all good romantic images it hovered on the boundaries of the unreal, creating a frission of excitement—of unresolved adventure," writes historian Barry Cunliffe.[76] It established a connection between islands and the unknown that would remain at the core of Western islomania for centuries to come. The association of islands with the mysterious became so strong that any unexplored place, whether or not it was surrounded by water, was assumed to be an island. The tendency to turn all unknown lands into islands is exemplified by the treatment of Scandinavia, which for a very long time was thought of as an island.[77]

When the Romans began to push their imperial frontier north, their legendary islands moved just ahead of their advance. They thought of the isles rumored to exist to the north and west of Gaul in utterly otherworldly terms until they conquered and named them the British Isles. Though the Romans never really looked for Ultima Thule, it remained for them a compelling vision, growing in significance as the empire itself declined and its boundaries became more circumscribed. It was for many Romans a symbol of much needed renewal, of new beginnings. Because the sea itself was associated with the beginnings of time and the islands of the far sea were viewed as unsullied by the depredations of history, the farthest isle was seen as providing a fresh start for an enfeebled empire. It was not just another world, but a "new" world where jaded Romans could expect to be regenerated. Ultima Thule, with its promise of new beginnings, was to haunt the European imagination for centuries to come.[78] Until the eighteenth century all new worlds were imagined to be islands.

As the Roman Empire collapsed in the early Middle Ages, Europeans turned inward.[79] The sea and its islands, however, remained their mythical geography. *Oceanus* was not so much wide as simply beyond the bounds of human existence. In a similar way, islands belonged to a different world, "favorite places for the most astounding and divine adventures."[80] The next time Europeans searched for the farthest island they would be seeking not imperial but spiritual regeneration.

MEDIEVAL ISLOMANIA

The purest form of potentiality is emptiness itself.

—Eric Hirsch, introduction to *The Anthropology of Landscape*

IT WAS THE SEA'S VACANCY THAT THE ANCIENTS found most disturbing. Medieval Europeans also viewed the waters to the west as a void, but eventually they turned this emptiness into potentiality, first as a spiritual asset and later as material opportunity. When they finally ventured into the Atlantic in the fifth and sixth centuries they did so in search of a desert in the sea, coveting empty rather than inhabited islands. The initial motivation for voyaging was religious. The Western quest for spiritual transcendence, born thousands of years earlier in the arid environment of the Middle East, was transferred to the oceans, the only place Europeans knew that matched, as writer Paul Shepard phrases it, the "sensory deprivation and awesome overload" of the desert.[1] Holy men sought out barren, unknown islands where they could experience the purest expressions of the will of a god of the heavens with no visible attachments to earthly things. The equation of the spiritual quest with a voyage offshore would motivate exploration for centuries thereafter.

"Landscape is the work of the mind," writes Simon Schama; and desert is something we project on a place.[2] It is more a perception than a description, for the term has been applied to an astonishingly wide variety of environments over the course of human history. It does not necessarily designate a hot, dry place, for geographers talk about snow and ice deserts, while the term "forest deserts" has been applied to the thinly populated rain forests of central Africa.[3] What all have in common, however, is perceived emptiness. In reality deserts are not deserted. The have flora, fauna, and a nomadic life all their own. People indigenous to the desert have a strong sense of place and attribute holiness to the landscape they call their home. But it was not nomads, but settled people from the desert's edges who endowed it with even greater sacredness. Having first encountered God in what seemed to them to be the vast emptiness of the desert, the ancient Hebrews associated it with holiness. They passed their sacred geography along to the early Christians, who made a practice of wandering in the desert.[4]

Deserts are among the world's most protean, impressionable landscapes, not only because they are subject to seasonal and long-term physical changes, but because they are so easily inscribed with images that originate from the outside and over which the actual residents have little control. The nomads of the Middle East would never recognize their homelands as envisioned by outsiders, but they were not the ones who have shaped the image of the desert that has been planted in Western minds. The great American and Australia heartlands were anything but barren landscapes to the aboriginal peoples who inhabited them, but European settlers perceived them as deserts, a description that endured against all evidence to the contrary.[5] As in the case of the Middle East, it was the perspective of the outsider that prevailed

The Desert Island

The image of the desert island has also been a product of the outsider, of sojourners rather than settlers. Some islands are by nature desertified, lacking water, flora, and fauna, and are truly uninhabitable. But most islands, even those with the most forbidding environments, are capable of sustaining life, including human life. Yet many of these have qualified as desert islands because they were perceived to have that quality which Western culture has for so long been associated with desert—namely wilderness.[6] In today's vocabulary, wilderness is thought of almost exclusively as a natural phenomenon, but prior to the nineteenth century wilderness was a spiritual rather than a physical condition. Sojourns in the wilderness were the source of many of Judaism's most important revelations. In the Christian tradition the wilderness was a place of Satanic temptation as well as divine inspiration. Even in this secular age an aura of sacredness clings to those places we designate as wild, especially now that the city has lost its association with holiness.[7]

Desert islands have loomed large in Western mythical geography. In the Judeo-Christian tradition, spaces apparently devoid of life are easily imagined as places of creation; and desert islands have been repeatedly colonized with dreams of revitalization, both personal and societal.[8] A desert island was the setting for the archetype of the self-made man, Robinson Crusoe, and films like *The Castaway* still depend on desolation to narrate modern individualism. Desert islands also invite us to contemplate human degradation, as in H. G. Wells's *The Island of Doctor Moreau*, Peter Benchley's *The Island*, and William

Illustration 4   Stranded man reading *Self Magazine,* cartoon by Jack Ziegler

Golding's *Lord of the Flies.* Recent television survivor series show us the best and the worst of ourselves. And the desert island cartoon has become a favorite medium for poking fun at absurdities of modern life. There, isolated by the surrounding sea and exposed to the glare of the merciless sun, contemporary foibles are hilariously magnified.

Today's castaway has little in common with the shipwrecked sailors of the Odyssey or Defoe's Crusoe. There is no hint of a heroic journey or the struggle to survive against all odds. There is nothing about the cartoon castaways' condition that suggests they are in any mortal danger or even minor distress. As far as we can tell, their experience has been neither traumatic nor transformative. They are recognizable versions of our urban selves, out of place but not out of character, funny rather than heroic, comic rather than tragic. Yet the desert island still functions in the same way as it did in medieval and ancient times. It strips everything to the bare essentials, removing the confusing clutter of history and geography, allowing us to see with excruciating clarity the human condition. Ironically, the symbolism of desert islands looms ever larger now that there are so few such empty places left in the world.

Cartoon islands also bear a striking resemblance to the ancient archetype of earth island. They are almost always drawn as a perfect circle, a symbol of wholeness. The single palm suggests the equally archaic notion of *omphalos,* the navel of the world, what Mircea Eliade would call a "sacred center," a place where earth is joined to heaven.[9] The cartoon island is a perfect illustration of a mythical geography still operating "long after geography had become scientific," but now serving different cultural purposes.[10] There was a time when desert islands were places both holy and hellish, the exclusive destinations of heroes and hermits seeking to demonstrate their virtues under conditions of extreme adversity. Today they attract more ordinary mortals wishing to connect not with what lies beyond but with what lies within. Once upon a time, the desert island represented the cosmos; now it symbolizes the ego.

Holiness is not something that comes first to mind when we think about desert islands today, but there was a time when their boundedness and isolation were associated with sacredness. To sacralize is to set apart. In virtually every religion, the *sacre* is a place separated from normal time and space. "At the level of experience," writes Yi-Fu Tuan, "sacred phenomena are those that stand out from the commonplace and interrupt routine."[11] The familiar and everyday cannot take on the aura of sacredness, which is accessible only by crossing temporal and spatial boundaries. This is the reason why going to church or synagogue on the Sabbath is considered sacred, while worshiping at home is not. The sacredness of any place is directly proportional to the effort it takes to reach it. The journey to the landscapes of the holy is always a ritualized ordeal.

Wild and Holy Islands

Islands have always been associated with wild, unpredictable behavior, not just of their inhabitants but as places. They have a way of vanishing overnight and also have been known to appear out of nowhere. Volcanic eruptions can just as suddenly obliterate as create oceanic islands. Rising or falling water levels have a similar effect. Today's global warming threatens the existence of hundreds of islands worldwide, but this is by no means the first time that lands have been drowned. But flooding creates even as it destroys, carving islands out of mainlands. Only a few millennia ago the British Isles were a part of the Eurasian continent. In the grand scale of evolutionary time, islands come and go in a blink of an eye.

Given their mutable character, it is no wonder that islands are the stuff of legends, the location for origin and extinction myths. Perhaps because so many of their drowned remains haunt the Mediterranean, it was easy for the Greeks to believe Plato's fictional tale of Atlantis. Though there is no evidence that Atlantis ever existed on Santorini or at any of the other sites that modern mythmakers have located it, the idea of the lost island, even the lost continent, remains credible. Wandering and levitating islands turn up in mythical geographies around the world. Evidence of drowned coasts and uplifted seabeds must have roused curiosity long before any scientific explanations were available. And when Europeans began to pay close attention to their own geomorphology in the sixteenth and seventeenth centuries, they were inclined to think in catastrophic terms, of sudden changes brought on by diluvial, seismic, and volcanic activity, with islands being one of the most mutable of all land forms.[12]

We now know that European geography underwent huge changes long before humans were there to witness these. The most recent transformation occurred at the end of the last Great Ice Age beginning about 10,000 B.C., drowning coasts, flooding estuaries, severing peninsulas and creating new islands. By 6000 B.C. the present shape of the British Isles was visible. The Baltic had opened up, and the archipelagos of Sweden and Denmark had formed. This was the first time that many northern and western parts of Europe were open to human occupation. By 8000 B.C. Europe was receiving its first migrants from the Mediterranean. They came by sea rather than land, and hugged the coast as nomadic hunters, gatherers, and fisher folk, at first camping rather than settling on headlands and islands. A few intrepid Phoenician traders followed them, setting up Europe's first port on the island of Gadir, at the mouth of Rio Gaudalete in what is now the location of the Spanish city of Cadiz. The Phoenicians are also known to have used islands along the African coast as trading posts; and they voyaged to the Canaries and may have made contact with both the Madeiras and the Azores, feats that would not be replicated for another ninety-three hundred years.

Between 7000 and 4000 B.C. agriculture came to Europe, partly by land but also by sea. First practiced on coastal islands and promontories, neolithic cultures gradually moved inland. But it would be a very long time before a continental identity would develop. It was the Atlantic coastal zone, "its cultures uniquely fashioned by being at the extremity of the world, bound together over vast distances by maritime networks," that played the most vital role in northwestern Europe's development in the centuries prior to the coming of Romans in the second century B.C.[13] Not only was the sea and the many rivers opening off it the main route for trade, but it seems that much of Europe's political and cultural development occurred at the edge of the sea on small islands where foreign traders were be tolerated by inland potentates who did not welcome them to their well-guarded interiors. The remains of many forts and burial grounds have been excavated on coastal peninsulas and islands, indicating the importance of the coast to the development of a more complex, settled society.

Pytheas the Greek voyaged in the fourth century B.C. in search of the "tin isles," now known as Britain. Of particular interest to him was the legendary Isle of Ictis, a source of this desired metal. The extraterritoriality of islands guaranteed that strangers could find a kind of safety there they could not expect if they set foot on the mainland. The isles of Gadir and Mogador off the coasts of the Iberian peninsula and Morocco also functioned in this way. Ictis was probably one of the small isles off the coast of Cornwall, perhaps Mount Batton at the head of the Plymouth Sound, which had been a trading place for centuries before Pytheas's time, or St. Michael's Mount, still today an island at high tide, though better known for its religious than economic functions.[14]

Islands with reputation for holiness existed all along the well-traveled coasts of the Mediterranean and the Atlantic because the boundary between water and earth had been suffused with sacred meanings in ancient times. Land and sea constituted two different worlds, requiring elaborate precautions for those who wished to pass from one to the other. The ancients associated the sea with chaos, while Christianity identified it with Satan. Islands were a kind of third place, partaking of both sea and land, liminal places that were the sites of rites of passage for travelers between earth and water. Entering or leaving the sea required therefore rites of passage protective of both the traveler and the host, and small coastal islands served as thresholds where peaceful coexistence was guaranteed. These were also thresholds between the natural and supernatural worlds, so it is not surprising that isles in the Mediterranean were long associated with cults. Their sacredness was easily transferred from paganism to Christianity and Islam. The islet of Hieronisos off Cyprus was the location of the cult of Apollo before Christianity turned it into a shrine to St. George. Pagan maritime pilgrimage routes island hopped along the Mediterranean littoral, offering seafarers spiritual as well as material comfort. These same stepping-stones were later used by Christian and Muslim merchants and pilgrims.[15]

Islands near to the Atlantic coast of Europe were also locations "sacred to the gods," liminal places where wondrous things were most likely to happen.[16] Long before Christians sought out coastal isles as places of special holiness, pagans were using them as sacred sites. Lavret, a small isle at the mouth of the Loire, was the location of a women's fertility cult; another, the Ile-de-Sein, was said to be the home of female priests, later condemned by Christians as witches.[17] In pre-Christian Europe, islands were thought of as having a sacred quality that predated their ecclesiastical uses. Barry Cunliffe writes: "particularly small remote islands, had a special quality. . . . Perhaps it was the idea of boundedness—the sea serving as the protecting perimeter—that was the attraction. The islands were liminal places, neither entirely of the land nor of the sea, which would have endowed them with unusual power in the minds of those who lived at the interface between land and ocean."[18] Christianity would appropriate this sense of holiness, building its shrines on precisely the same spots where pagan temples once stood.

As medieval Europe turned in on itself, the perceived gulf between land and sea widened, and offshore islands retreated in even greater obscurity and mystery. Much of the geographical knowledge of the ancient world was lost and replaced by biblical geography, which held tightly to the old idea of an *Orbis Terrarum* cut off by a raging *Oceanus*. Agriculturally based feudal Europe turned its back on the sea, treating it as an alien place. It would be a long time before ordinary people would return to the sea, and when they did it was with less confidence than had the neolithic argonauts, who had populated Europe from the sea thousands of years earlier. Like other documented cases of peoples, including islanders, who lose their seafaring habits, medieval Europeans became ever more landlubberly and seafaring. There was only one group among them that ventured into the waters of the Atlantic. It was not merchants or warriors in search of wealth and glory who did so, but rather a group of wholly otherworldly men, who turned to the sea not because of its abundance but its barrenness.

The Appeal of the Desert

The Near East, the font of so many of our mythical geographies, gave us two of our most powerful symbolic landscapes, the garden and the desert. The two have defined one another ever since, a binary of order and wilderness deeply embedded in the Western way of looking at the world.[19] No doubt the very difficulty of the environment of the arid Near East had much to do with the idea of the garden as something that must be carved out of wilderness and protected against its depredations. Eric Leed speculates that the story of the Garden of Eden originated as a "myth told in the tents of nomads," but it is also likely that it was settled people of the fertile crescent who, having seen their efforts at agriculture repeatedly ruined by overgrazing, soil erosion, and the kinds of diseases associated with settled populations, had the strongest memories of once green and fertile lands and retrospectively shaped these into a powerful myth of paradise lost.[20] But the arid regions of the world were not the only places were the binary took hold. It traveled well beyond its place of origin. As a powerful component of Judeo-Christian tradition, the desert was transported to the well-watered landscapes of Europe and ultimately the New World. It crossed sea as well as land, ultimately finding a home on islands as well as continents. Ironically, the water that surrounded islands enhanced their association with the desert.

The religious significance assigned to the desert by Judaism and later by Christianity had no counterpart in either Greek or Roman culture. For the Greeks everything of significance took place within the polis, the place of human settlement. They found all they needed to orient and inspire themselves within the city walls or in their own cultivated gardens and sacred groves. Scenery and uncultivated nature did not interest the Greeks. Although their gods dwelt atop the bare peaks of mountains like Olympus, they were able to locate their sources of sacredness closer to home.[21] Barren, untamed places, whether they be mountains, the sea, and uninhabited islands, were associated with barbarism.[22] In this very centered society, everything remote was strange and unappealing. They did not seek the wilderness. And when they found themselves on wild islands their first impulse was to return home as quickly as possible.

This tradition was sustained by the Romans, who also regarded the city as the source of all order, the *omphalos* of their world. The countryside belonged to a lower order of things, a place of recreation, a sojourn but not true home. They too preferred formal walled gardens to direct contact with nature. Their empire was a network of cities, a series of sacred centers rather than a continuous territory everywhere invested with special meaning. Like the Greeks, the Romans abhorred the empty and uninhabited: they rarely strayed from the beaten path and had little curiosity about the edges of the world except when they were advancing toward it with their legions. They might be fascinated with the myth of Ultima Thule, but they mounted no concerted effort to locate or settle it.[23] Like the Greeks, they were landlubbers.

Europe owed its fascination with deserts not to the pagan ancients but to the Judeo-Christian tradition. The Jewish people's relationship to the desert had been a long and tortured one. They were not nomads, but their repeated exiles and sojourns in the desert had produced their closest encounters with a divinity who was associated more with heaven than with earth. While the gods of the pagans were associated with specific places, the God of the Jews was at home anywhere and everywhere. His essence was historical rather than geographical.[24] The Israelites were his chosen people, but he made sure they paid for their sins by extended exiles in inhospitable places. It was in the wilderness that he revealed himself to them; and time and again it was the desert that was the source of Jewish trial and redemption.

Beginning as a Jewish sect, Christianity inherited this exilic tradition. Jesus himself had wandered in the wilderness, setting an example for his followers to turn their backs on home and family. For Christians the desert was also the place of both punishment and salvation. As a persecuted minority that refused to acknowledge the pagan gods, Christianity's earliest sacred sites were outside the walls of the Greek and Roman cities. From the earliest days the sacred geography of Christianity was decentered, a series of isolated, one might even say insular sites, in places remote from civilization. Its earliest missionary successes, such as St. Paul's visit to Malta, were insular.[25] As Christianity became more established, it developed by creating what amounted to a series of islands of holiness, bishoprics located in what seemed to the church leaders a sea of paganism.[26] The monastic movement developed in precisely the same archipelagic manner; and cathedrals were also islands, vertical masterpieces, *omphalmi* connecting heaven and earth.[27]

In contrast to Roman civilization, medieval Europe developed in a very decentralized manner. Not only did it have a plethora of sacred centers, but its holiest sites were peripheral, located somewhere to the east.[28] By far the most powerful and mysterious places lay far from home, the reason why travel, including exile, was so central to the attainment of spiritual wisdom and revelation among Christians from the very beginning.[29] The first demonstration of the spiritual attraction of marginal places occurred in the fourth century when the deserts flanking the lower Nile became the locus of an extreme ascetic movement that has come to be known as the desert fathers. These men chose the ordeal of the desert because it offered them an escape from a settled existence burdened with worldly temptations. True to the ideal of the Christian *viator,* these men wished to leave behind the lower material world of women and family to emulate Christ in his journey into the wilderness. Among the desert fathers, travel out from the centers of civilization became travel both up to higher levels of spirituality and back to an uncorrupted world. They devoted themselves to *fuga mundi*—flight from the world—and sought to sever themselves from all human contact in their quest for God.[30]

Eric Hirsch notes that in many religions, holiness is located at the margins, "and it is interesting that sacred sites and places are sometimes physically empty and largely uninhabited, and situated at some distance from the population for which they hold significance."[31] Christian dualism, which made such a sharp separation between heaven and earth, placed the sacred not only above but beyond. The association of distance with transcendence, which is common in many religions, was particularly accentuated, with the result that from the very beginning the faithful were encouraged to leave behind their ordinary lives, including home and family, in order to find spiritual perfection.[32] By the Middle Ages the journey would become the major metaphor for Christian life and even those who never left home came to think of themselves as *viator* moving through time if not through space toward a union with God. It was natural for a transcendental religion that had never been quite at home in the world to valorize movement rather than settlement as holiest of all vocations.

The most extreme of the desert fathers stripped themselves of all worldly things, wandering and perishing as they believed God had willed them to do. They were to be found in caves or perched on pillars, hermits starving and scourging themselves, many dying alone, forgotten by all but their merciless

God. Others formed small monastic colonies where they exhibited their holiness to the curious, ultimately becoming the object of a more organized kind of religious travel, the pilgrimage.[33]

The flight to the desert would wane in subsequent centuries once Christianity became more established and gained an urban base. The church hierarchy continued to be suspicious of hermits and mystics, but could never extinguish the impulse to equate holiness with movement away from the world. Even after Rome was established as its administrative hub, the church continued to look beyond the pale of settlement for collective and personal salvation. Saint Augustine's distinction between the City of God and the City of Man would remain a central tenant of the Christian faith throughout the centuries. Christian otherworldliness found practical expression in the monastic movements, which assigned the highest marks of holiness to the celibate life. It also drove a wedge between the clergy and the laity, the monastery and the parish, and reinforced a difference, already present in the pagan world, between holy men, who could leave the world behind, and impure sessile women, bound to a lower earthly existence.

Fuga Mundi: Flight from the World

As Christianity spread north and west into Europe it had to adapt to a quite new topography. It faced the problem not only of an unfamiliar natural environment, but of a landscape already invested with pagan meaning. The church solved this problem by incorporating some pagan understandings of mountains, trees, and islands into its own sacred landscapes, but it also invested the new terrain with the mythical geography it brought with it from the Near East.[34] In early medieval Europe the forest became the desert. When European Christians took up the ascetic practices of the desert fathers they adopted the impenetrable woods as their hermitage, attaching to it the supernatural meaning of wilderness. In the first centuries of Christianization the forests of Europe were filled with male recluses doing penance for their worldly sins.[35] Many of them were Irish.

The pagan Irish had long used exile as a form of punishment. In a society organized so completely around families, distancing offenders from kin was not only the harshest punishment conceivable but a way of protecting the community itself.[36] A tradition of exiling to islands, landlocked and sea moated, existed both there and in pre-Christian Scandinavia.[37] The early Irish church would adopt exile as a form of punishment for the violation of its laws. Many were sent into exile, while others left home as penance, as a means of purging themselves of their sins. Men were more likely to be punished with exile than women, and in the fourth and fifth centuries Europe was flooded with Irish males who became known as the *peregrini*. The ordeal of going "overseas" was thought more efficacious than exile within Ireland itself. Crossing water symbolized a threshold and the kind of spiritual cleansing the exiles were seeking. It seems that Irishmen often paused on offshore islands before venturing into the interior of England or Europe. Bardsey Island off the St. David peninsula in Wales, where as many as twenty thousand Celtic saints are said to be buried, is famous for having "enjoyed an almost limitless reputation for sanctity." It was even called a second Rome "in virtue of so great a concentration of holiness within so small a compass."[38]

Dozens of islands on the coasts of Ireland, Wales, Normandy, and Scotland eventually acquired similar reputations. Nendrum, now known as Mahee Island in Strangford Lough in Ulster, served as a mission station to Ireland. Today it is an isolated place, but in the fifth and sixth centuries it was connected to Cornwall, France, and even to the Mediterranean.[39] To the list of Irish holy isles must be added Inishmurray, Sula Sgeir, Lindisfarne, Caldy, and Scatley Island at the mouth of the Shannon River. There were similar sanctuaries off the coasts of Brittany, Wales, and Scotland. Some of these existed prior to the founding of inland hermitages, but others served as retreats for established mainland monasteries.[40]

E.G. Bowen writes in his study of Celtic culture that although asceticism in the Eastern Mediterranean was marked by a movement into the desert, in the West it was marked by the creation of innumerable island sanctorium."[41] Initially, coastal islands were simply way stations to the deserts of the European forests. Later, when the papacy cracked down on the *peregrini* because of their undisciplined habits, continental wildernesses became off limits. The penitents returned to Ireland and found another, even more enticing form of exile, this time *in oceano desertum,* the desert of the sea.[42] "At first they were satisfied with little isles in their native lakes and rivers, not far from the monasteries forming the *civitas.* Then they began to retire to numerous islands of the Irish coast, and when these were no longer places of solitude, a voyage in frail boats was to search out some desert isle in the ocean."[43] In what became known as the "white martyrdom," the sea became the spiritual desert, the last refuge of holy wilderness in Europe.

Some of these seaborne penitents simply pushed off from the western shore in small skin boats, trusting to God to do with them what he willed. Destinationless wandering was the ultimate form of pious travel; and those who opted for *fuga mundi* were often bitterly disappointed when their flights from the world, particularly their flight from women and family, failed. A man called Baitan asked Saint Columba for a blessing before setting out to find his desert in the sea. Columba gave his opinion that Baitan would fail and be buried in "a place where a woman would drive sheep over his grave," which turned out to be true. The Abbot of Durrow took to the sea on three separate occasions, becoming known as Cormac of the Sea (*Cormac Leir*) before finally settling down and

Illustration 5   Monks cells and graves on Skellig Michael

becoming known as Saint Cormac. But none was more fascinated with the desert in the sea than Brendan, the abbot of Clonfert in Galway. He apparently launched a series of voyages, for his name is associated with various islands, including Culbrandon, one part of which was known as "the corner or treat of St. Brendan."[44]

Tales of white martyrdom were eagerly consumed and emulated. Of course, the experiences of those who floundered were never recorded, but in time a series of island hermitages came into being. Most were located off the western coasts of Scotland and Ireland, but there is evidence of retreats in the Firth of Forth as well as on isles north of Scotland. Some of these have the names of saints associated with them; and many remained religious sanctuaries for centuries. On one isle an *ermita insulanus* was reported to be living in the twelfth century. As late as the sixteenth century, insular hermits were receiving alms from the Scottish kings.[45]

This new kind of desert father was to leave us a fascinating archeological record. The ruins of tiny beehive huts on now remote uninhabited islands off the coasts of Scotland and Ireland are a testament to their movement. The anchorites populated rocky outcrops like Skellig Michael, where they eked out a solitary existence, living in caves or stone huts, tending tiny gardens and surviving on birds' eggs and fish.[46] At first they refused companionship, but in time they formed small colonies that took on the attributes of monasticism. Initially closed off to the world, they also eventually accepted the visits of pious folk, even women, who brought food to them and regarded them as living saints, believing them to have, like their forest-dwelling forerunners, healing and magical powers.[47]

Of course islands were not for everyone. They initially attracted only those willing to risk encounters with the strange and the unknown in search for God. But more ordinary believers sought out the holy isles when pilgrimage routes to Rome became disrupted. The Scots and Irish were forced to create their own indigenous pilgrim ways, which led westward and involved visits to islands known for their saints and other marvels.[48] Among the stations of the new maritime pilgrim routes were Skellig Michael, the Isle of Aran, St. MacDara's Island, and Inishmurray, some of which were still operating as holy sites into the mid-twentieth century.[49] The anchorites' beehive huts became what Peter Harbison has called the world's "first and oldest bed and breakfast establishments."[50]

Once the original anchorites' retreats became monastic communities, there was no way to stop the increasingly heavy traffic of pilgrims, traders, and wandering scholars who were attracted to the islands. In time, many of the holy isles became like small cities, some of the richest and most sophisticated places to be found anywhere in Europe. Islands like Saint Columbo's Iona were renowned for their arts and learning. From these places flowed missionaries who moved from island to island before taking Christian civilization inland to the British mainland and ultimately to the continent. It was from the island of Lindisfarne on England's east coast that the Irish launched their mission to England.[51]

By the eighth century these holy isles constituted a desert in the sea in name only. They had become worldly, often very powerful communities, with solitaries confined to their farthest edges. In the absence of towns in Ireland, the monasteries were the functional equivalent of cities, although, when a hermitage became a monastery, it reserved some cave or remote beehive hut for solitaries. On Iona these are memorialized in place names like *Cladha-an-Disseart* (Burying Ground of the Desert) or *Port-an-Disseart* (Port of the Desert), but no one would any longer confuse the holy islands with the wilderness.[52] Their wealth was known throughout the Western world, and when the Vikings came looking for plunder in the early eighth century their first targets were holy islands rather than the much poorer mainlands.

Spiritual island hopping and the maritime pilgrimages that followed ultimately extended beyond the coastal waters of Ireland and Scotland, and on to the Faerøe Islands, to Iceland, and, as some would have us believe, even to Greenland and the northern coasts of America. What is certain is that Irish monks led the way in the initial settlement of North Atlantic islands, including

Iceland.[53] By the eighth century what might be called a sea of monastic islands came into existence. These holy isles were in contact with the continent, but also constituted a world of their own, trading among themselves, spreading culture as well as religion. The monks had learned arts of navigation unknown to other Europeans. They created a seaborne world that was rich materially as well as spiritually, one of the reasons they would later attract Viking and other raiders.

The desert in the sea came to an end with the Viking incursions of the eighth century, which expelled the monks from the far islands of the North Atlantic and severely threatened the monastic existence of the Irish and Scottish coasts. The anchorites were once again forced to find a new desert, and this time they turned to inland holy isles, two of which were in Loch Lomond in Scotland, others on Lough Derg and other Irish lakes.[54] The Lough Derg holy isle, ultimately known as Station Island, had originally been associated with a local hermit by the name of Dabhoec, but later, under the careful management of the Augustinian order, became identified with the greatest of all the Irish celebrity saints, Patrick. From the twelfth century onward, Station Island lost all semblance of desertedness to become a classical pilgrimage site.[55] Still, the fact that what became known as St. Patrick's Purgatory was an island in a lake far from anything meant that getting there amounted to a considerable ordeal; and the fact that the purgatorial pilgrimage involved crossing water reinforced the otherworldliness of the place, ensuring its reputation for sacredness up to this very day.

Saint Brendan's Island

Even when the monks pulled back from their outposts in the North Atlantic in the eighth and ninth centuries, the European imagination continued to wander offshore. The islands they left behind lost none of their numinosity; their emptiness only confirmed their reputation as places where, as Claude Kappler notes, "marvels exist for their own sake outside the laws that generally prevail."[56] Holy isles were about to take on a whole new life in the minds of Europeans, especially those who had never been to sea or set foot on an island.

By the eighth century, the *peregrini* had been replaced by the *navigatini* as Christian superheroes. Travel by water was regarded as the ultimate ordeal, adding to voyagers reputation for having special qualities. The pagan Celts had their shamans, whose spiritual visits to otherworldly islands were told in stories called *echtra*. By the eighth century these were being displaced by another kind of voyaging tale, the *immram,* in which the destination was no longer supernatural. They featured heroic men "rowing about" in a real sea filled with islands that belonged to this world rather than to the next. In the Christianized versions of the *immram,* saints replaced warriors as central figures. They went to sea in search of God rather than glory, but they encountered there many of the same monsters and demons that had tested their pagan predecessors. The most famous of these Christian adventure stories, *The Voyage of Saint Brendan,* was "the culmination and high point of the otherworld and voyage tales of the *echtra* and *immrama* types," Peter Harbison writes in *Pilgrimage in Ireland.*[57]

The *Voyage of Saint Brendan* may well have been based on the actual journeys of the sixth-century abbot of Clonfert, who is known to have lived on the west coast of Ireland and roamed the islands seeking his desert in the sea. Within a hundred years of his death, oral tales about him were in circulation, and by the tenth century these were in Latin texts of multiple editions. It may also be that his story, which involved visits to many different islands, reflected the memory of maritime pilgrimages that by then had been disrupted by Viking raiders. By the time the story became text there may even have been a cult of Saint Brendan.[58] In the twelfth century islands named after him would appear in various *mappaemundi* and would remain a feature of European maps for centuries to come. Saint Brendan's islands would make their own journey in the vast empty sea, turning up in various places, at times confused with the Fortunate Isles.[59]

What Brendan's story lacked in geographical detail it more than made up for in its power to evoke that strange mixture of pagan and Christian beliefs that constituted the worldview of the Middle Ages. As we have seen, desert islands were closely associated with the supernatural, with extraordinary events, heroic adventures, and divine revelations, with mythic beginnings and endings. Although no longer physically accessible after the eighth century, these holy isles continued to function on maps and in stories as inspiration for the faithful and as popular entertainment for those who never had any intention of ever going offshore. The fact that they remained unvisited only added to their credibility among believers.

The Voyage of Saint Brendan is the story of a monk's quest for a Promised Land of the Saints reported to exist somewhere to the west of Ireland. Brendan and his companions wander for seven years in an open boat wholly accepting the will of God, knowing that in the end Brendan will return to be buried in the land of his father. The tale recounts many adventures, including landing on Fish Island, which turns out to be the back of a whale, evoking the well-known legends of sea monsters. But many of the islands encountered have monastery-like establishments, suggesting that the story is based on distant memories of pilgrimage routes long since disrupted. But the appeal of the Brendan tale derives as much from its ability to conjure the mythical geography of the Holy Land as to any references to real times and places. The story evokes a biblical temporality and geography that would have been familiar to any believer. The passage of time is marked by holy days (Easter, Christmas,

Illustration 6   Fish Island, Voyage of Saint Brendan, from Caspar Plautius, *Nova Transacta Navigato* (1621)

Pentecost), and all the persons encountered (Paul the Hermit and Judas) are biblical rather than contemporary. The thick description of nature that makes travel literature interesting to us is entirely absent. As one translator of the *Voyage* notes, although the tiny boat encounters some rough seas, "one does not feel the salt spray. . . . [O]ne does not see the scudding clouds or wilt under the pitiless sun. . . . It takes forty days to reach an island, but the reader does not feel them pass."[60]

It is the absence of exact chronologies and precise locations that sets *The Voyage of Saint Brendan* apart from modern travel tales. Nowhere in the account do we get a naturalistic description of the islands themselves. Their shape is invariably symmetrical, circular in the manner of the classical *omphalos*. At one point the voyagers encounter what is described as "The Crystal Pillar," what might appear to us to be an iceberg, but to the medieval reader is a symbol of heaven rather than a natural feature. Because travel outward in space was also travel back in time, anachronisms abound. The islands' flora and fauna are all found in the Bible. The Island of Smiths is easily identifiable as hell; and the Promised Land of Saints has all the stock features of terrestrial paradise.

The purpose of the story is clearly allegorical rather than descriptive. Coming as it does after the maritime pilgrims route had been closed, the *Voyage* is best understood as mental pilgrimage to a mythical geography that had lost none of its appeal for being inaccessible.[61] These were islands that Christian culture lived *by*, not *on*. Geographical description mattered much less than cosmological credibility. Brendan's voyage is not one of discovery, but rather a reassuring journey through a landscape familiar to any informed believer. Although it is a sea voyage to the west, its itinerary is that of the deserts of the Middle East. It removes its audience from the constraints of real time and space to allow them access to biblical times and places. The sites evoked are not those of the Atlantic Ocean but the Sea of Galilee, for Brendan and his shipmates could not but remind the reader of Christ and his disciples crossing troubled waters.[62]

The power of the tale is more memorial than historical or geographical, and any attempt relate it to actual events or places is bound to fail because what we have here is not a physical journey but a mental pilgrimage. Brendan's islands were all the more appealing because they exist outside both time and space, as empty of human history as they were of natural geography. It was this emptiness that allowed the transference of the events and places of the deserts of the Holy Land to the Atlantic. That these were islands that no European had occupied in living memory (perhaps at any time) made them all the more powerful in the minds of Christians.

It is not surprising that Saint Brendan's Isle should be one of the first islands to appear in a medieval *mappaemundi*. It was soon followed by a host of equally legendary islands that gradually filled the previously empty spaces of *Oceanus*.[63] Saint Brendan's Isle was prominently displayed in maps of the time because the *mappaemundi* were meant to illustrate biblical geosophy rather than provide precise locations or directions. Medieval measures were imprecise and numbers were used for their symbolic rather than for their quantitative value. In Brendan's voyages, it takes forty days to reach virtually every location, testifying to their religious significance rather than their exact location.[64] Like the medieval paintings and stories, *mappaemundi* lack a single point of temporal or spatial perspective that would allow the viewer to differentiate between the near and far, or between then and now.[65]

As with the case of medieval painting, the faithful were invited to see the world through God's eye.[66] Medieval cartography was not so much untrue as it was a means of revealing a different kind of truth. As Mary B. Campbell has pointed out, the medieval traveler was more concerned with "the divine and human than with the natural or ecological," accounting for the fact that the features highlighted on *mappaemundi* are "almost always 'places where' someone did or said something." rather than a objective description of space as such.[67] The stories were simultaneously instructive and entertaining. "Wandering survived in literature, though the religious emphasis of the earlier centuries often gave way to entertainment, parody, and poetry," notes Kathleen Hughes.[68]

Legendary Islands of the Western Sea

By the High Middle Ages the once empty western seas were filling up with imagined islands. By then there were very few places on the continent sufficiently isolated to be able to sustain that sense of the *sacra* that had existed there in earlier, more sparsely inhabited centuries. As a consequence, we find the holy and the hellish moving offshore, carried there by the popular media of the age, folk legends and oral tales, but also by the most sophisticated Latin travel stories frequently illustrated by fanciful *mappaemundi*. Celtic lore made major contributions to this process. The eighth-century *Voyage of Bran to the Island of Women* mentions one hundred and fifty isles, while the contemporary *Voyage of Mael Duin* contributed an additional twenty nine. They were full of the most extraordinary creatures, monsters but also female sirens, clearly the projection of fears and desires generated by males who may never gone to sea or set foot on an Atlantic island.[69]

The twelfth century renaissance of classical learning brought back to consciousness the Fortunate Isles and thus lent further credibility to homegrown tales of legendary islands. It was easy enough to substitute Christianity's devils for paganism's demons, and to transpose the attributes of heaven above or Eden itself to the green and pleasant islands pagans thought to exist just beyond the horizon. Locating both paradisical and hellish other worlds at sea was longstanding pagan practice. The Greeks and Romans had imagined their dead heroes at peace on islands to the west of the Pillars of Hercules. The Celts and the Norse also located their dead offshore; and certain islands off the coast of Brittany were associated with dead souls in the pre-Christian period.[70] These islets were near enough not to be forgotten but far enough to prevent unwanted hauntings. The walls of tombs and cemeteries also served to keep ghosts at bay, but water worked even better, providing a convenient threshold between mythical geographies of the living and the dead.[71]

From the twelfth century onward this stock of imagined isles was immensely expanded from an unexpected source, the vast inventory of fabulous isles associated with the mythical geography of the Far East, from the Indian Ocean and from China's seas. Some of these dated back to ancient times, when Alexander the Great's expedition to India brought back tales of exotic and wondrous isles in that region of the world. To these were now added a multitude of islands reported by European travelers to Asia from the twelfth century onward. As trade between Europe and China opened up along the Silk Road and through India, the East again became the locus of European imagination. Marco Polo brought back a muddled account of a great island we now know as Japan, together with reports of some 7,540 other isles, all so fabulously rich that their inhabitants, who occupied grand villas and castles, did not even bother to covet these treasures. The appeal of Polo's tales were immensely amplified by his ghostwriter, Rusticello of Pisa, who was steeped in the literature of medieval chivalric romance in which islands were the location for noble adventures. During the Middle Ages the mythical geographies of the east were relocated to the West. As David Beers Quinn puts it, "new geographical ideas were largely old ideas shifted westward." The fabulous islands that Europe now imagined to lie beyond its shores arrived there "largely through transference, through the exchange of verbal and visual images from an Old World context to the New."[72]

From Polo onward, the realm of the fabulous moved offshore in a decisive manner.[73] In part this was a result of trade connections that opened the lands of Asia and Africa to Europeans, dispelling some of the interiors' more mysterious qualities. As the fourteenth-century Portuguese discovered the Canaries, Madeiras, and then the Azores they divested these isles of their mythic associations with the Fortunate Isles. The West African coast ceased to be a mythical geography, and when Vasco da Gama rounded the Cape of Good Hope and reached India in 1498 the effect was to disenchant the subcontinent. But while exploration demystified some landfalls, it stimulated imaginings of what lay just beyond the horizon. Alvise da Ca do Mosto, a Venetian who sailed for Portugal and helped stake its claim on the Cape Verde isles and the coast of Senegal, convinced himself that he had found earthly paradise at the source of the Senegal River.[74] However, it was islands that lent themselves most readily to paradisical imagery, and even if the Canaries and the Madeiras proved not to be places of peace and plenty, new blessed isles appeared elsewhere, moving, like Saint Brendan's Isle, to yet another point in the great empty sea, always just beyond the horizon.

Islands became the destination for knights-errant from the Arthurian legends onward. In the late Middle Ages there was less and less room for feudal heroics on land, so islands in the far sea became places where fame and wealth might still be attained. In an era of monarchical consolidation within Europe itself, it was much easier to imagine oneself as king of the isles than as a continental sovereign. Dom Henrique Bethencourt, the self-styled king of Canaries, was known as the Tristram of the Island. In 1499, another islomane, Pedro Gomez du Coninha, the grantee of the island of São Tomé off the coast of Guinea, announced his intention of turning it into a city to rival the glories of Rome.[75] King John II of Portugal was only too happy to feed the fantasies of his landless nobles by doling out fiefs on yet undiscovered islands. Don Quixote offered the Island of Baratania to Sancho Panza in return for his loyalty.

Europe's Insular Moment

If voyagers could not find the islands mentioned on late medieval and Renaissance *mappaemundi* it was simply assumed that they were temporarily lost in the vast ocean space rather than nonexistent. It has been noted that "the death of an unwanted island was a lingering one," and it took the Isle of Saint Brendan some thirteen centuries to disappear from the sea charts.[76] In the absence of reliable longitudes and latitudes, islands could not be given a fixed location; one effect, Denis Cosgrove writes, is that their "geographical indeterminancy also increased their imaginative resonance."[77] No matter how many islands might be discovered, there was always the farthest island, Ultima Thule, to dream about and to think with.

By the fourteenth and fifteenth centuries the interiors of Europe were being mapped with somewhat greater precision. But if geography was about to take on new life on the continent, geosophy had its renaissance offshore. While portolan charts gave ever great definition to coasts, the empty ocean remained open to speculation. Everything unknown was imagined to be an island; and by the late Middle Ages the *mappaemundi* illustrating one great earth island had to compete with a new kind of cartography that concentrated exclusively on offshore islands. Known as *isolario,* these island books were produced in large numbers in Venice, itself a city built on islands with an island empire stretching across the Mediterranean.[78]

The *isolario* were not meant for navigational purposes. P. D. A. Harvey described them as a "disorderly mixture of fact, fiction, and fantasy, compiled from personal observation, hearsay, and a variety of historical sources."[79] Islands were depicted as qualitatively different from mainlands, and, while they no longer belonged to the otherworld, they retained elements of the supernatural that made them all the more intriguing to contemporaries. By the fifteenth century, islands had attained a special place in the European imagination, a fact reflected in the phenomenal popularity of the *isolario.*[80] Of all the various land forms available to meditation, islands were regarded as the best to think with.

We equate insularity with narrowness and constriction, but the Renaissance found it exciting, indeed liberating—an exit from the totalizing cosmology of the Middle Ages in which there had been little room for the appreciation of variation and difference.[81] Islands, previously seen as inferior fragments of earth island, were now perceived as complete in themselves, alternative worlds of their own. Insularity thus provided a space for the expression of the kind of questioning of received truth that was now stirring within Renaissance culture. The *isolario* gave free play to the impulse to imagine worlds different from anything that had ever been known before. Until the Enlightenment positioned islands within the realm of nature, insularity gave free reign to European subjectivity.[82]

In many ways this was a continuation of medieval geosophy. Now, however, one earth island was insufficient to represent different views of the world that jostled one another in Europe's geographical imaginary. One great macrocosm was replaced by many different microcosms. In the *isolario* each island was depicted as a world of its own, onto which could be projected any of the diverse desires and fears that were being generated within Europe itself. Islands of seductive women appeared alongside islands of devils. The *isolario* allowed Europeans to think of the world as much more heterogeneous than the one represented on the old *mappaemundi*.[83]

By the year 1400, islands had become the favored ways of representing and knowing the world at large. The image of the sea as a desert did not disappear immediately. A rising tide of Christian millenarianism in the fifteenth and sixteenth centuries reinvigorated biblical geosophy. Mythical geography now had a new lease on life, even as Europeans came to know the world better than ever before. Discovery of new islands took on enhanced significance as signs that the Second Coming was close at hand. It was with the understanding that the end was near that Columbus set off westward in 1492 into what he was sure was a sea of islands stretching from Europe to Asia. His voyage was no *fuga mundi*, no escape from the world, but an effort to reconnect *Orbis Terrarum*'s eastern and western shores, thus bringing closer the end time as foretold in Revelation. Each island he encountered strengthened his faith that the moment was near when the earth would once again be made whole and the threatening sea would be no more.[84]

CHAPTER 3

ISLANDS AS MENTAL STEPPING-STONES
IN THE AGE OF DISCOVERY

Fictions are the bridges for discovering facts.

—Dora Beale Polk, *The Island of California: A History of the Myth*

LONG BEFORE EUROPEANS DARED STRAY BEYOND SIGHT OF LAND, they were imagining an ocean they had never sailed, filled with islands they had never seen. The movement of the mind always prepares the way for the movement of the body. John Allen tells us that "no exploratory venture begins without objectives based on the imagined nature and content of the lands to be explored."[1] The European Age of Discovery in the fifteenth and sixteenth centuries was founded almost entirely on illusions that had been nurtured over hundreds of years by landlocked people who had no real knowledge of what lay beyond the edge of their world. Valerie Flint tells us that the "most apparently fantastic of Columbus' ideas were *precisely* the ones which allowed him to make the most important of his real discoveries."[2]

For centuries Europeans had been so fascinated with that which lay beyond their shores that they had become convinced that they knew as much about the ocean and its islands as they did about places on the mainlands.[3] By the fifteenth century their mythical geography had indeed become their reality. What had once been an oceanic void had by that time been filled with islands. Thus, as explorers set out on the high seas they were venturing not into some great unknown, but into a space with which they were all too familiar. The challenge for Europeans was to defamiliarize what they found so as to come to grips with the true nature of the worlds they were encountering.

When Europeans began to explore it was not with the intention of discovering new worlds but of recovering old ones. As far as they were concerned, the old world consisted entirely of islands, the great earth island and its vast eastern and western archipelagos. Setting off with the expectations of finding a world of islands, Europeans believed all the lands they encountered to be insular. So powerful was their islomania that it would be a very long time before they grasped the fact that they had inadvertently found not one sea but several and that some of the lands found were not islands but continents. As long as Europeans persisted in thinking about the world archipelagically, they were bound to find only islands.

Today's explorers are always looking for something new, something previously unknown. They are supposed to be the first to find, the first to know. But this was not the case in the fourteenth and fifteenth centuries. The very idea of something new was unthinkable at the time. The ancients had no concept of discovery because they thought they lived in a finite, eternal world that contained all that which had been or ever could be known. That which they did not know was simply temporarily lost and ultimately retrievable. People of the Middle Ages also operated within a temporal and spatial framework in which nothing was wholly unknown. In the fifteenth and sixteenth centuries discovery still meant to "uncover," "disclose," or "reveal"—what today we would call recovery.[4]

Exploration did not involve looking for something new, but of searching for what was already known. When the ancients used the term "new world" they did not mean what we now mean. The Romans believed that Ultima Thule, the "farthest island," was such a place, but it held out the promise of renewal rather than a wholly new start. For medieval voyagers, travel out meant travel back. Lacking the modern notion of progress, in which the past is constantly transcended, they could conceive of the new only in terms of the old. This view would persist long after contact with the Americas. David Beers Quinn reminds us to "remember that the New World was strange before it was entirely new." It would be thirty years after Columbus before the term "new world" took hold, and longer still before its flora, fauna, and peoples began to be understood on their own terms. For centuries, Europeans would try to assimilate what they found in the Americas and Australia to what they were familiar with back home.[5]

Neither the Norse nor Columbus were out to find the continents that we now know as the Americas because the very idea of a continent was unknown at the time.[6] We do a grave disservice to history when we endow medieval and Renaissance voyagers with modern intentions. They belong to an era of philosophical rather than scientific exploration during which the object was not to observe nature with the intention of opening up new knowledge but to penetrate the veil of appearances to recover deeper, eternal truths.[7] The enterprise the voyagers embarked on is better described a *quest,* defined by Geoffrey Ashe as something "more profound than a search. It is a spiritual adventure."[8] A quest is as much a mental as a physical act, and, though often associated with movement, it was not so much the actual distance traveled but the cognitive and psychological experience that really mattered. A quest involves a journey of mind and spirit "to and often beyond the boundaries of human experience."[9] Discovery of the new can be a consequence of the quest, but it is not its original intention.

When the Irish monks set off to sea to escape from the world, they established a precedent for waterborne quests that would persist for the next thousand years and more. Though we honor Columbus for his "discovery" of the material reality we call the New World, he was not a modern explorer. His was not a scientific expedition, but a spiritual quest. As part of a long line of inspired Christian *viator,* Columbus was, as Pauline Moffatt Watts puts it, "journeying through time and space of a tainted cosmos in search of a redemption that would occur with the termination of that cosmos."[10] He was voyaging in what he thought to be a finite universe of space and time, a world that he believed to be quite small and in a time span that he was convinced was very short. He had no attention of opening up vast new lands or initiating a new era in human history. Quite the contrary, this late medieval man believed that each step of his journey brought mankind and the earth closer to the end time described in Scripture. Columbus's initial motivation was not conquest, for the object of the first voyages was commercial trade with Asia. Columbus was not venturing into empty spaces, but on a sea that was believed to be immensely full of islands that would make excellent trading posts with the mainlands of the easternmost parts of the Old World.[11] His ambitions would grow over time, and, in the end, everything he touched would be transformed beyond recognition. But this was a consequence, not the motivation, of his westward journey.

The Raging River Becomes a Navigable Sea

Before Europeans could venture westward, the waters to the west had to be reimagined as something other than a limitless river encircling and constantly threatening earth island. The ancients had no concept of a far shore of *Oceanus.* They feared venturing into a place that provided no landfalls, no sure points of departure or return. Latin Europeans continued to regard *Oceanus* with enormous dread, while the Norse, whose name for the raging river was *Uthaf,* were equally wary even after they managed to sail all the way to Newfoundland around the year 1000 A.D. It was not until the fourteenth and fifteenth centuries that what had become known by that time as the Western Sea could be imagined as something bounded, as something that could be crossed.

By that time the notion of a spherical world had been accepted, but as long as there was a void between the western and eastern edges of earth island transit seemed impossible. Ptolemaic maps, reconstructed in the fourteenth century, added to the uncertainly by leaving so much of the intervening space empty. The recovery of ancient geography meant that some parts of the world were better mapped than before, but the Ptolemaic globe was three-quarters vacant, a kind of vacuum that gave new life to speculation and a reinvigoration of cosmography but added little to empirical geography. The cosmographers, says Frank Lestringant, were "free to inscribe on it [the globe] the delimitation of new invented or discovered lands; a form, at once closed and open, full and lacunary, that represented the ideal construction in which to house, with their approximate and disparate localizations, the 'bits' of space that navigators brought back from their distant voyages."[12] It would be a very long time before either the interiors of large landmasses or the seas themselves would be well enough known to release them from the grip of human imagination.

Vacuity invited intense islomania; and it was this that filled the waters with innumerable islands, lessening the fears of the void had prevented ordinary Europeans from venturing offshore. Seas had to be reimagined before they could be crossed; and they had to be renamed before men dared venture there. But by the fifteenth century fear was being displaced by certainty. As James Hamilton-Paterson describes it, Europe was by then gripped by "an anxious desire to frame a linked and archaic series of voids into distinguishable oceans."[13] Just as calling the open spaces of Australian "plains" and the grasslands of the North American "prairies" would later give settlers the courage to enter them, reimagining *Oceanus* as a bounded space, a sea rather than a river, created desire where only fear had existed before.[14] Even when the far shore was beyond the horizon, even when it was only in the mind of the voyager and not yet found on any chart, the mental boundary was sufficient to calm fears and inspire voyages. Nothing had changed in the nature of the waters themselves. The new seas were every bit as wild and deadly as the great river *Oceanus,* but, once the idea of bounded waters filled with innumerable islands was in place, the way for intrepid voyagers was open.

The Romans became comfortable with the Mediterranean once they defined it as *mare nostrum* (our sea), imagining it to be a relatively calm bay, bounded by lands on three sides, its opening protected by the Pillars of Hercules. Before the Norse could begin their remarkable voyages westward in the tenth century they had constructed their own *mare nostrum* as another great bay, extending from the Norwegian coast to what we would now call Baffin Island, Labrador, and Newfoundland. Yet this was not so much a geographical as a cosmological breakthrough, for the great accomplishment of the Norse was extend the boundaries of earth island, to reshape the old world in such a way as to encourage exploration. The Norse did not so much break the bounds of earth island as enlarge it in such a way that it made them feel safe when out of sight of land.

Illustration 7   Skalholt Map by Bishop Thordu Thorkaksson, 1670

They came to understand the North Atlantic as their *mare nostrum* by imagining it as an enclosed space, protected to the north by an extension of the Norwegian coast and to the south by the northern horn of Africa. In an Icelandic manuscript dating from about 1300, based on a twelfth century original, we are given a Norse geography lesson in which a great peninsula extends from Norway down to Greenland. "To the south of Greenland lies Helluland and then Markland; and from there it is not far to Vinland, which some people think extends to Africa."[15] The Norse retained the idea of a great river, which they called *Uthaf*, circling earth island, but they felt protected against it by the landmasses which enclosed the great bay. Guarded by Greenland to the north and Vinland to the south, and effectively plugged by two islands, Helluland (Baffin Island) and Markland (Labrador), the Norse version of *mare nostrum* felt sufficiently safe to encourage feats of navigation which seem terribly dangerous when traced on modern maps. It is only when we consider Norse mythical geography that we can grasp false assumptions that lay behind their extraordinary achievements before and after the year 1000 A.D.

The pagan Norse were no less anxious about the sea than were other Europeans.[16] They had their own stock of monsters and demons, but they sailed on waters that were free of the holy and hellish islands of biblical geography.[17] The sagas include mythical creatures that come from both ancient and Christian traditions, but these were composed only after the Viking conversion to Christianity.[18] Even then Norse voyagers seem to have been more interested in the natural rather than the supernatural features of the regions they visited. In contrast to tales like the Brendan voyage, the Norse sagas focus on scenic features, indifferent to the symbolism that so fascinated the Christian reader. They are full of practical information about safe harbors, stands of timber, grazing lands, and the sweetness of the Vinland morning dew, things that held no interest for monks but were of great importance to Norse farmer/seafarers.

But the Norse were infected with their own strain of islomania. Islands, imagined as well as real, provided them with bridges across troubled waters. Their mental maps were full of such places, and their cartographers wrote: "England and Scotland are one island, but are separate kingdoms. Ireland is a large island. Iceland is also a large island, to the north of Ireland. These islands are all in that part of the world called Europe."[19] And Europe itself was an island or rather a part of an island large enough to engulf and protect the smaller isles belonging to it. It was the notion of surrounding coasts that gave the Norse the courage to venture as far as they did, but they also took comfort from the islands that constituted a barrier between them and the vast *Uthaf*.[20]

The Norse stayed within what they imagined to be a great sheltering bay filled with familiar islands, "all part of the world called Europe." They stopped at what they thought was the edge of the world. Their stay on Newfoundland was brief, and by the fourteenth century they had abandoned Greenland as well, retreating to the safety of the one great island, Iceland, where they felt completely safe. Despite the fact that they voyaged farther than any other Europeans, their ventures confirmed rather than overturned existing geosophies. In this respect it can be said that they were the most accomplished explorers of an old world rather than discoverers of a new one.

It was other Europeans, influenced by the notion of the world as a sphere, who came to reimagine the river as a sea bounded by the western and eastern edges of *Orbis Terrarum.* The notion of the round planet, never quite lost even in the Middle Ages, became the object of intense speculation, with much debate about the distances between the western and eastern edges of island earth.[21] Once the world was conceived of as a sphere it became possible to imagine reaching the east by going west, though it would be a very long time before anyone would dare to act on that untested idea. What was required for that to happen was something to bridge the void between Europe and Asia, and that something turned out to be the mythical islands that proliferated in the later Middle Ages and the early Renaissance; these served, as James Hamilton-Paterson writes, "to blot up an excessive of vacancy, until something more solid turned up."[22]

It took still longer for that something—new continents—to be recognized for what it was. The notion of a single earth island, consisting of three parts, did not dissolve into the idea of separate continents until the sixteenth century; and it was not until the nineteenth century that the interiors of these large landmasses were sufficiently known to dispel the idea that they were archipelagic. Beginning in the Middle Ages and lasting through the eighteenth century, islands were to carry the cognitive and psychological burden of bridging a sea that still seemed alien and threatening to most Europeans.

Fictions as Bridges

Earlier, when those preeminent seafarers the Phoenicians and the Carthaginians had roved the seas, there had been little room for fictions. They almost certainly knew the Canaries, which are close enough to be seen from North Africa, but they may also have made contact with the Madeiras and Azores.[23] It is probable that the Phoenicians exaggerated the dangers of the sea in order to ward off rivals; and the Greeks and Romans made no efforts at verification, content to pass on legends of Fortunate Isles and the Islands of the Blest to posterity.[24] By 1400 what had become the Western Sea was filled to the brim with imagined islands, some centuries old but most of much more recent origins. To the old stock of pagan and Christian legendary isles had been added a host of new islands, many of them imported from the Far East. As David Beers Quinn has noted, "new geographical ideas were largely old ideas shifted westward."[25]

The loss of ancient learning during the Middle Ages only intensified speculation, opening up a blank space onto which all kinds of fantasies could be projected. The ancients had always projected the strange and the fantastic to periphery, beyond the edge of the known world, and the Middle Ages, influenced by Celtic myths as well as by classical legends, only accelerated this tendency.[26]

Placing the strange and monstrous beyond the pale made life at home seem safer.[27] Thus, as plagues and peasant revolts made life in late medieval Europe more fraught, there was a tendency to project outward both all that which was feared as well as all that which was desired.

In the fourteenth and fifteenth centuries ancient visions of the Fortunate Isles jostled for position with newer fictions like the Isles of Saint Brendan. The latter had appeared either as an archipelago or as a single island on maps from the High Middle Ages onward. Initially thought to be off the west coast of Ireland, it appeared on Bartholemeo Pareto's map of 1455 on the latitude of Portugal, north of Canaries and Madeiras, which were still marked as the Fortunate Isles. Once the Azores were explored, the Isle of Saint Brendan moved west.[28] By that time the myth of the Fortunate Isles was fading, and the introduction of slave labor stripped the Canaries and Madeiras of any association with blessedness. As one historian of these imaginary isles has put it: "Familiarity bred disallusionment. Islands abounding in marvels would have to be sought further out at sea."[29] Ultimately, the Isles of Saint Brendan moved again, this time north, where in the sixteenth century they came to rest just off the coast of Newfoundland. The isles were still being searched for there in the eighteenth century.[30]

The notion of roving islands was not at all strange in an era that had few fixed coordinates of either time or space. Space was perceived in the fifteenth century as heterogeneous rather than uniform, fluid rather than fixed. According to biblical geology the earth was alive; and, like the rest of nature, geography was animated, so that the idea of islands moving about was by no means as strange to contemporaries as it seems to us. "The strange, the fantastic, and the unreal were familiar and to that extent real," according to Quinn.[31] The association of islands with movement was already established in ancient accounts of Ultima Thule, which had been reported to be to the north of Britain by Pytheas the Greek in the fourth century B.C. Though other ancient geographers expressed doubts about its existence, Ultima Thule became for the Romans a kind of outer limit, and so, as each new island was discovered, it moved farther beyond the horizon of exploration. Ultima Thule also came to be associated with new worlds that would appear at the end of time. According to Seneca's famous prophecy, it would disappear with the temporal ultimate: "There will come an age in the far-off yearswhen Ocean shall unloose the bonds of things, when the whole broad earth shall be revealed, when Tethys shall disclose new worlds and Thule not be the limit of the lands."[32]

Biblical geography held a similar view of the end time, when the sea would disappear and islands would reunite with mainlands; and so Ultima Thule continued to hover at the edge of earth island, changing position each time voyagers pushed the boundary of the known world farther north or west. In Roman times it was associated with the Shetlands and Faerøes. By the early Middle Ages it had moved northeast again, becoming associated with Iceland. But when that island was brought into the orbit of the familiar, the ultimate island moved still further west, first to Greenland and then to Vinland, picking up an association with evergreen forests.

Thule's peregrinations continued in the later Middle Ages, when it became confused with one of the fabulous evergreen islands that had been reported to exist in the Indian Ocean, the Isle of Tylis. As there was no notion of continents lying between Asia and Europe there was nothing to hinder its movement east and south, and Ultima Thule ended up at the latitude of Gibralter located closer to Asia than to Europe. "Thule was always the next place," Robert Fuson notes, and in its last incarnation on maps it appeared as one of islands off the coast of Asia.[33] It was only when the American continents came into focus that Thule ceased to be the imagined marker of outer limits and disappeared from the West's mental maps, thus indirectly confirming Seneca's prophecy that in some "far-off years," when a new world stood revealed, it would no longer serve its function as an outer limit.[34]

Another legendary isle that changed its position was Hy-Brazil, which began its career off the coast of Ireland in Celtic legend in sixth century. In Gaelic its name meant Isle of the Blest; and over time it took on the coloration of both pagan and Christian mythology. In a chart of 1325, Hy-Brazil appears as perfectly round, though divided down the middle, a shape it would keep throughout its long history. It loomed particularly large in the fifteenth century, when Bristol sailors made a concerted search for it. Failure to locate Hy-Brazil did not diminish its luminosity, however; the failure only pushed the search farther to the west and north, where searches continued right up through the seventeenth century.[35] Hy-Brazil eventually came home to the Irish coast, where it remained on some charts until the 1870s. Even after it no longer existed on any map, sightings were still reported. T. J. Westropp, an Irish observer, was convinced he had seen it three times: "Just as the sun went down, a dark island suddenly appeared far out at sea, but not on the horizon. It had two hills, one wooded; between them, from a low plain, rose towers and curls of smoke." There still exists a Brazil Rock off Cape Sable, Nova Scotia.[36]

But the strangest voyage of all was that of the Island of the Seven Cities, also known as Antilia. Medieval legend told of seven bishops who, escaping the Islamic invasion of Spain in the eighth century, had found an island to the west where they had established seven fabulously rich cities. Antilia first appeared on a Venetian chart in 1424, and was sufficiently believable to trigger several Portuguese and English expeditions. It came to loom very large in the mental maps of those who thought a westward passage to Asia possible. Toscanelli believed it to be a stepping-stone to Asia; based on his speculations, Columbus made it one of his intended stopping places in 1492.[37] After that it moved from its midocean position to become identified with the islands of the West Indies, where it got ever smaller. But before it disappeared entirely from the maps it lent its name to a part of the Caribbean archipelago.[38]

But that was not the end of the story. In the early sixteenth century, the search for the fabulous Seven Cities moved inland, inspiring expeditions in the 1530s by Hernán Cortéz along the western coast of Mexico. Although nothing was found, Cortez named the peninsula now known as Baja "California" after a legendary island of Amazonian black women said to be rich with gold. This was the origin of the legend of the Island of California, which was to persist long after the search for the Seven Cities was called off.[39] Even after it was proved that California was really part of the mainland, mapmakers insisted on depicting it as a paradisical island. The Spanish believed they had found there a version of the Islands of the Blest. Sir Francis Drake also mistook it for an island, naming it New Albion, and until the mid-eighteenth century the Island of California remained on the sea charts. Even today the name still evokes fantasies of a place apart, graced with abundance and pleasure.[40]

Ultimately the image of paradisical islands would move westward, coming to rest by the eighteenth and nineteenth centuries in the South Seas. Yet this did not clear the Atlantic of its accumulation of legendary islands because, even as exploration proceeded, legendary islands multiplied. Ironically, discovery of new lands had the effect of expanding the frontiers of mythical geography. As Donald Johnson has put it, "it was when the geography of tradition gave way to the geography of observation [that] the phantom islands reached their highest form of cartographical expression."[41]

The Expansion of Terra Incognita

The history of exploration suggests that discovery has the paradoxical effect of expanding the sphere of the unknown. As John Kirtland Wright asserted many years ago: "Though the ages men have been drawn to unknown regions by Siren voices, echoes of which ring in our ears today when on modern maps we see spaces labeled 'unexplored,' rivers shown by broken lines, islands marked 'existence doubtful.'"[42] It is the "unknown island" that excites Jose Saramago's fictional voyager. Despite the skepticism he meets at every turn, he remains undeterred in his quest, exhibiting a passion that reminds us of all the Irish monks and Italian mariners who had preceded him.[43] Wright noted that "the most fascinating *terrae incognitae* of all are those that lie within the minds and hearts of men."[44] And no places have had a longer or more intense relationship with the unknown than have islands.

The sixteenth century added a whole raft of yet unknown islands to North Atlantic charts; Mercator's map of 1569 alone added five.[45] Some conformed to the dream of the Fortunate Isles, places of peace and plenty. But others, like Santanzes (Hand of Satan), a large island thought to lie north of Antilia, expressed the darker side of Europe's islomania. While many islands were imagined as sirens, luring sailors to their shores, the Santanzes were believed capable of reaching up to seize passing ships. An Isle of Demons was also reported in the Atlantic in 1555, finding a variety of locations before it finally disappeared in later centuries.[46] The Galapagos were named the Las Encantadas, the enchanted isles, by the Spanish. A reputation for cursedness clung to them well into the nineteenth century, when Herman Melville, visiting them in the 1840s, described them as "evilly enchanted."[47]

The failure to find the legendary islands, blessed or cursed, shown on early maps in no way diminished the urge to seed the empty sea with new ones. Frobisher claimed to have found Buss Island in 1578, and it was searched for as late as 1934.[48] We can add to this list Frislandia, Green Island, Estolandia, Mayda, Jaquet, Fonseca, the Los Jardines, and many more. Several were still on the British Admiralty charts of 1807, though each had gotten smaller over time. The history of these "lost islands" always seems to follow the same pattern. First they appear just over the horizon, growing in size and significance in the first stages of exploration, then moving to the periphery, shrinking and roving from one place to another before finally disappearing from maps, if not from minds.[49]

This was the fate of the Isles of Saint Brendan, which, when exploration opened up the Atlantic, initially migrated all the way to Newfoundland's Bonavista Bay, finally ending up in the marshes on the coasts of South America.[50] There still exist places called Sanborandon which, being both Edenic and inaccessible, keep alive today the myth of the Promised Land of Saints.[51] In the Middle Ages and the Renaissance, the fact that a place was unknown enhanced rather than diminished its reality in the minds of contemporaries. After all, they inhabited a world in which the greatest of all realities, God, was unknown and unknowable. In an age less attached to material things, illusions and fantasies took on a much greater reality than they do in our own.

Europeans filled their maps with unknown islands, betting that they would surely turn up some day. Apart from the detailed *portolan* that sailors depended on to navigate coastal waters, medieval *mappaemundi* were not for finding specific locations, but for confirming the truth of biblical geography. The theme of loss was familiar to Christians, who believed the earth had been degenerating since the Fall and the Flood, and was now losing more and more lands to the encroaching sea. Islands were the emblematic lost lands, and a confirmation of the truth of biblical geography. Henry Strommel, who has documented the numerous "lost" islands that remained on the charts long after the search for them has ended, notes that "remote or uncharted islands have exercised a peculiar fascination over the imagination."[52]

But in a world that was perceived as finite and static, nothing was ever really gone, only temporarily displaced. All those islands and peoples who had been scattered by the Flood existed somewhere in the distant present when they would all be gathered together again as promised in Revelation. Thus, as the biblical end time neared, the significance of islands loomed ever larger in the minds of Christians. No one attached more importance to them than Columbus, however. Without those islands in the near Atlantic that he knew so well, he would never have acquired his skills as master mariner. But of ever greater import were those islands he did not know. They were what lured him westward.

Islands in the Mind of Columbus

Columbus's mental world was a mix of Christian and classical elements.[53] His Biblical geography located the navel of the world at Jerusalem, for throughout the Middle Ages the European cosmographical imagination was oriented almost exclusively to the east, the site of Christianity's holiest places, including Eden as well as the Holy City. The East was also the preferred location of biblical beginnings and endings. There was located the place of Genesis and the forces of the Apocalypse, Gog and Magog. But with the closure of the eastern Mediterranean by the Turks in 1453, access to both sacred place and time was cut off. Now, for the first time, speculation turned west. "The roundness of the earth was the knowledge by which Christendom began to revive the pagan idea of the west," writes Loren Baritz, "though the east lingered as a place while the west, for the Catholic nations, became mere direction."[54] Columbus's vision of a westward route focused exclusively on the Far East. Neither he, nor any other explorer, had any notion of the west as a place lying somewhere between the two edges of earth island.

A desire to recapture Jerusalem and to hasten the Second Coming of Christ had obsessed late medieval and Renaissance millenarians like Joachim of Fiore. But now that the Holy Land was cut off by the Turks, millenarian hopes were directed increasingly westward, especially to China and the Indies, where the resources for reconquest might be acquired. The desire to reopen trade with Asia by water had already engaged the Portuguese in an exploration of the African coast and would ultimately take Vasco da Gama around the Cape to India. The westward passage looked the riskier enterprise, and it was only through almost fanatical persistence that Columbus managed to gain the support of the Spanish monarchs. He did not promise them discovery of a new world but rather a re-

covery of access to the old world.[55] Columbus could imagine no other destination but the far side of earth island, no worlds but the old world. It would be a
very long time before anyone would conceive of new continents or plural seas.[56]

But Columbus was not only a space explorer; he was a time traveler. Going
west had always been associated in pagan minds with going back to some more
primordial past. In Christian geography west also came to stand for new beginnings and the chance to recover that which had been lost through the Fall and
the Flood. Columbus had been deeply influenced by late medieval millenarianism and believed the Second Coming to be close at hand, and, like all Christian
viator, he was on a sacred journey, one that would take him not only to the ends
of the earth but to the end of time itself. As told in Revelation and reiterated by
Saint Augustine, islands, the symbols of the fallen condition of the earth and
mankind, would play a crucial role in this divinely ordained drama. The final
days would be brought near when all the lost islands of the world were found
and their peoples converted to Christianity. Augustine had written: "God will
prevail, it is said, against them and wipe out all the gods of the peoples of the
earth, and they will adore him, each one from their own place, all the peoples
of the islands. And indeed, not only the peoples of the islands, but the universal orb of the earth."[57]

Having read Marco Polo's account of a vast archipelago of more than seven
thousand islands stretching eastward from the coast of China and the Indies,
Columbus was well aware of the immensity of this task. Yet it only seemed to
amplify his millenarian vision. The legendary wealth of these isles would also
allow the fulfillment of the long-standing dream of the recapture of Jerusalem,
another step toward the Second Coming. Dreams of treasure mingled in
Columbus's mind with a passion for conversion. Above all, Pauline Moffatt
Watts argues, he saw himself on a divine mission and sincerely believed that the
final stages of "the journey of the *viator,* which had begun in the deserts of the
Old Testament prophets, was surely almost over."[58]

It is certain that Columbus knew the legends of Antilia and Saint Brendan,
and accepted the archipelagos described by Polo as a reality. He also believed in
all the fabulous islands mentioned in the Bible—Tarshish, Carthyr, and Ophyr.[59]
Together, these provided a mental bridge across the expanse of the sea. Mandeville's entirely fictive and Marco Polo's highly imaginative accounts of Asian archipelagos created a mental bridge between the two edges of earth island. Because
the distance between Europe and Asia was already vastly underestimated in the
late-fifteenth-century maps by Toscanelli and Behaim, those who ventured westward believed that they might easily island hop to the riches of Asia, picking up
not only trading partners but converts along the way. And true to these predic-
tions, Columbus's first landfall was an island, leading him to believe that he had

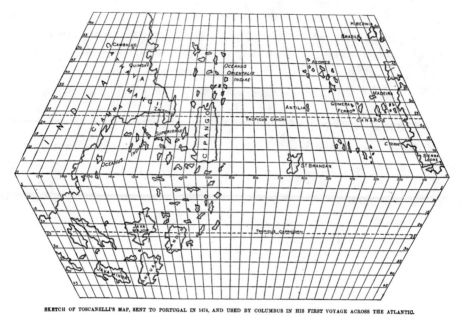

SKETCH OF TOSCANELLI'S MAP, SENT TO PORTUGAL IN 1474, AND USED BY COLUMBUS IN HIS FIRST VOYAGE ACROSS THE ATLANTIC.

Illustration 8   Reconstruction of Toscanelli's Map of 1474

reached the periphery of the Indies, a conviction that he was never to relinquish and that accounts for the name of the Caribbean archipelago.

The actual maps that Columbus carried with him have been lost, but we know that his own mental map was so full of islands that he could never view the Americas as anything but insular. Everything he encountered was interpreted in terms of what was already known. Upon encountering Hispaniola, he proclaimed: "This island is Tarsis, is Cythia, is Ophir and Ophas and Chipango, and we named it Espanola."[60] He paid little attention to the geographical particulars of the islands, but assimilated all, regardless of size and shape, to existing stock of legendary isles. Early maps of the islands portray them in geometric shapes, often rounded off to the circular forms that had always been associated with the insular. It would be centuries before fact would displace fantasy, and even today this mythical geography has not been entirely displaced.

Nor was Columbus any more attentive to the natural features of the world he had stumbled upon. He tended to assimilate everything to the categories of European flora and fauna, emphasizing similarity and ignoring difference. Like all men of his day, Columbus was wholly theocentric, believing nature to be merely an instrument of divine will without a purpose or history of its own. God caused volcanoes to erupt, waters to rise, and islands to emerge and disappear in mysterious ways. He had created the earth as a stage for the working out of the human drama, but its features were, according to Leonardo Olschki, no more than "an accessory element of the narrative, being merely a frame for human life, activity, and events."[61] Islands took their special significance and interest not from their natural features, but from the fact that they were places where divinely inspired events had or would happen. The strangeness of the Americas did not prompt Columbus to observe more carefully, but rather to speculate more grandly. It only reinforced his conviction that he had arrived in a special place at a propitious time. In effect, islands provided him with a stage on which to enact his predestined role as the messenger of the millennium.

Noting how difficult it was to persuade Columbus to change his mind about what he had encountered, the Spanish clergyman Las Casas said of him: "How marvelous a thing it is how whatever a man strongly desires and has firmly set in his imagination, all that he hears and sees at each step he fancies to be in his favor."[62] Columbus was not alone in his belief that he had reached the eastern margins of earth island. During his first three voyages he set foot only on islands and never fully explored the mainlands of Central America, which he encountered only on his last visit. It would take decades before those who followed convinced themselves that what they were encountering was truly a New World, and even then they would depict it through old-world lenses.[63] Not until the eighteenth century did cartographers finally agree that the Americas were wholly separate from Asia. And so it took a very long time for earth island to dissolve into continents. And even when the mainland was finally reached and colonized, the Americas continued to be thought of as a vast archipelago, passage through which would surely lead to Asia.

It is said that Columbus discovered America, when in fact he never acknowledged the existence of a new landmass apart from earth island. Of course, the discovery of continents was not his object in the first place. Columbus's recovery of islands was sufficient to bring him fame among his contemporaries, and he chose to place golden islands on his coat of arms as a symbol of his accomplishment. Yet in one very important respect Columbus was convinced that he had reached a new world, as much a feat of time as space travel. He felt confident in declaring himself to be the discoverer a "new heaven and a new earth" because according to his biblical geography the end of the earth was associated with the end of time. By crossing the sea to recover lost peoples and lost islands for Christianity, he believed he had played a special role in bringing the Second Coming closer. Now that the islands had been reclaimed, the earth would again become whole, and the seas vanish. Columbus felt himself to be a divine messenger, if not a prophet in his own right.[64] Placing himself at the center of a divine drama, he cast islands in the most important supporting roles, consistent with biblical geography.

Mapping Old Worlds on New

In the late Middle Ages and Renaissance periods, space had no existence apart from time. Travel out in space was to be seen as travel in time, backward and forward. Europe had once located its golden ages of the past in the East, but all that had now changed, allowing the West to be the repository of ancestors. This was a major reason why Native Americans were initially seen as "lost tribes," as survivors from a golden age that Europeans had long since left behind. Given the prevailing view that the earth and its peoples were degenerating, there was every reason to expect that these people had preserved some superior physical and spiritual characteristics of the common ancestors. And for a time, it seemed to Columbus and others that they did. Assimilated to an image of ancient pagans, they were initially praised as noble savages, only to be denounced almost immediately as savage primitives. Either way, being "out there," they were automatically assigned to the "back then," distanced from Europeans not only spatially but temporally. From this point onward Native Americans were denied contemporaneity, assigned to some other phase of history, or, worse still, cast out of history entirely, becoming peoples without history.[65]

Because European voyagers had set out to recover an old world, it took a long time before the notion of a new world sank in. For the first two centuries of contact, explorers refused to acknowledge the newness of the New World, insisting on assimilating both to familiar categories, including the biblical narratives. From the start, Europeans held highly ambivalent, unstable views of the peoples they encountered in the Caribbean and the mainlands of the Americas. In a similar way, the newly discovered islands of the Caribbean were immediately assimilated to the world as Europeans knew it. They were seen as lost worlds despite the fact that they had been known to their inhabitants for centuries. Displaced in time as well as space, remote islands lost their place in history and drifted into a static limbo that allowed them to become the repositories for any desire or fright that might be projected their way. The siren calls of the Atlantic produced very mixed feelings among those who heard them. The powerful symbolic content of the islands repelled as well as attracted. Often personified as seductive females, islands were Calypsos beckoning to male voyagers in ways that no other land form was able to do.[66]

For most of the Age of Discovery, maps were based more on speculation than on observation. They served not to locate places, but to confirm beliefs, especially religious beliefs, about the world at large. It was not that islands were by nature less daunting to Europeans. The uncharted or the fog-bound island terrified sailors. Bermuda, where so many ships foundered in the sixteenth century, was named by the Spanish the "Devil's Islands" and was believed until the seventeenth century to be inhabited by demons. There was nothing comforting about the shores of islands. Coasts are always a danger to ships, and beaches a point of vulnerability to those onshore. For centuries, shores were places to be avoided.[67]

"It is the map that precedes territory," observes Jean Baudrillard, and the first thing Europeans did when they arrived at any new place was exactly what they had done throughout the Middle Ages: name it and mark off boundaries, effectively islanding it from surrounding territories.[68] In the case of islands, Europeans invariably removed themselves from their shores, building, in the fashion of Robinson Crusoe, forts and other enclosures, creating islands within islands. Until the eighteenth century, natural boundaries by themselves were never enough to provide Europeans with the security they were seeking. They built fences even before they planted crops or bred animals. In the tropics, thick windowless walls made the settlers feel psychologically safe even as they contributed to their physical misery.[69] Importing old world landscapes had a similar effect of domesticating a world that initially defied description. At every step of the way, exploration and colonization depended on fictions, on an illusory familiarity.

It would be several centuries before Europeans would learn to live on islands as they found them. As long as they insisted on approaching nature as symbol rather than reality, they would suffer the consequences. But explorers and colonizers found what they wanted to find, another example of mythical geography trumping physical reality. Islands were often perceived as perfect circles, symbols of wholeness. Maps tended to represent islands like Hy-Brazil or Antilia in idealized ways, as circular or rectangular, stressing similarity at the expense of difference. The South Atlantic island of São Tomé, first sighted by the Portuguese in 1470, was pictured for more than a century as perfectly circular despite its teardrop shape.[70] The cosmic features once associated with earth island were now transferred to a variety of islands. Geographical particularities were ignored in favor of symbolic and geometrical forms originating in ancient and medieval cosmologies. Islands were no longer seen as fragments, but whole to themselves. As such, they now took on the mythic functions that could no longer be sustained by the image of a single earth island. In this respect, the medieval tendency to assimilate everything to a single closed cosmos was replicated in the proliferation of insular microcosms.[71]

Inventing Islands and Continents

Exploration expanded the boundaries of the known world, disrupting the medieval and Renaissance cosmography by both extending the horizon beyond the edge of the sea and disconnecting it from the heavens. All this coincided with the findings of Copernicus and Kepler indicating that planet earth was not the center of the solar system, causing the heavens and earth to take on a very different meaning. The old vertical scales were displaced, if not immediately replaced, but even more important was the way horizontal space took on a whole new significance. Space became infinitely extendable, centrifugal rather than centripetal. The horizon was no longer associated with the edge of the world but became a moving frontier to explore and conquer.

The vast extension of space had the unanticipated effect of increasing the felt need for knowable, bounded places. In the course of the sixteenth and seventeenth centuries, the vastness of the oceans became known, but this produced a felt need to divide them into seas. Previously perceived as an utterly other place belonging to demons and monsters *Oceanus* now became a multitude of bounded seas that could be mastered. Edmundo O'Gorman writes: "Instead of the ocean appearing as dividing land into separate masses, it is the land that appears as dividing the waters into separate oceans."[72] Seas became more like huge lakes, something that could be crossed using the mental stepping-stones provided by islands.

It was also at this moment that the earth island was reconfigured into a series of continents. The term "continent" was first used in the modern sense in the sixteenth century to mean. "a portion of th' Earth, which is not parted by the Seas asounder."[73] It was also at this moment that the understanding of the island as land surrounded by water emerged. The *Oxford English Dictionary* tells us that before the sixteenth century the word was "formerly used less definitely" to describe peninsulas, wooded copses, blocks of buildings, even people living separate from others. "The concept of insularity, in the sense of discontinuity, ceased to be the property applicable to the great landmasses," says Edmundo O'Gorman.[74] For the first time, islands were defined exclusively by water, no longer to be confused with landlocked places.[75] When the old concept of earth island ceased to be believable, when the old center no longer held, the scramble was on for something which could provide an orientation, a sense of direction in this brave new world. The shift from thinking of the world as a single cosmos where every part was analogous to every other part, to the notion of a globe of infinite linear extension, characterized by difference and discontinuity, was a long, drawn-out affair, not complete until the eighteenth century. It would take a long time before continents would provide this. In the meantime, the search for something to replace the old cosmos would focus on islands.[76]

The newly invented telescope and the microscope would ultimately give access to a world of the infinitely large as well as the infinitely small, further decentering both earth and man. Now that the human body could no longer be the measure of all things, the need for something comprehensible, something that could be grasped in the mind's eye, became even more overwhelming. In a world of ever vaster spaces, islands gave shape and meaning to the vast expanses of uncharted seas that exploration had revealed.

In the sixteenth century, islands came to be seen as worlds in their own right. The world had become simultaneously both larger and smaller, and islands, easily seen as microcosms, took on the burden of representing the world at large. Fears of empty spaces, triggered by exploration and amplified by the collapse of the old cosmological order, were relieved to some degree by filling the oceanic voids with islands, which were understood to be microcosms in their own right.[77] Previously, islands had been seen as fragments, evidence of a fallen world that would be made whole only at the end of time. Now, in the wake of the collapse of medieval geosophy, islands came to be emblems of wholeness. In the sixteenth and seventeenth centuries, Europeans would look offshore for images of paradise and utopia they despaired of finding closer to home.

Even as European territorial monarchies were absorbing the islandlike enclaves within their newly established boundaries, the archipelagic imagination was working overtime offshore. The autonomy enjoyed by the feudal aristocracy had eroded, as had that of the church. Growing volumes of trade were also undermining the insularity of chartered towns, but the ideal of the insular refused to die. It was simply displaced into those spaces outside Europe, beyond the reach of monarchs. In the process of external colonization, Europeans pursued the same strategies that had proved successful in the prior five hundred years. It was the same coalition of nobles, priests, and merchants who, with royal charters in hand, settled first the islands of the near Atlantic and then the far Atlantic. Aristocrats, having lost their power and domains at home, planted a new feudalism on islands. Religion spread through the same cellular replication that had accomplished the Christianization of Europe. And new American towns were created by charter, just as in the old world. Everywhere they went, Europeans sought out islands; and when they could not find them, they created them.

By going offshore, Europe was slowly but surely taking on its modern identity as a continent rather than as a part of something previously called Christendom, which included parts of Asia and Africa. Europeans came to see themselves for the first time as the center of their own world rather than as a part of a much larger entity. "In discovering America," writes John Eliott, "Europe had discovered itself."[78] It was from the far shores of America that it began to see itself as something more than the Cap de Asia, as a continent in its own right.[79] It was in this same moment that Europe began to construct its own sense of geographical destiny, no longer focused on the Middle East and the Mediterranean, but pointing westward, off- rather than onshore. As Europe came to have a new geographical and historical understanding of itself, its littoral and offshore islands also took on a whole new meaning. The coastal regions of France and Spain became more powerful than their interiors; and the English began to see their islandness as an asset rather than a liability. In the next three centuries the future seemed to belong to the seas and islands.[80] European civilization was about to become an Atlantic civilization.

CHAPTER 4

SEARCHING THE SEAS FOR
ISLAND EDENS AND UTOPIAS

A map of the world that does not include Utopia is not worth even glancing at.
—Oscar Wilde, *The Soul of Man under Socialism*

THE AGE OF DISCOVERY DID MORE THAN EXPAND the size of the known world. It created a still greater realm of the unknown.[1] But its greatest effect of all was on the European imagination itself. Because, as John Kirtland Wright observed, "the most fascinating *terrae incognitae* of all are those that lie within the minds and hearts of men," this contributed to yet another form of islomania.[2] Europeans were not only discovering new lands, but producing them. The Age of Discovery would bring forth the notion of continents for the first time, but it would also give new meaning to islands. Two new categories—paradise and utopian islands—were to emerge between 1500 and 1800. As was the case with the legendary isles of the past, they were projections of mainlanders' fears and desires. Paradise islands stood for what Europeans most feared losing in the new age of conquest and colonization; utopian islands represented what they most hoped to gain in the brave new early modern world. As Henri Baudet put it so felicitously, images of paradise symbolized the "no longer," while utopia presented a dream of the "not yet."[3] As islands of the mind, not to be confused with real places, paradise and utopian islands represented the purest expressions of European longings for the next four hundred years.

The moving frontiers of exploration opened up a liminal space that came to be filled with a new genre of imagined islands. For almost four centuries insular paradises and utopias proliferated, adding to the huge stock of legendary islands already present in European minds. As long as Europeans lacked the scientific instruments to chart the seas with precision, their existence could be doubted,

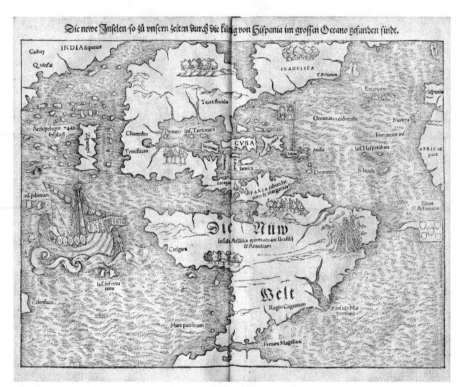

Illustration 9   Sebastian Muenster's Map of New Islands, 1544

but never disproven. Sebastian Muenster's rendering of what he called "new islands" in 1544 is typical of the lively imagination operating at the time. He in-
serts a huge island that he calls Die Nuew Welt but leaves the mythical
Fortunate Isles and Hesperides in place. Chipango is allowed to remain close to
the position Toscanelli assigned it, making it appear to lie just off the west coast
of the new island. It is clear that Muenster was still thinking archipelagically
rather than continentally. And so too were virtually all his contemporaries.

Even as some parts of the ocean were thoroughly explored, the utopias and
paradises simply moved to other regions, always plausible, always just beyond
the horizon. Not until the nineteenth century would the sea search be called off.
But by then paradise and utopia had either moved onshore or been transposed
to a temporal dimension.

Ancient Paradise

Paradise belongs to those sacred lands and timescapes that mankind has conjured up as an otherworld, where the limits of ordinary existence do not apply

and where, as Jean Delumeau writes, "the human soul tries and will always try to set its heart on the impossible."[4] It belongs to that category of sacred places that are always thought of as being "out there," occupying their own separate space or time, inaccessible and therefore incorruptible.[5] As Yi-Fu Tuan has pointed out, the root meaning of *sacer* is separateness.[6]

Notions of paradise are found in virtually all cultures, and they usually contain certain common elements. All express a generalized sense of longing focused on a place or time where plenitude, freedom, peace, and immortality are imagined to exist. "The nostalgia for paradise is among the most powerful nostalgias to haunt human beings," writes Harry Partin. "It may be the most powerful and persistent of all."[7] Paradise's inhabitants are presumed to live in a kind of childlike innocence, nurtured by an environment that provides them with everything they need. Toil and trouble are absent, and so too are disease and death. Paradise is often imagined as a primordial condition, associated with origins, but it is just as frequently linked with regeneration, with new beginnings. However, earthly paradise is almost always to be found in an "elsewhere," either in some very remote place or in some remote time, an "elsewhen."[8] Paradise has been located in all kinds of times and places, but all have one thing in common: inaccessibility. Today, Western Christianity has placed it beyond this world in the heavenly afterlife, but for most of European history there has been an earthly paradise located in some distant place or time beyond the reach of ordinary men and women.

The term itself derives from the Persian *pairi-daeza,* meaning a walled enclosure. The first paradises were royal parks and pleasure gardens.[9] The Greeks took up this idea and passed it on to the Romans. The first paradisical gardens belonged to kings, but it was not long before other powerful and wealthy persons emulated royalty. Ordinary people also resorted to the sacred groves and holy springs that constituted the sacred landscapes of ancient Greece and Rome. And in time, paradise was incorporated into cityscapes in the form of pleasure and leisure gardens.[10]

The idea of paradise had not existed before the neolithic agricultural revolution and the urban civilizations it produced. Hunter-gatherer societies do not produce visions of paradise because they do not exhaust the bounty of nature itself. It was only when settled agrarian peoples used up the forests and lands that the idea of paradise emerged to represent what had been lost. Walling off nature as a garden memorialized a more peaceful, abundant existence now lost forever. As civilizations began to take up more and more of the earth's surface, even this was not sufficient to sustain the ideal. The vision of paradise migrated to ever more remote places, first to mountains and later to islands, where it was possible to imagine an abundance of flora and fauna beyond the destructive grasp of mankind. The ancients left the mountains to the gods, and they were the last places to remain forested; islands, because they too were beyond the reach of mainland civilizations, sustained a vision of unspoiled nature even longer than onshore locations.

The Greeks did not begin to project paradisical visions onto islands until they had denuded their own mainland landscapes.[11] In an effort to protect this last vestige of untainted nature, they imagined the isles to be surrounded by ferocious seas and terrible monsters, ensuring that these remained a place apart. "The Greeks placed almost all their fabled, carefree regions next to equally terrible ones," Ernst Bloch reminds us. "Monsters lurk in front of fragrant groves, there are dangerous waters around the islands of the Pheacians and that of the Blest."[12] The Romans had their Elysian Fields and Isles of the Blest, but they located these safely beyond the Pillars of Hercules. Heroes might journey there, but never with the intention of occupation. An even safer storage were the golden ages of the past, however. In the ancient world, paradise was invariably associated with bygone days, with the distant past rather than with the future.[13]

Christian Paradise

Consistent with their cyclical notion of time, the Greeks and Romans stored their visions of paradise in the past. However, the Judeo-Christian tradition suggested that better worlds lie somewhere in the future or in some remote and inaccessible place in the present. Jews and Christians traditionally placed their vision of earthly paradise, Eden, beyond the reach of ordinary mankind, sometimes on a high mountain somewhere to the far east, sometimes on an island in the far seas.[14] Medieval Christianity also had its celestial heaven, its hell, and an intermediary place it called purgatory, all of which were also assigned geographical locations in the medieval cosmos.[15] But it was the location of Eden, the earthly paradise, that occasioned the most intense interest and speculation.

As Christianity grew more worldly in the twelfth and thirteenth centuries, interest in biblical geography increased. In what Jacques LeGoff has called the ensuing "spatialization of thought," places like paradise and purgatory, which had been abstractions, took on specific geographical locations.[16] Until then the faithful had been satisfied by accounts of visionary journeys by souls who left their bodies in order to bring back reports from otherworldly places, but in the later Middle Ages these lost credibility and were replaced by travel accounts that purported to be by real people traveling in the real world.[17] Accounts, whether wholly fictionalized, like that of Sir John Mandeville, or more realistic, like that of Marco Polo, which claimed to have come close to finding Eden somewhere in the distant present, assured Europeans that, however difficult it might be to reach, much less occupy, earthly paradise was a real place. Eden began to appear on the *mappaemundi* of the later Middle Ages, but always at or beyond the edges of earth island and always behind insurmountable walls or surrounded by fire (see Illustration 3). Christians might approach paradise, but they could go no farther. "Although entry is forbidden, the search for its location and the sojourn in its eternal surroundings are Christian and permitted," Ernst Bloch writes.[18] Christian pilgrims were encouraged to think they might whiff its fragrances and glimpse its glories, but only to remind them of their own postlapsarian condition and the fact that their best hope for paradise lay either at the end of time on the occasion of the Second Coming of Christ or in the afterlife in heaven above.

Until 1400 Eden was much more likely to be associated with mountains. The Old Testament located it in high places closer to heaven. Mountaintops were the only places thought to have escaped the Flood. When Sir John Mandeville claimed to have found it on a high mountaintop that had survived the Flood, his fiction set off an era of quests that would not end until the eighteenth century.[19] Dante located his paradise atop Mount Purgatory in the Indian Ocean, and Columbus imagined to be at the headwaters of the Orinoco, on a high place shaped like the nipple of a woman's breast.[20]

As Europeans became more worldly they showed a noticeable tendency to think of Eden as a real place, once lost but now recoverable.[21] Increasingly it was identified with islands rather than mountains. The closure of the Middle East in the fifteenth century by the Turks set off a number of seagoing quests, increasingly in a westerly direction. The initial response to isles in the milder climes of the Atlantic was almost always to see them as Edenic. The fact that no detailed pictures of earthly paradise existed made it possible for almost any island to be envisioned in that manner. The Portuguese were so certain they had rediscovered Eden in the Azores that they named the first children born there Adam and Eve.[22] Images of plenty and bliss were easily transferred to other legendary islands such as Saint Brendan's Isle, Hy-Brazil, Antilia, and several others.[23]

Eden began to disappear from *mappaemundi* in the fifteenth century, but this did not diminish its credibility because now it was assumed to belong to the expanding realm of *terra incognita*. In fact, the plausibility of paradise was ensured by the lack of precise geographical knowledge at the time. During its long history, it had been located and relocated many times. Such movement is typical during moments of major social change and ecological transformation when places once thought of as pristine were despoiled and the ideal was forced to move on to new, more distant locales. In the later Middle Ages, the location of paradise shifted more frequently, moving from India to East Africa, and then to the coast and islands of West Africa, the Canaries, Madeiras, Azores, and the

Cape Verdes. Having failed to find it in any of these places, the European imagination shifted westward, and Eden took up residence in the New World.

Paradise Found

From the fifteenth century onward islands became "the last refuge of all original happiness, wisdom," writes Baudet.[24] Now paradise was allowed to exist in the here and now, and the noble peoples who were imagined to inhabit it became the objects of intense curiosity. Earlier quests for paradise had stopped short of possession, kept in check by the belief that paradise existed in some other inaccessible time or place. But now the idea that paradise could actually be realized in the here and now unleashed unfulfillable desires that western civilization has been contending with ever since.

No longer located in some distant time or place, the search for Eden became "the partner of the other more obviously economic projects of early colonialism," Richard Grove writes.[25] But paradise found quickly turned into paradise lost when the isles that seemed so desirable on first contact were found to harbor deadly diseases, environmental disasters (including extinctions), and hostile local populations that Europeans were not prepared for.[26] However, because this experience so closely paralleled the story of the Fall in biblical Eden, it only reinforced the sense of loss and the longing that was at the root of European expansion in the first place. Each lost Eden reinvigorated the quest for paradise elsewhere. In seas filled with an endless supply of unknown islands, it seemed that the search would never run out of new possibilities. It was only when the Atlantic had been thoroughly explored that the quest turned to the Pacific, where it finally exhausted itself in the nineteenth century. Yet the search for island paradise never really expired; it has taken on new life for the benefit of the modern tourist trade.

Each tropical island encountered seemed at first to fit the description of paradise. Glimpsed at a distance from ships, they all seemed to match the visions that Europeans had brought with them across the Atlantic. At first sight the islands seemed so fecund as to free men forever from toil. They were also the object of the sexual fantasies of the males who first spotted them. Paradisical places like the fabled Island of California were often populated with desirable women. Since Homer's time, islands had been colonized by patriarchal fantasies, imagined to be populated by beautiful females intent on seducing male wayfarers.[27] In the first phases of European expansion, new worlds were invariably imagined as feminine. America constituted "virgin" lands and was personified by a nude female figure in a feathered headdress.[28] Often the islands were identified with Mother Nature herself, an image of abundance that added immensely to their allure.

The search for paradise was invariably sexually charged. The peoples living on tropical islands were thought to be living in a conditions of prelapsarian innocence, which the explorers wished to recover for themselves. But they were also sexually powerful, a threat to good Christian explorers bent on converting their inhabitants. Contact with native women was seen as a dangerous temptation; and it is not surprising that island women, at first seen as innocent and virginal, soon came to be portrayed as voracious Amazons, cannibals, and witches, a source, like Eve, of all kinds of troubles.[29]

Island Edens also conjured fears of corruption, something that Christians had always associated with abundance. Jackson Lears writes that "American bounty was enticing, but also emasculating, perhaps worse." The female figures encountered in its landscapes were full of ambiguity.[30] This was particularly true for Protestant explorers, influenced by an asceticism that saw paradise as something to be earned, not found. They preferred barren isles to tropical ones. Captain John Smith talked of building "a Garden upon the top of a Rocke Ile."[31] It was the same reason Crèvecoeur praised Nantucket, which in his view had just the right balance of resources and scarcities to keep men happy but busy, comfortable but virtuous.[32]

Paradise Lost

For most of the early modern period, islands had the first claim on paradise. In time, however, the American mainlands came to be identified with Eden, a place, in John Donne's words, "that shall never grow old, the kingdom of Heaven."[33] But even the enormous power of the myths that Europeans brought with them could not block out reality forever. By the seventeenth century, islands that earlier explorers had identified as paradisical had taken on a different aspect. They had become integrated into the rapidly expanding circuits of commercial capitalism, their space and time coordinated with that of the continents. They were all too accessible and vulnerable to the corruptions of the world. Paradise found turned out to be paradise lost; and ever since then, the Atlantic islands have been haunted by experiences of exploitation, bloodshed, and extinction.

Island populations were particularly vulnerable to the importation of disease. The flora and fauna were no less fragile, and, beginning with the Canaries, Azores, and Madeiras, islands were case studies in ecological disaster—denuded, eroded, and ultimately rendered uninhabitable. Where sugar plantations replaced forests, rainfall lessened, and water became a problem. Even Columbus was aware of this disastrous impact, and the ecological problems already identified in the eastern Atlantic only increased when sugar production was transferred to the

Caribbean islands.[34] Europeans were quick to exploit and then abandon islands, but slaves, indentured servants, and prisoners, who constituted the vast majority of the Caribbean's inhabitants, had no choice but to endure the increasingly difficult conditions there. Images of hell, already associated with islands in ancient and Christian imagery, were readily available to those seeking to describe their experiences with ecological devastation.[35] The same isles that had been locations for paradise were now stand-ins for hell.

Ambivalence best expresses the early modern attitude toward islands. The same islands were often described in wholly opposite terms. William Strachey described Bermuda as "the Devils Islands . . . feared and avoyded of all sea travellers live, above any place in the world," but in the next sentence he talked of them as God's "meanes of our deliverance."[36] Shakespeare incorporated both the paradisical and the hellish elements into the island of *The Tempest,* making of it a "barren place, and fertile."[37] Defoe's shipwrecked hero, Crusoe, repeated Prospero's feat of transforming barrenness into productivity, but only by retreating from the shore and building his own island within the island.[38] Sixteenth-century shipwrecks on the Bermuda islands gave them a particularly sinister reputation. Sylvester Jourdain, reporting on a 1609 catastrophe, described them as "a most prodigious and inchanted place, affording nothing but gusts, stormes, and foule weather; which made every Navigator and Mariner to avoide them as they would shunne the Devill himselfe."[39] There were similar accounts of New England coasts, where any shore continued to be thought of as a wild, desolate place, haunted by sea monsters, well into the nineteenth century.[40]

By the eighteenth century, paradise was less likely to be something found than created. The old idea of paradise as manmade garden, as *hortus conclusus,* was revived. As the rapacious plantation economy turned Caribbean isles into moral and ecological wastelands, the paradisical element still present there was preserved by fencing or walling off the land and enclosing nature's bounty.[41] Plantation owners who could afford to return home took the flora and fauna with them, creating botanical gardens and hothouse paradises in Europe itself. Zoos were similarly designed to bring paradise to Europe. "Europe brought home to Europe the stock of the world's diversity. The new things arrived in waves, with increasing speed, from the middle of the sixteenth century," notes Richard Drayton. "In a hundred years, there was no way back to Eden, no means of reinaugurating a Golden Age."[42]

English gentry, many of whom had made their fortunes in the sugar islands, turned their country seats into little Edens, blending Christian with classical pagan elements. In the eighteenth century, gardening became a passion among the landed classes. Max Schulz tells us that "for a brief fifty years the English garden functioned symbolically and literally, as a paradise; but it was a *hortus con-*

clusus without Angel of Annunciation, Blessed Madonna, or immortal child. It is a New Eden in which are installed latter-day Adams and Eves in knee breeches and afternoon gowns, who fear no divine exclusionary restrictions."[43] Even as the industrial revolution turned cities into living hells for the working classes, the European and American middle classes created what Yi-Fu Tuan has called a "modest Eden" in the newly developing suburbs,[44] The Victorians created their own *rus in urbe,* insisting that every home have its garden. Ultimately bourgeois civilization would make of every home a "scaled-down Eden. "Today, Europeans and Americans still want to believe islanded domestic life can be Edenic, though most of us now also look elsewhere, to tropical islands in winter and summer retreats in summer, for a taste of paradise.[45]

Enter Utopia

It is easy to confuse the paradise and utopian islands of the early modern period, but their origins and purposes were actually very different. Utopias jostled with paradises for a place in the vast *terra incognita,* but they represented a dream not of what had been but what could be. The Renaissance and Reformation unintentionally broke the spell of tradition and opened up a small space within which to consider alternative ways of organizing society. Utopian thinking existed in the ancient world, but was overshadowed by Christian millenarianism and peasant arcadianism in the Middle Ages. When it reemerged in the sixteenth and seventeenth centuries, it took a distinctly new form.

From the beginning, this new utopian mode of thought fastened on islands. The relationship between islands and utopia is in many ways as perverse and unnatural as between islands and paradise, for utopian thinking did not originate on islands or ever have much appeal to islanders themselves. Its origins were exclusively continental, the product of Europe's internal upheavals. Yet the legacy of this peculiar moment lives on in the utopian visions that we still persist in imposing on islands, even when the original meaning of utopia—literally, "nowhere"—is ignored. The original island utopias of Sir Thomas More and his imitators were not meant to be achieved. It would not be until the nineteenth century that anyone tried to realize utopia in the here and now. They were conceived of and understood to be useful fictions; and it was this that gave them their appeal to a Europe struggling to understand its postmedieval condition.

The name Utopia was invented by Sir Thomas More in 1516, and its meaning remained relatively constant from the sixteenth through the eighteenth century—a good place that is also no place. In 1619 Johann Valetin Andreae produced his vision of Christianapolis, modeled on Plato's Republic but set on an island. This was followed by Francis Bacon's *The New Atlantis* (1627),

Illustration 10   Sir Thomas More's Utopia, from Ambrosius Holbein's "Map of the Isle of Utopia" in John Frobenius's edition of *Utopia*, 1518

Tomasso Campanella's *The City of the Sun* (1637), James Harrington's *Oceana* (1656), all set on islands or islandlike landscapes. These masterpieces spawned in turn dozens of now forgotten imitators like Philipp Balthazar Sinold, who published *The Happiest Island in the Whole World or the Land of Contentments* in 1749.[46]

The utopias of this period were so realistic as to make them believable to contemporaries who, understanding so much of the world to be yet unknown, could easily believe that they could be realized, if not here and now, then somewhere and somewhen. "If a utopia is merely or primarily reflective of an existing reality it is trivial," note Frank and Fritzie Manuel. "On the other hand, when the imaginary world is cut off from all relationship with reality, it becomes a vaporous fairy tale, formless and pointless. The great utopia startles and yet is recognized as conceivable."[47] In an era when so much was unexplored, so much unknown, utopias were entirely in the realm of possibility, even probability.

Of course what is conceivable differs from society to society, period to period. During its long history, utopian thought has used just about every available place and conceivable time to project the ideal worlds that are utopianism's gift to human culture. Just where or when the image of the good place appears is not arbitrary, however. In the ancient world utopian places were invariably associated with golden ages of the past that might yet be regenerated. The Greek imagination did not extend very much beyond the boundaries of its own immediate world, the polis, and the utopias of the ancient world were imagined almost exclusively as cities or citylike places.

It was Judaism that oriented utopian thought from the past to the future, introducing a linear notion of time, which was taken over and further developed by Christianity. Jews and Christians projected their good places forward rather than backward in time, but because they believed themselves living on God's time, the arrival of utopia was beyond human control. In this millenarian tradition, better worlds are always God-made rather than manmade. Millenarianism is capable of projecting utopian images, but these are located beyond the individual human life span in the afterlife of heaven or at the end of time, when, at God's discretion, a New Jerusalem will appear.

The vision of a New Jerusalem clearly owes something to the ancient traditions of associating utopia with cities. In both pagan and Christian thinking, utopia differed from paradise insofar as it was imagined as a city rather than a garden. While it contained certain paradisical elements, the early modern utopia was not the product of nostalgia for something that had once been, but a longing for something yet to be. Furthermore, it was not God-ordained or natural, but manmade.[48] Paradise was associated with origins, with the simplicity of a life free of laws and rules. Its order was inherent, the result of innocence uncorrupted by the advances of civilization, including knowledge itself. Utopia, on the other hand, was the product of civilization, of the application of knowledge and effort. It is invariably imagined as a city rather than a garden, the product of man rather than nature.

Sir Thomas More's Utopia lives not on God's but on man's time. It is very much a manmade rather than a divine creation. Though More was in every respect a Christian, he was no millenarian. His idealized place exists neither at some mythic beginning nor at the end of time, but outside of time, wholly in space, and this is what constitutes the novelty of all the island utopias of the period 1500–1800. It is therefore the fact that More's utopian island exists in its own unique distant present that sets it apart from both ancient and medieval dream worlds. His vision is contemporaneous, existing somewhere in *terra incognita* of the yet-to-be explored oceans. It is this location on an unknown island that gives it credibility and accounts for its appeal to early modern readers, who found the nowheres as believable as somewheres. Neither before nor after were utopias to be so highly spatialized, a condition that can be explained by the fact that at this historical moment *terra incognita* offered so much latitude for utopian thinking.

Frank and Fritzie Manuel note that "imaginary societies are situated along the general path of actual conquests, discoveries, and explorations."[49] Utopias appear to have had an affinity for frontiers and edges, for thresholds and unmapped spaces that are betwixt and between. The relationship between utopia and exploration was close but complex. It seems that access to unexplored places triggered imaginings of utopian places. This had occurred in the time of Alexander the Great, when his conquests opened up India and its seas to the Greek imagination. It was then that Euhemerus conjured up the fabulous island of Panchaia and that Imbulus wrote of a voyage to the Island of the Sun. In the early modern period, each time the horizons of Western culture moved, utopias proliferated, but always just beyond those frontiers. Perhaps this was because in the process of exploration, between the opening up of new territories and their actual mapping, a kind of third space was created that was somewhere but nowhere, accessible to the imagination before it was colonized by real time (history) and real space (geography). As we have already seen, islands had long been perceived as thresholds. Their status as liminal place, somewhere between land and water, made them particularly attractive to both religious and utopian thinkers.

Their extraterritorial status is not the whole explanation of how islands became the favorite location for utopias from the sixteenth through the eighteenth century. Nowheres are always the product of somewhere. Even when they negate geography and history, they are its progeny, clearly reflective of a specific moment in time, taking their shape from the society that gives them birth. Early modern utopias were the product of special circumstances. They did not occur in static societies or among people who had accepted their lot.[50] Contrary to what one might expect, it was not the exile or the immigrant who showed the greatest utopian propensity. The poor and the displaced may have been prone to millenarianism, but not utopianism. Nomads, who were constantly on the move and knew no frontiers, had no need of paradises or utopias because they had no yearning for elsewheres.[51] Nor did societies that were deeply rooted or centered produce utopias. Great empires showed little utopian propensity. Chinese civilization, which sees itself as the center of the world, considered itself its own utopia. The same had been true of Rome. The utopian propensity was very active in the young United States when it saw itself as marginal, but clearly atrophied when the United States became an imperial power; and this was also the case with the Soviet Union, where the utopian impulse died when it came to see itself as a core rather than as a periphery.[52]

It is equally clear that utopias proliferated in times of crisis, when dissatisfactions with the status quo triggered imaginings of alternatives. Yet the utopian propensity did not show itself everywhere in Renaissance and Reformation Europe. It did not come out of rural settings where arcadian myths had long gripped the imaginations of the European peasantry. The image of the Land of Cockaign, with its gluttonous drunken revels and orgiastic sexuality, was the poor people's dream, and very much at odds with the kind of civilized urban enjoyment of life that characterized More's Utopia.[53] As Northrup Frye has pointed out, "The great classical utopias derived their form from city-states and, through imagining, were thought of being, like city-states, exactly locatable in space."[54]

Voyage to Utopia

When the urban ideal faded with the collapse of Rome, the ideal of civilization retreated within the walls of the monastery or was imagined to exist in some far-off place like Jerusalem. During the Middle Ages one had to travel in order to find civilization. "Striving to perfect oneself morally involved topographical displacement," notes Aaron Gurevich.[55] It was much easier for Christian Europeans to imagine utopia at a distance than closer to home. Therefore is not surprising that when modern utopian thought emerged in the sixteenth century, it expressed itself in the form of travel tales.[56] Thomas More renewed an ancient narrative form that, as Louis Marin summarizes it, begins with "a departure and a journey, most of the time by sea, most of the time interrupted by a storm, a catastrophy which is the sublime way to open a neutral space, one which is absolutely different."[57] Until the nineteenth century, virtually every utopia took the form of the voyage tale, relying on an unmapped place, usually an unknown island that existed in some unchronicled time, to present a vision of society startling, yet conceivable.

The classical utopias of the early modern period all rely on the fiction of the odyssey, building on a tradition going back to the Greeks, but also enriched by the medieval legends and fictions of spiritual journeys undertaken not so much to discover or to colonize but to recover and bring back deeper truths, personal or collective. These pilgrimages invariably involved danger and difficulty, often across waters to islands or other inaccessible places.[58] All spiritual journeys are, writes Eric Leed, "roundtrips, rather than exiles or migrations."[59] According to Victor Turner, they are rites of passage "going to a far place to understand a familiar place better."[60] The purpose of religious pilgrimage had been to behold more clearly sacred truths that will never reveal themselves closer to home. The purpose of the secular utopian voyage was similar, namely to grasp social truths obscured in the here and now.[61] What Victor Turner says of pilgrimage applies equally well to the voyages to utopia. "The peripherality of pilgrimage shrines and the temporal structure of the pilgrimage process, beginning in a Familiar Place, going to a Far Place, and returning, ideally 'changed' to a Familiar Place, can be intimately related to van Gennep's concept of the rite of passage, with its stages of separation, margin or *limen,* and reaggregation."[62] The narrative of the journey to utopia removes the reader from his or her milieu to a strange but vaguely recognizable place. Not only the time but the space of the ordinary world has been left behind. The island provides the perfect setting because it is detached from all historical as well as geographical connections, allowing the reader, as in a dream, to enter fully into its imagined reality.[63]

Unlike modern scientific expeditions which bring back down-to-earth information, the object of utopian voyages was inspired images. The specifics of place mattered as little to the utopian travelers as they had to the holy *viator* like Saint Brendan. Utopian travel accounts were scenically sketchy.[64] The reader's gaze is directed to the archetypal rather than the particular, but what these accounts lacked in detailed description they made up for in the power of their images.[65] In the case of the pilgrimage, the enduring image was that of the sacred cosmos; in the utopian voyage it was that of a social cosmos. The island acted as a lens, focusing the mind of the traveler.

The voyage tale was a mental rite of passage, carrying Europeans away from their everyday world into the unfamiliar realm, returning them with a vivid image of a better world.[66] Like all the great Christian pilgrimage sites, the classical utopias were located on the geographical periphery, remote and inaccessible except through the imagination. Just as holy islands derived their special meaning from temporal as well as spatial displacement, so did the island utopias. Their remoteness and isolation allowed them to function as microcosms capable of symbolizing all the world's problems and possibilities. No other land form served in the same way during the early modern period.[67] A mainland, even a peninsula, would not do. More's Utopia was itself an artificial island, created when King Utopus opened up a channel in a peninsula.[68] And not just any island would serve this purpose. Utopian isles are shaped to fit the predetermined dimensions. All were imagined to have a symmetry rarely encountered in nature.

The islands' natural boundaries were never sufficient in and of themselves. The island of More's Utopia is fortified, and there is but one access point. Just as a pilgrimage site jealously protects its integrity by ritually marking its boundaries, so every effort is made to see that the presence of strangers does not disrupt the fixed routines of the community. In Bacon's New Atlantis, all strangers are segregated residentially, placed in a condition of quarantine for the duration of their stay. They wear a distinctive costume, eat a different diet, and are closely supervised by their guides. At the end of the stay there are equally elaborate rites of departure, ensuring that the spatial and temporal boundaries of utopia remain the same as they were at arrival, uncontaminated by the visit. Visitors are allowed to take nothing away except what they arrived with. Special rites ensure that their presence left no mark on either the geography or the history of utopia. It is as if the visit had never happened, ensuring the community is unchanged and that the traveler takes back a pristine, timeless vision of utopia, uncontaminated even by his or her own presence. But the rite is not complete until the voyager has been reintegrated into his/her own community, thereby marking that mental distance between utopia and home that confirms the reader's sense of having been somewhere, even if nowhere, bearing witness to the social truth in the same way the pilgrim bears witness to divine truth.

David Harvey has called these "utopias of social form," contrasting them with later utopias that incorporated a temporal dimension. "Put crudely, spatial form controls temporality, an imagined geography controls the possibility of social change and history."[69] All early modern utopias were static, though by no means backward looking. Human labor was their foundation, and the work ethic their redeeming feature. Their social and political structures were hierarchical and authoritarian, and slavery was acceptable. They all kept the traditional household structure, sustaining patriarchy, together with gender and generational differences that were the signatures of Renaissance and Reformation society. Consistent with the mores of the time, sexual conformity within marriage was seen as a key to human happiness.[70] They were clearly products of their own time, though they existed outside history in the distant present.

Early modern utopias appealed to a strife-torn society yearning for harmony and stability. Utopian islands offered what Frank Manuel aptly describes as "calm felicity," the dream of a world where neither the encroachments of time nor space are visible. Since Plato, utopian thinkers had never been anything but realists, providing contemporaries with a perfected version of that which already existed. Early modern utopias had no concept of change or a vision of a radically different future. Thomas More provided a vision of what the Renaissance city-state could be if its basic features were fully realized. The conditions of Campanella's and Bacon's utopias were also up-to-date technologically but not socially or politically progressive. In More's Utopia there is no hint of historical progress and no sign of the dynamics of commercial capitalism, state formation, and religious schism that were already altering Europe beyond recognition. The absence of these things constituted their appeal to contemporaries.

The Good Place Becomes the Good Time

The conditions that produced early modern utopias would not last forever. In the late eighteenth century, islands and utopias parted because by then the space of *terra incognita* had been substantially diminished; most of the world's islands had been so completely explored that they could no longer serve as a screen onto which timeless social or religious ideals could be confidently projected. It was now the continents that provided blank spaces to be colonized by utopian thinking. In the nineteenth century, utopia would appear on the inland frontiers, though it was not long before these interior spaces were also colonized and effectively closed to the utopian imagination.[71]

However, even as space closed, time was opening up. By the nineteenth century, history was no longer dictated by biblical narratives. Time now stretched into what was to become the "deep past," while the future opened wide to speculations that previously had taken only spatial form. Utopian thinking moved inland, becoming landlocked, but also less spatialized, becoming a sometime rather than a somewhere. As Frank Manuel tells us, "Whereas before the nineteenth century utopias are invariably stable and ahistorical, ideals out of time, they now became dynamic and bound into a long prior historical series . . . good place becomes good time."[72]

And now, for the first time, utopia was imagined as a real possibility, as something that could happen. In the early part of the nineteenth century thousands of utopian communities were established in Europe and the Americas. These were often landlocked islands in a sea of hostile political and social forces, but they did not see themselves as insular. Dreams of static order gave way to fantasies of universal progress. Rather than closing themselves off to the world, utopians imagined themselves as providing attractive models that would soon be adopted worldwide. In the belief that they were at the cutting edge of history, utopians did all they could to diminish the isolation that their enemies imposed on them. Instead of retreating to some distant present, utopians became enthusiastic bridge builders to the rest of modern society.

Nineteenth-century utopias tended to appear more frequently on land than on sea frontiers, always on the move, just one step ahead of encroaching urban civilization. But when realized, utopia tended to disappoint and produce dystopia. For this reason utopia ultimately moved to the one place it could not be contaminated by reality, namely the realm of the future. Time ultimately replaced space as the safe storage for dreams; and as long as the idea of progress remained the secular faith of Western civilization, the future provided a home for utopian ideals. But by the end of the nineteenth century, doubts about progress had surfaced and in the twentieth century even the future was off limits to utopia. When George Orwell wrote this century's great dystopian novel *1984* (published in 1949), he did so on the bleak Scottish island of Jura. At that time, no place, even an island, was capable of sustaining the dream of a better society.

Today, utopian thinking struggles to survive at the margins of public attention. Visions of a better, more peaceful life still cling to islands, which John Fowles calls the "original alternative societies."[73] Sometime in the 1980s a young woman named Cynthia Bourgeault was drawn to Swans Island, Maine. She loved its dimensions, where "in this minute, excruciating finiteness you see the real scale of things, the passage through time that is the other component of our identity here on earth, again marked and honored in community." But what she found when she moved there was too much of a good thing, a community of longtime residents that gently but firmly excluded those, like herself, who had come "from away." She learned that "acceptance must be earned; a place in the community must be won," a price that, in the end, she found she could not afford. "I myself discovered the beautiful shimmering image of island community to be a mirage." After six years she left Swans, but not without deep regrets.[74] In effect, Cynthia Bourgeault had recapitulated the history of modern Western utopianism. She too became disillusioned with her island dream, though not necessarily with the vision of utopia itself. That survives, as it has always done, to take up residence in another place or in another time.

CHAPTER 5

ISLANDS IN THE MAKING
OF ATLANTIC CIVILIZATION

The events of history often lead to the islands. Perhaps it is more accurate to say that they make use of them.

—Fernand Braudel, *The Mediterranean
and the Mediterranean World in the Age of Philip II*

EUROPEANS HAD VOYAGED WESTWARD IN FULL ANTICIPATION of finding old worlds, and it was a very long time before they fully comprehended what they had found was something quite new. Sixteenth-century maps still represented the sea as filled with islands, the Americas being the largest of those that lay between Europe and Asia. Europeans were still acting on ancient and medieval cosmographies, but unwittingly they had created something that had never existed before, namely an Atlantic basin that belonged for the next three centuries not just to them but to Africans and Native Americans, to Sengalese and Cape Verdeans, to Nantucketers and Philadelphians. For a period of time there existed what Felipe Fernandez-Armesto has rightly called an Atlantic civilization, belonging as much to the sea as the land, as much to islands as to mainlands.[1]

To grasp what this lost Atlantic civilization was like we might want to recall precolonial Polynesia, a Pacific civilization where the inhabitants saw themselves as living in a sea of islands, connected rather than divided by water, a kind of aqueous continent that stretched for thousands of miles in many directions. "Their universe comprised not only land surfaces, but the surrounding ocean as far as they could traverse and exploit it," writes Epile Hau'ofa. Though Westerners think of islands as small places, to the Polynesians their island world "was anything but tiny."[2] To them, the sea was home, a place rather than an interval between places. Connected to the sea around them, islands were not perceived as either remote or insular. They were also fully a part of the history taking place offshore as well as onshore.

We have difficulty grasping such a world because we think of the sea as a void rather than a place and we treat islands as if they are always small, remote, and isolated whatever their size and proximity. We also have a tendency to think of islands as backward and less developed regardless of their economy or social organization. But these current understandings should not prevent us from recovering a sense of that sea of islands that between 1500 and 1800 constituted the core of a flourishing Atlantic civilization. For almost three centuries islands constituted the center rather than the periphery of what was then a leading edge of world economic, social, and cultural developments. The later rise of the power of continents should not be allowed to obscure the degree to which islands influenced the course of early modern history.

Taking History Offshore

The medieval vision of an earth island girdled by a great river had faded by the sixteenth century. It was then that the old world's three parts became the first three continents: Europe, Africa, and Asia. The modern notion of the seas was born at the same time, Edmundo O'Gorman writes. "Instead of the ocean appearing as dividing the land into separate masses, it is the land that appears as dividing the waters into separate oceans. The concept of insularity, in the sense of discontinuity, ceased to be properly applicable to the great landmasses, and instead of unsubmerged land appearing as two gigantic islands, the ancient Atlantic Ocean now appears as two gigantic lakes."[3]

Islands also came to be understood in new ways. Previously used to describe any isolated place, whether on land or sea, islands came to be defined by water. The *Oxford English Dictionary* tells us that before the sixteenth century the word island was used to describe peninsulas, lands surrounded by marshes, wooded copses, blocks of buildings, even people living separated from others. By the sixteenth century, however, sea-girt islands were coming into their own as a distinctive landform. Perhaps the first use of the word in its modern sense was recorded in 1555, when Antonio Galvano, writing about a failed ancient project to dig a canal from the Nile to the Red Sea, noted that it would have made Africa "an Island all encompassed with waters."[4]

Medieval geosophy was giving way to modern geography, and land forms had begun to acquire a distinct character which would ultimately distinguish them not just from the seas but from one another.[5] But it took several centuries before the contrast between islands and continents became absolute, and even now a certain ambiguity remains. It was not until the nineteenth century that Australia was finally mapped as a single large island, and only in the twentieth century did it join the club of continents. Confusion still lingers about what to call Australia; schoolchildren there are taught that they live in "the-world's-largest-island-the-world's-smallest-continent."[6]

During the early modern period, European attention was focused far more on islands than it was on continents.[7] Not only did islands continue to loom large politically and economically, but they exerted a fascination that larger landmasses could not yet begin to match. Not until the nineteenth century did continents begin to hold sway metaphorically as well as literally, a fact that we ignore at the risk of distorting the history of the early modern world. Islands played a far larger role in the period 1500–1800 than at any other time before or since. They were crucial to economic and political development but no less significant culturally. Islands were not only the lands that Europe principally explored, claimed, and colonized, but those it imagined and fictionalized.

We have lost sight of this because in the Western historiographical canon, laid down in the nineteenth century, history is presented as if it begins and ends at the edges of continents, and dwells almost exclusively on their interiors.[8] All that which lies beyond the shores is either prelude or aftermath of the grand continental narratives. Continents have a tendency to appropriate everything into their temporal and spatial domains. It is said that Columbus voyaged from Europe to discover America, but, as we have already seen, his points of departure and arrival were largely archipelagic. A similar continental claim has been made for the Vikings, forgetting that their most important settlement was on the island of Newfoundland. This might seem a quibble if it were not for the fact that so much has been made to ride on these myths. Were we to accept the fact that 1492 has no direct relevance to the continents we now know as the Americas, all received wisdom about history and geography would have to be radically revised, if not wholly abandoned.

We have seen just how much the late Middle Ages and Renaissance were preoccupied with islands. For a very long time European explorers and settlers were not much interested in interiors of continents. Even the Spanish, who carved out the largest land empires, were initially confined to coasts and islands. The French and the English moved inland by rivers, so it was almost as if the oceans were invading the continents. Seventeenth-century English colonists were advised to settle near navigable rivers "that which bendeth most toward the North West, for that way you shall soonest find the other sea."[9] The vision of an archipelagic America was laid to rest only in the nineteenth century, though explorers never gave up completely on the idea of a polar passage, which was, in fact, achieved in the early twentieth century.

But what if we were not so attached to the myths of continents, less enamored of a continental telos that would have us believe that everything moves inevitably in favor of great heartlands, begins and ends at their boundaries? Instead of seeing continentalism as the culmination of history, it might be possible to imagine other scenarios in which waters play more important roles than lands, becoming historic places in their own right. There is every reason to do so because, as J. H. Parry has demonstrated, "The Great Age of Discovery was essentially the age of the discovery of the sea," reminding us that "for the most part, the explorers sought not new lands, but new routes to old lands."[10] Waters that had been obstacles gave unprecedented access. Before the fifteenth century, Daniel Boorstein reminds us, "the Ocean led nowhere; in the next centuries people would see it led everywhere."[11]

In the revised narrative, history moves off- rather than onshore. It would embrace the archipelagos that form, like Pacific Oceania, a sea of islands, rather than islands in the far sea. What might be called an Atlantic Oceania was indeed like a continent, except that its parts communicated by water rather by land, by far the more efficient and fastest means of transportation in the period 1500 to 1800. Movement was unimpeded, and interisland movement was frequent. Atlantic Oceania even had its own languages, the pidgins, which allowed its people to communicate at least as effectively as the continentals.

In the rewriting of history, it would not be territory itself but *access* to territory that would be of central economic, political, and social importance. In this telling of history the extraterritorial, including seas and rivers, but also islands, would come into their own as agents rather than as passive objects of continental imperatives. After all, the notion of the world mapped onto clearly bounded territories is a very modern notion. The Middle Ages, as Michael Biggs notes, was "essentially a mapless world" know as a "succession of places."[12] Distance was calculated in terms of the time it took to travel from place to place rather than in precise measures of space. States were not centralized or unified as tightly bounded territories. Sovereigns reigned over a scatter of lands, often far distant from one another, more like an archipelago than a continent. This condition continued throughout the early modern period, and it was only in the nineteenth century that contiguity of territory became the mark of a developed nation-state.[13] Until then, archipelagos of territory, whether landlocked or seagirt, were just as attractive to sovereigns as more unified and centralized lands.

During the early modern period, political development proceeded archipelagically. One might even say that the initial stages of Western modernity were far more a matter of islands than continents. This perspective not only changes our sense of periodization, but cuts us adrift from the mainlands of history itself. It not only alters the when of Atlantic history but its where. In this respect, it poses an enormous challenge to a Western historiography which, born in the age of continents, is marked by a territorial bias that subordinates smaller land forms to larger ones, just as it favors larger nations over smaller ones, privileging what it likes to call its core over what it perceives as its periphery. Taking an archipelagic perspective therefore not only illuminates the places but the peoples that the continental bias has deprived of history. But it also throws new light on what we call the mainlands.[14] We need to accept John Pocock's invitation "to let our mental vision travel out into a diffusion of pelagic cultures lying beyond 'Europe' and 'civilization' as conventionally imagined."[15] This is the only way to recapture the relationships of lands, oceans, and islands, and to see Atlantic civilization not as an appendage of European civilization but as something with its own history and geography, forged as much offshore as onshore.[16]

Island Empires

The discovery of the Americas was unintended, and it was not until the seventeenth century that Europe figured out what to do with the New World. As Robert Lopez once perceptively remarked: "Indeed, for a moment it looked as if Europe would reject the unresolicited gift of 1492."[17] Europe was absorbed by its own internal problems and would soon be fissured by the Reformation. The Black Death a century earlier had solved the overpopulation problem, making it very difficult to get people to settle the New World. Those first to cross the Atlantic were looking for a quick return on their investment and an equally quick return home. During the sixteenth century it was gold and silver that lured men offshore. And even those who came to settle did not want to work the land.[18]

The Spanish were lured inland by gold and silver, but their settlements were in many ways exceptional. The French and English launched similar searches for treasure, but when these proved unsuccessful they had to settle for fish and furs. These enterprises did not involve permanent settlement until the seventeenth century, however, and when that finally happened it was on islands, not mainlands. Fishing required no continental connection at all, while the fur trade was in the hands of Native Americans, making inland settlement irrelevant. Fishermen had set a precedent for the use of islands early on by camping there in the summer months. Newfoundland and islands along the New England coast served this purpose well in the sixteenth century, but never led to permanent populations. Islands had the advantage of being accessible to the mainlands, but also fortifiable against the Native Americans onshore.

Islands therefore became forward bases in both fishing and fur trading. Sable Island, a whaling station off Nova Scotia founded by the Marquis de la Rock, became the first French colony to last more than a year. But its colonists were minor criminals rounded up for the purpose of labor, and in 1603 they turned on their guards and escaped their island prison, thus ending the enterprise.[19] The English also looked to islands, first to Roanoke and then Jamestown, for their first permanent settlements. But the colony on Roanoke Island was a failure, and Jamestown came close to disaster because of disease and the aristocratic colonists' lack of skills and deficient work habits. It was only when a suitable export crop, tobacco, proved profitable that the inland dimension of the Virginia experiment was assured.[20]

Just how insular Europe's designs on the New World continued to be is illustrated by the fact that in the eighteenth century islands were still seen as more valuable than mainlands. While the Spanish tended to withdraw to the mainlands, other European powers competed tenaciously for the vacated isles. Even tiny islands were coveted and fought over far more than large territories. St. Luca changed hands so many times—fourteen—that today it is a French/English hybrid. The population speaks a French patois but drives like the English on the left side of the road.[21] In the treaty negotiations with the British in 1763 that ended the Seven Years War, the French were more interested in holding onto the tiny sugar-producing island of Gaudeloupe than in keeping the vast territories of Canada.[22] Ambivalent attitudes toward mainlands would persist right up to the nineteenth century.

Islands had always been of strategic advantage to Europeans. Beginning with the Crusades, the islands of the Mediterranean had been their stepping-stones. As Fernand Braudel described it, Europeans moved "crab-wise from rock to rock," rarely going far inland.[23] Many eastern Mediterranean isles remained under their indirect control until the fifteenth century, when the Venetians had important colonies on Crete, Corfu, and numerous other islands. The Venetian intention was not control of territory but control of trade, and they became the envy of and the model for their neighbors.[24] It was on islands that they developed immensely valuable sugar plantations. Sugar production began in Syria and Palestine, but, when control of these areas was lost in the fourteenth century, the technique was moved to Cyprus, and then to Crete and Sicily. There it became associated with slavery, so that when in the fifteenth century the Genoese took sugar production to the Canaries and the Madeiras they imported Africans as the newest slave supply. Columbus introduced sugar in San Dominique in 1493. From there sugar and slavery spread in tandem throughout the Caribbean.[25]

Imperial archipelagos also had roots in the western Mediterranean. The Catalans invaded Majorca in the thirteenth century, turning it into an entrepôt of free trade and low taxes, which attracted a polygot population of Christians, Muslims, and Jews. The Aragonese entered the competition for islands in the next century, picking up isles on the North African coast that gave them access to the sub-Saharan gold trade. At the same moment, Genoese communities were spreading throughout the Mediterranean islands, constituting yet another loosely constructed trading empire. Islanders themselves were active in colonization, the Majorcans being at the forefront of exploration and settlement. In this period, intrusions on the mainlands remained "shallow and feeble," a measure of how European imperialism was a seaborne operation from the very beginning.[26]

When the eastern Atlantic islands began to attract European attention in fifteenth century, their discovery and colonization was another multinational enterprise, with Majorcans and Catalans, together with the Portuguese, taking the lead. By the mid-fifteenth century there existed what Felipe Fernandez-Armesto has called the "Atlantic Mediterranean," projecting itself gradually south and west from the Canaries and Madeiras to the Cape Verdes and Azores. There were by then not only Italians, Spanish, and Majorcans, but French and Flemish involved in trade and colonization.[27] And these archipelagos were now connected with northern nodes of trade and exploration in Ireland and England. There is evidence that Columbus sailed on Portuguese ships to Galway and Bristol, and that he may even have gone to Iceland.[28]

The expansion further west was therefore not such a great leap, physically or imaginatively, as we have been lead to believe by those who see 1492 as representing a great historical turning point. On the contrary, its late medieval origins are now reasonably clear. Europe's maritime technology and navigational experience had been honed by centuries of experience, but no less significant was insular romanticism and the late Medieval millenarianism, without which the westward thrust is inexplicable.[29] Europeans did not possess sufficient military power to open the overland trade routes to Asia closed to it by the Turks. In effect, they took the only option open to them, going offshore and becoming, as J.S.R. Phillips puts it, "commercial empires held together by novel supremacy at sea, by holding strategic points" but avoiding continental commitments until the nineteenth century.[30] "The Sea is the only Empire which can naturally belong to us. Conquest is not in our interest," wrote the Englishman Andrew Fletcher in 1698.[31] None of the great ancient empires of the Greeks or the Romans had relied as much on sea power; nor had the Asian powers bothered to militarize their adjacent seas. But now Europe used the one resource that gave it an advantage, namely skill in shipbuilding and navigation, to create something quite unprecedented, what Charles Boxer correctly called seaborne empires but could just as well be described as island empires.[32]

For the first three hundred years of island empires it was the Atlantic Oceania, not the continents, that were the prime object of European desire.[33] It will be remembered that the initial objective of the voyages of discovery were the riches of the old world of Asia. Initially, Europe thought that islands "were best if they were inhabited, preferably by docile and industrious people," writes J. H. Parry.[34] Europeans sought and found such islands in the Indian and later the Pacific Oceans, but the results of their Atlantic explorations were at first disappointing. Some islands there were inhabited, but the inhabitants were judged insufficiently docile or industrious. Beginning with the Canaries they were brutally conquered, the populations extinguished; and, with these extinctions, the original sense of place and history was erased, to be replaced by new, hybrid identities.

For most of the early modern period, islands afforded strategic advantages that no landlocked outpost could offer. They, not inland places, were the initial points of trade on the African, American, and Asian coasts.[35] When European interest turned to the extraction of resources, islands offered some of the most lucrative opportunities. Beginning with the Azores and Madeiras, islands were first areas to be stripped of their native timber, animal and plant populations.[36] The next step was the importation of European herds and crops, altering forever the ecology of these places. The production of sugar using slave labor, already perfected on Mediterranean isles, was first transferred to the near Atlantic islands and then to the Caribbean. And islands were to remain the preferred locations for plantation economies for almost three hundred years.

Empires of Access

"When we think about the expansion of Europe we often conflate an oceanic presence—or a bounded presence on an island or a littoral—with continental territorial control," writes Elizabeth Mancke.[37] As she rightly notes, control of the seas and islands was not just a prelude to territorial possession but ends in themselves. These are best defined as *empires of access,* not empires of possession. The interiors of the Asian, African, and American continents were neither known nor coveted until the nineteenth century. What was desired was access to the goods (including slaves) that were produced on the continents, not the continents themselves. This was best achieved by control over coasts and coastal islands. The success of just such a strategy in the Mediterranean in the late Middle Ages led to its extension to the African coast in the fifteenth century and its ultimate projection to all the world's regions by the end of the eighteenth century. Europeans were content to let the peoples of the interior, whether they be African slavers or Native American fur traders, control their end of the business. Indeed, they preferred it that way.[38]

The empire of access was empire on the cheap. Even the strongest Renaissance kingdoms were weak and poor by world standards. Their legitimacy was dependent on dynastic claims over peoples who were linguistically, culturally, and ethnically heterogeneous, and over territories that were not contiguous. In short, their domains were more like archipelagos than like continents. Borders mattered much less in polities where allegiances were organized hierarchically rather than horizontally, where sovereignty was attached to persons rather than to territories.[39] In a world of vertical rather than horizontal perspectives, Europeans at every level were willing to accept authority from "above," even when this power was from the "outside." Loyalties to foreign rulers, which would be quite unacceptable in the modern territorial state, were routinely accepted until the nineteenth century, when the rise of the nation-state finally severed sovereignty from individuals and vested it in clearly defined lands and peoples.

Early modern kingdoms did not possess the kinds of standing armies necessary to control territory outside their own domains and certainly not that overseas. They were used to wielding power at a distance, handing out islands as feudal fiefs and concessions rather than ruling them directly. Anthony Pagden has described the most powerful empire within Europe, that of Charles V, as being more like "a modern multinational corporation than a state."[40] Crowns did not yet possess a monopoly on armed force and continued to rely on private individuals and groups as extensions of sovereign power. Granting charters, fiefs, and special powers was the way in which European expansion had proceeded in the later Middle Ages, and this would continue to be the practice up through the eighteenth century. The Portuguese found they could keep Madeira going only by encouraging the settlement of Flemings.[41] To achieve their goals, kings readily indulged the "insular romanticism" of the nobility, freely handing out fiefdoms on islands that were only presumed to exist. Columbus may have thought he would be rewarded with Antilia, which he fully expected would be one of the stepping-stones to India.[42] Monarchs could afford this generosity because the supply of unclaimed isles seemed inexhaustible. It was a cheap and easy way of extending patronage; and Columbus was only one of many islomanes to be encouraged by such a strategy, which worked well as long as the reality of the Atlantic isles was still obscured by the legends conjured up by enduring insular romanticism.[43]

In the absence of a standing navy, the licensing of seagoing privateers also allowed kingdoms to make claims with little or no cost to themselves. In the long term, a distinction between noble adventurers like Ralegh and ordinary pirates would have to be drawn, but that did not happen until the late seventeenth and early eighteenth centuries when freebooting began to complicate internal European politics and monarchies found it necessary to place tighter controls over their surrogates on the seas as well as on land.[44] This was done haltingly and re-luctantly, however, for none of the kingdoms had the money or the power to substitute their own armies or navies, especially when this meant diverting them from European affairs. By the mid-eighteenth century, however, European states felt they had no choice but to make the settlers pay for their own protection. When new taxes and laws were imposed, the loyalties of the colonists was sorely tested. The result was that the loosely held continental parts of the empires of access broke away. Today, all that is left of the original European imperium is a handful of islands and islandlike enclaves.[45]

Islands of Capital

The politics of Atlantic Oceania remained largely feudal in nature, but their economies were anything but medieval. While land continued to be the basis of European status, wealth, and power at home, this was not the case of the At-lantic world. It was access, not possession, which offered the greatest rewards for commercial capitalism that gained its greatest momentum on the sea, not on land. This was an extraterritorial economy in which money was to be made in transactions among widely scattered markets. Merchants invested in inventory, not directly in production. In a system that resembles in some ways the just-in-time production schedules of the current global capitalism, merchants left it to the producers to shoulder the costs of the instruments of production, labor dis-cipline, and time lost when demand fell and the labor force was idled. In Eu-rope itself trading goods were produced by the putting-out system, which relied on the labor of tens of thousands of mainly rural people working out of their own small cottages. Urban merchants warehoused both raw materials and fin-ished products in what we called at the time "factories," but they preferred to keep actual production at a distance, like islands in the far sea.[46]

Under this form of protoindustrialization, production of everything from cloth to guns and pots and pans increased enormously without disturbing the geographical distribution of Europe's population, the old rural social structure, or the neofeudal political order. The merchant capitalists operated from within urban enclaves in their homelands or abroad under charters issued by foreign rulers. Commercial capitalism functioned extremely well in this archipelagic en-vironment. Having no territorial ambitions of its own, it was satisfied in play-ing off one sovereign power against another. Profits were made by attempting to calculate when to release or withhold inventory, or by controlling markets ac-cording to mercantilist principles.

Islands were particularly significant in the Atlantic slave trade. Access to sources of slaves required no possession of territory, something that was in any

Illustration 11   Aeriel view of slave trading Bance Island, west coast of Africa

case beyond the power of Europeans to achieve against the overwhelming strength of inland African kingdoms and the deadly effects of tropical diseases. It cannot be said that the African coast belonged to any European nation during this period. The Dutch and the English successfully competed with the Portuguese as supremacy in the carrying trade changed hands several times.[47] Places like Goree and Bance Islands were used to hold and "season" human inventories, natural prisons in this era of forced labor. One of the most successful of these operations was in Cape Verde Islands, whose slave markets had the reputation of being pricey but delivering value for money. Bentley Duncan writes that its slaves were considered a better buy because "the most unfit, the most sickly . . . had already been culled." Cape Verde slaves had "endured the trauma of their first sea passage, their bonds with the mainland were already loosened; their incentive for escape was weakened, and the opportunity to do so much diminished."[48]

A similar strategy of access also applied to the third leg of the infamous Triangular Trade, namely the plantation economies of the New World. Europeans had had their sugar islands in the Mediterranean since the Middle Ages, but the favored location in the seventeenth century became the islands of the Caribbean, where the soils and climate proved right for the crop and the geography crucial to the control of the largely slave labor force. As long as Europeans controlled the waterways, islands' extensive coastline guaranteed them access while denying their captives exit. The same thinking applied to places where white convict labor was imported. It is no wonder that some of the first permanent colonies, staffed with prisoners, were islands. The greater the proportion of coast to interior the better, for smaller islands like Barbados had no hinterlands to escape to. But even larger islands like Jamaica were preferable to the mainlands, and so began the long and tragic association of islands with imprisonment, something that still exists today.

In the seventeenth century, when sugar was king, the Caribbean islands were the world's richest prizes, changing hands frequently as the European powers fought over them. But this competition should not hide the fact that island economies were multinational affairs. Ships under foreign flags were tolerated by local authorities as long as duties were properly paid and authority ritually acknowledged. Even when mercantile measures were tightened in the eighteenth century, the new rules were easily evaded. Smuggling was endemic on islands, where the abundance of coastline was an invitation to free trade. The same sea moats that made islands so attractive to plantation development made them virtually free ports for most of the seventeenth and eighteenth centuries. The defenders of free trade like Adam Smith saw this as an advantage and associated islands with freedom and prosperity.[49] Islands once valued for their wondrous qualities were coming to be seen in much more mundane material terms. Islands were now thought to be the geography most conducive to commerce and therefore to prosperity. The *Encylopaedia of Britannica* of 1797 assured the English of their natural advantage over all continental nations: "Another considerable advantage arises from its accessibility on every side, by which it is open to receive supplies from other countries, and has the convenience of exporting its commodities and manufacturers to all markets, and in comparison of the continents, at all seasons."[50]

Merchant capitalists treated the plantations in the same way they dealt with their hinterland producers in Europe. They rarely invested directly in the production process, leaving its windfalls and risks to the plantation owners. They were no more eager to be in possession of these places than were the royal authorities, who left planters with an enormous amount of power, not only over the lives of their workers, but over themselves. Indeed, by the later eighteenth century, many of the sugar islands had, like the coastal colonies on the mainlands, developed separate identities, still recognizably European but claiming liberties that even the most privileged subjects of the home country would not have dared to assert. In many ways, the power of local authority remained alive and well in the New World up through the eighteenth century.[51]

The settlers continued to operate under the assumptions of the empire of access longer than did their countrymen back home. When, in the second half of the eighteenth century, monarchies became more absolutist in their territorial ambitions and more competitive with one another, they began to exercise a greater measure of control over the New World.[52] This was first met with appeals to honor "ancient liberties" by those holding royal grants. Liberals like Adam Smith supported the colonists' exemption from mercantile controls on the basis that this was consistent with the principles of free trade.[53] But the monarchs saw only the threat to their authority, and ultimately American settlers were forced into armed rebellion. Revolts fared less well on the islands than on the continents however. Most of the islands or parts of islands, with the exception of Haiti, remained yoked to their former masters.[54]

The People of the Great Western Sea

Size and distance are relative matters, and the archipelagos of early modern Atlantic Civilization did not feel small and remote to islanders themselves. Given considerable free rein, settlers came to regard the sea as belonging to them, drawing the world closer, expanding rather than foreclosing their horizons. During this three-hundred-year span it was land, not sea, that created the greater sense of remoteness and limitation. It was the continents that appeared on maps in narrowed or shrunken form, filled with blank spaces, while the oceans remained crowded with islands, large and small.

Between 1500 and 1800 the sea and its islands loomed large in the European imagination. Indeed, the maps of the sixteenth century exaggerated not only the number but the size of islands. Just as the mythic island of Antilia had earlier been represented as so large that it could easily be mistaken for Cipangu (Japan), so now known islands were represented as "monstrously swollen, enlarged out of all proportion to the continental land masses," Bentley Duncan notes. The Madeira archipelago, which is about the size of Long Island, was portrayed as the size of the present New York State. "The huge islands emphatically assert their presence in the mid-Atlantic and furnish graphic testimony to both the psychological and practical significance of islands to men of former times."[55] On the great Venetian sea chart of 1539, the Carta Marina, the sea is full of monsters, and the islands appear as disproportionately large and fascinating.

In an era before standard measurement, scale was much less precise than it is today. Yet this is not sufficient to explain why islands were so outsized in early modern cartography. "Smallness is a state of mind," Epile Hau'ofa reminds us.[56] Of course the meaning of islandness varied enormously. For the African slave or the English convict the same shores that offered unlimited horizons to their

Illustration 12   Section of Olaus Magnus's Carta Marina (1539) showing Iceland and Greenland

masters were prison walls. But for a majority of Atlantic islanders it is probably safe to say that the sea was not a limit to but an extension of their possibilities. It has been said of the multiethnic and polyglot merchants of Funichal in the Madeiras that they were "men of true 'Atlantic' outlook, at home on two or three continents."[57] Insularity, as it was then understood, did not mean narrowness and provinciality, but stood for openness and cosmopolitanism.

It is no accident that this was the moment when the English, having cut themselves off from their continental connections, began to think of themselves archipelagically. As Jeffery Knapp has argued, the sixteenth-century English came to see themselves as a chosen people whose insularity was proof of spiritual strength, who would make of this a virtue and conquer the Atlantic "by means of littleness."[58] Colonies in America allowed John Donne to think of "this Iland, which is but the Suburbs of the old world, a Bridge, or Gallery to the new."[59] As they turned westward, first conquering Ireland and then planting themselves on the coasts and islands of North America, the English created what might be called a greater British archipelago.[60] They liked to contrast their island empire, which they believed conducive to liberty, commerce, and prosperity, with the continental empires they associated with despotism and economic backwardness. Separation by sea, once seen as a curse, was now a blessing.

Island empires were viewed as the wave of the future, the highest form of civilization yet known to man. In his *Naucratica: or Naval Dominion* (1798), Henry James Pye compared the new Atlantic to the ancient Aegean and proclaimed it a triumph for humanity equal to, perhaps even greater than that of the Greeks.

> By love of opulance and science led,
> Now commerce wide her peaceful empire spread,
> And seas, obedient to the pilot's art,
> But join'd the regions which they seem'd to part,
> Free intercourse disarm'd the barbarous mind,
> Tam'ed hate, and humaniz'd mankind [61]

"Europe's experiments in conquest, colonization, and commerce clung like a ship's barnacles to the littoral of the world ocean or sought out offshore islands surrounded by sea moats," writes Stephen Pyne.[62] These coasts and islands came to constitute a distinctive world, with its own dynamics. To be sure, this Atlantic sea of islands was to have a much stronger continental flavor than its Pacific counterpart, but it would be wrong to think of it as European for it had pronounced American and African elements. When the Chinese published a guide to the Atlantic in 1701, they lumped together Europeans, Africans, and Americans as "the people of the Great Western Sea," thus capturing more accurately than later continentalist perspectives the true nature of Atlantic civilization.[63]

We have already seen how islands and islanders contributed to all the voyages of discovery, not just as captains and crews, but as the victuallers of the ships that invariably put in at the islands on both the outgoing and return voyages. Without this dynamic sea of islands offering psychological security as well as material support for the triangular trade that was at the heart of commercial capitalism, these voyages would have been not have been possible.[64] As the leading historian of the eastern Atlantic islands has put it: "The islands made signal contributions to the Atlantic world in general. If there had been no islands, seventeenth century maritime commerce would have been distinctly different, and navigation itself appreciably more difficult and more hazardous."[65]

Islands were also crucial to the peopling of the New World. The reluctance of Europeans to leave their homelands and settle the New World voluntarily meant that the process of the Europeanization of the Americas came much later than most of us realize.[66] Islands were particularly subject to overpopulation because, without hinterlands to absorb their surpluses, the only way to survive was to leave. Often it was young men who would leave their wives and children behind to sign onto a passing vessel, especially the lucrative whaling ships. With the money earned at sea, they might then establish themselves on some other shore, later sending for their families. They might even return in old age, a pattern that still today prevails on many islands that lack the resources to support their younger populations.[67] It was not really until the nineteenth century that the newly discovered continents became what Alfred Crosby calls "NeoEuropes."[68] Islands were the first NeoEuropes, but they did not remain so for long. Non-European peoples, especially Africans, dominated most Caribbean island populations, and cultures were quickly creolized. Together islanders and mainlanders made a new Atlantic civilization. It has been described as a "great community extended north and south [that] was frigid and equatorial, African and Europe, black and white, and it wedded the Old World to the New World."[69]

In the sixteenth and early seventeenth centuries, peoples of the African, European, and American littorals often had more in common with one another than they did with the residents of their own hinterlands. Coastal Africans who had a long history of interaction with Europeans have for good reason been called "Atlantic creoles." Many were free people who found their way to the Americas voluntarily, constituting a distinct group quite different from the enslaved Africans from the interior who were later imported to stock the plantation economies. "Black life in mainland North America originated not in Africa or America but in the nether-world between the continents," writes Ira Berlin.[70] Atlantic creoles were prominent in the New Netherlands but also in New Orleans and the Chesapeake region. They farmed, traded, and even owned slaves. They often intermarried with Europeans and Native Americans living in the coastal regions or on the barrier islands of the Atlantic coast. On Kent Island in the Chesapeake there existed a triracial community that managed to hold its own until finally overwhelmed by the Maryland white planter elites later in the seventeenth century.[71]

William McNeill has noted that it was in this period that sea frontiers superceded steppe frontiers "as the critical meeting point of strangers."[72] The peopling of the Americas was as much an Atlantean as a European project. Many of the first settlers on isles and coasts of the Americas were themselves islanders.[73] Even when continents were settled, colonists (with the exception of the Spanish) tended to turn their backs to the interior, preferring to face outward to the sea. "God performed no miracle on New England soil. He gave the sea," writes Morison.[74] For most of the seventeenth and eighteenth centuries New England was as closely connected with the Caribbean and with the Madeiras and the Cape Verdes as with the British Isles. The Azores were particularly closely connected to New England through whaling, a connection that did not weaken until the later nineteenth century.[75] The thirteen mainland British colonies were originally more archipelagic than continental. Connected by sea rather than by land transport, they too belonged to the greater British island empire that stretched from the Shetlands to the Falklands. In the course of the late seventeenth and early eighteenth centuries it even seemed as if the colonists were being drawn ever more to the sea rather than into the interiors of the continent.[76]

There was nothing at all insular about the islands or the islanders. Many, like the Cape Verdeans, learned, by necessity, to feel more at home on the South and North American continents than in their native isles. Ties of trade stretched from the salt islands of the South Atlantic to the fishing outports of Newfoundland. The Yankee cod fleet would sail first to the Cape Verdes to pick up salt before heading for the northern fishing banks.[77] People from the Hebrides adapted easily to Cape Breton Island; and Nantucket was closer in many ways to the Azores than it was to Massachusetts.[78] Islands were to islanders like oases are to desert nomads. And for most of the early modern period, islands were like ships, their populations more like passengers than permanent residents. The summer fishing islands were often occupied by men of several countries who elected an "admiral" from their own ranks to rule for the season.[79] Most island populations were as polyglot as the crews of the ships that paid them call, owing their loyalty and identity more to the sea of islands than any of the continents.[80] They were truly the people of the Great Western Sea.

Eclipse of the Island Empires

It was from its mastery of the seas, not lands, that Europe experienced its first great economic boom, 1500–1800. The wealth accumulated through its archipelagic empires of access would find its way back to the continent, partly to be invested in land and the neo-feudal aristocratic societies that land supported, but also partly to capitalize new industrial enterprises that would ultimately undermine the old order of things. It could be said that events led from islands to continents, but in the end it was the mainlands that had the last say in island affairs. While islands participated in the independence movements of the late eighteenth and early nineteenth centuries, they were less able to defend their autonomy than were the continental colonists. The Haitian revolution proved to be the most democratic of all the Atlantic revolutions of the late eighteenth century, but its success was bittersweet. The black Jacobins were isolated, and Haiti's economy was destroyed, leaving the new island nation vulnerable and impoverished.

It was not islands but continents that were destined to dominate economically as well as politically and militarily. Most of the Caribbean islands remained European possessions until the twentieth century, more rather than less controlled. The modern nation-state was less generous in dispersing its authority than the old monarchies had been. Sovereignty was no longer attached to a person, but to a territory. Boundaries had become fixed, and authority from beyond was ensured by conquest and territorial possession. Atlantic and Pacific islands alike were affected by this new phase of imperialism, which disconnected them not only from one another but from the world at large.

In the late eighteenth century the boundary between land and sea became more definite. The new nation-states concentrated their energies on their own interiors. The rebellious North American settlers declared themselves to be "continentals," and Tom Paine used the argument that if God had meant them to remain British subjects he would never have placed an ocean in between them and the home country. Edmund Burke thought that, short of draining the Atlantic, there was no way that the Americans could be denied independence.[81] The sea, that thing which for three centuries had tied the world together, was no longer seen as doing so. And its islands, which had been perceived as bridges, also lost their power of connectivity.

It was not so much that commercial ties had weakened or that distances had gotten somehow greater. Now the sea was perceived a vast moat, and the islands were taking on an aura of insularity that has haunted them ever since. In the age of industrial capitalism and the nation-state, history turned its back on Atlantic civilization, forgetting that it had ever existed. The nineteenth-century progressive imagination turned inward to focus on roads and bridges, ignoring waterborne forms of transportation. No longer stepping-stones to the future, islands retreated into the mists of history, to remain in obscurity until much nearer our own times.

CHAPTER 6

SCIENCE DISCOVERS NATURE'S
ISLANDS AND ISLANDERS

An island is certainly an intrinsically appealing study object.

—Robert MacArthur and Edward O. Wilson,
The Theory of Island Biogeography

FOR CENTURIES EUROPEANS HAD BEEN FASCINATED with islands, not for their natural features but for their divine and mythological attributes. It was assumed that everything in nature had a divinely determined meaning and purpose that people could determine by the study of scriptures and ancient texts without the need for close observation of the islands themselves. Because everything in nature was symbolic, island scenery held no interest. In medieval and early modern travel accounts "natural scenes are usually invoked for their heavenly or hellish qualities," Peter Coates notes in his work on Western attitudes toward nature, "Rugged places are seen as hell; gardens invested with heavenly qualities."[1] Before the modern era the eye was the least trusted of the senses, which were viewed, according to Eric Leed, as "avenues of sin and corruption," turning man too much to the world and away from God.[2] Little effort was made to record natural details until eighteenth- and nineteenth-century science privileged sight and, with it, close observation. For the first time the island became what MacArthur and Wilson would call an "intrinsically appealing study object," making it the favored place for the new natural and human sciences, a mecca for zoologists, botanists, geologists, and anthropologists.[3]

This explains why the islands that are linked forever in our minds with science—the Galapagos—were neglected for so long before Darwin visited them in the 1830s. Discovered by accident by the Spanish in the sixteenth century, they were christened the Las Encantadas, a name sufficient to ward off learned visitors for the next two hundred years. Known best to whalers and other mariners who stopped there for water and to capture giant turtles to stock their larders, the islands' reputation in the seaborne world was as cursed isles. Herman Melville, who visited them in the 1840s, described them as "an archipelago of aridities, without inhabitation, history or hope of either in time to come."[4] His description owed more to biblical geosophy than to scientific geography, but he was probably closer to the view held by most contemporaries than was Darwin himself.

Disenchanted Islands

Living in an enchanted world created and still governed by divine will, most early modern Europeans and Americans continued to regard the earth as "a kind of gigantic living creature."[5] Their universe remained profoundly geocentric and anthropocentric, endowed with animate qualities irreducible to temporal or spatial quantities. Time was measured differently in every village, and there were no standard measures for distance. People lived by the rhythms of nature and made no distinction between it and themselves, for they understood the human body to be analogous to earth's body, a microcosm to its macrocosm. The earth was born, aged, and died in the same way as man. In the biblical understanding that prevailed until the eighteenth century, everything was interpreted in terms of decline. The proof that the earth was aging and would ultimately pass away was seen in its wrinkled surfaces and ugly eruptions. Mountains were like "Warts, Tumours, Wenns, and Excrescenses [that] are engendered in the superficies of men's bodies."[6] Such a blemished world evoked none of the aesthetic appreciation that was to be lavished on mountains in later centuries. On the contrary, it was the ugliness of earth, oceans, and islands that was repeatedly remarked upon during the sixteenth and seventeenth centuries. Beauty lay elsewhere, in the heavens or in other unseen worlds inaccessible to the senses.

"Animistic beliefs do not necessarily promote reverence for nature," notes Peter Coates.[7] In the case of Christian culture, nature worship had always been associated with paganism and satanism. It was not until the eighteenth century that attention began to turn toward the natural as opposed to the supernatural world, not so much because Christianity lost its influence but rather because religion's understanding of the world had undergone an epochal transformation. The metaphor of the living creature had given way to the mechanistic understanding of the world as machine, set in motion by God at the first creation and running on its own until the end of time according to its own set of natural laws. Henceforth, it became possible to worship God though nature, thereby legitimating the natural sciences in ways that had been inconceivable earlier.

Referring to the cursed Galapagos, Melville wrote that "in no world but a fallen one could such lands exist."[8] But this was already a fading opinion among educated people because what in the previous centuries had been perceived as a degenerative condition was now optimistically interpreted as an improving one. A more beneficent God had placed at man's command a plenitudinous world capable of fulfilling not only all his needs but his dreams. Earthly features like mountains, seas, rivers, and islands, which had been seen as symbols of God's wrath and obstacles to the progress of mankind, were reinterpreted as contributing to human happiness. Mountains were now seen as sources of mineral wealth, and rivers as highways. Islands that were once navigational hazards became convenient stepping-stones, while oceans ceased to be seen as sources of disease, their shores becoming locations for health spas.[9] What had been ugly suddenly became beautiful. Henry Moore anticipated the new aesthetic of mountain glory when he wrote in 1662: "Even those rudely-scattered Mountains, that seem but so many Wens and unnatural Protuberances upon the face of the Earth, if you consider but of what consequences they are, thus reconciled you may deem them ornaments as well."[10] What earlier had been referred to as this "little dirty Planet" was now seen in an entirely different light. At the end of the eighteenth century an observer of this change could write that "the dreary and dismal view of waste and universal ruin is removed, and the mind is presented with the pleasing prospect of a wise and lasting provision for the economy of the nature."[11]

By the mid-nineteenth century, "science, more than any other intellectual force, exorcised the curse that seem to hold the Galapagos Islands spellbound. No longer could any place in nature hold evil or withstand change," Edward Larson writes.[12] Nature was finally coming into its own as something worth paying attention to as a reality rather than as symbol. It was ceasing to be understood as a set of heterogeneous qualities and becoming a uniform thing that could be measured and quantified according to certain universal standards. The idea that islands were made of a different stuff than mainlands, or that each ocean behaved very differently from every other was giving way to a concept of universal natural laws acting the same in every place and at every time. Natural history was slowly disentangling itself from biblical history, while human history was also coming into its own as autonomous from divine will. The age of miracles had finally given way to the age of achievements during which mankind would fulfill its potential through the mastery over the bountiful natural world that God has so generously provided.

The western world was experiencing the consequences of a revolution in temporal and spatial scale that had begun in the sixteenth century. The closed, centripetal world of the Middle Ages was disintegrating as both the infinitely small and the infinitely large became accessible to a learned public. The invention of the microscope in 1593 and the telescope in 1608 had the unanticipated consequence of destabilizing the geocentric and anthropocentric universe that had prevailed up until then. The Age of Discovery had begun the process of unmooring the earth from the heavens by extending the horizon far beyond the point that the sky and the oceans met. By the seventeenth century, scientists were exploring deep space; and by the eighteenth century time was also losing its finitude. "A long—or indefinite—time-scale was the logical correlate to the previous century's acceptance of infinite—or indefinite—space," writes Roy Porter.[13]

Now that the immensity of the universe was established, time as well as space burst their previous bounds. Having challenged the biblical geography and history that had set the beginnings of time at Creation only six thousand years earlier, speculation about the age of the earth and of mankind accelerated. While they could not agree on the antiquity of man or the age of the earth, eighteenth century scientists could assent to James Hutton's 1785 conclusion that time "is to nature endless and as nothing." In a stunning paper, "Theory of the Earth," which opened the way for the modern earth as well as human sciences, Hutton declared that he could detect "no vestige of a beginning—no prospect of an end."[14]

The story of the earth could no longer be told in the condensed dramatic terms of biblical geography, with its fixed beginning and sudden finale. The idea that the world's features were the product of divinely inspired one-of-a-kind events like the Flood was discarded for understandings that emphasized ongoing natural processes that began deep in the past and would continue far into the unforeseeable future. Now that divine will was no longer active, it was not necessary to assign supernatural meanings to any event or any place. Beginnings did not have to be seen as an act of creation or endings as willful destruction, for nature did not operate by such intentions. The focus shifted from catastrophic events to gradual, almost invisible processes that had been happening in the same way for millions of years. This made it possible for scientists to deduce from what they saw happening in their own time causes of changes that happened much earlier and also to predict future events.

It was now possible to look at the world in an entirely new way, as a gradual, ceaseless evolution. Mountains were now understood as constantly eroding, but at the same time being thrust up by forces operating deep within the earth. Islands were subject to the same general law of nature. The appearance and disappearance of islands, once seen as proof of divine intervention, now had a natural explanation, as explained by Alexander von Humboldt. "Islands, which the action of submarine fires have raised above the waters, are decked by degrees in rich and smiling verdure; but these new abodes are often laid waste by the renewed action of the same power, which caused them to emerge from the bottom of the ocean."[15]

Now that islands were everywhere subject to the same natural laws, they ceased to belong to that mythical geography that for so long had placed them on the periphery. The Atlantic archipelagos were the first to become disenchanted. It was already clear by the eighteenth century that paradise was not to be found there. Then, when the Pacific isles turned up empty, paradise disappeared from the distant present and was relocated to the deep past, and it became the subject of historical as opposed to geographical speculation. Islands in the Pacific now became objects of scientific expeditions rather than locations for armchair speculation or fictional treatment. For the first time islands and their inhabitants passed from the realm of the supernatural into the category of the natural. "Explanations in which miracles were central had yielded to more naturalistic viewpoints," notes Porter. "Mother Nature had been objectified."[16]

Travel Makes Truth

Islands had previously belonged to the fluid indeterminate world of the sea, always appearing and disappearing, hard to pin down. They were more easily imagined than located with great precision. As we have already seen, islands moved about on early modern maps, changing size as well as position. Islands found were easily lost, adding to their reputation for being the most mysterious of all land forms. Western navigators had long used a compass and sextant to determine latitude, but until the eighteenth century precise longitudinal location eluded them. In waters that were new to them they had to rely on local pilots and indigenous maps to find their destinations. Columbus had been dependent on local knowledges in the Caribbean; and, despite all his skills as a navigator, Captain Cook was only too happy to rely on local informants and their charts to guide him through the far reaches of the Pacific.

The problem of determining precise longitude was that it required accurate measurement of time, and until the eighteenth century this could not be kept with any great accuracy at sea. The result was that captains navigated by a combination of latitude, dead reckoning, and personal experience. Ships tended to crowd into well-known sea-lanes, where they were vulnerable to attack. If they missed the longitude they were seeking, their voyage could be extended by weeks and even months as they searched back and forth, their crews ill and starving, sometimes mutinous. The search for a way to determine longitude had become obsession with British naval authorities who had seen whole fleets wrecked on treacherous isles. The loss of two thousand men on the Scilly Isles in 1707 prompted Parliament to pass the Longitude Act in 1714, which established a handsome prize of twenty thousand pounds to be awarded to the first to prove an accurate method. Astronomers were convinced that a way could be found to use observation of the heavens for this purpose, but, in the end, it was the humbler profession of clockmaking that showed the way. John Harrison, a mechanical genius of lowly origins, overcame the devious resistance of some of England's most powerful scientists to secure his claim to the prize. By inventing a clock that could remain accurate under any condition, even the roughest seas, he made possible the accurate calculation of longitude. As Dava Sobel put it so memorably: "He wrested the world's whereabouts from the stars, and locked the secret in a pocket watch."[17]

By the end of the eighteenth century, it was possible to plot with reasonable precision the location of coasts and islands that had only been guessed at earlier. Sea charts were now cleared of monsters and fantasy islands, though a few of the latter were to linger well into the nineteenth century. Maps became less decorative and more practical, but what they lost in aesthetic value they more than made up for in utility. Geography had finally supplanted cosmography, and accuracy now required that cartographers ease themselves out of their armchairs and venture out to measure and locate. The prestige of geography now depended on fieldwork, for truth was now the product of firsthand observation.[18]

Once discovered, islands now remained fixed in place. This made it possible for scientists to replicate one another's observations and experiments at particular locations. Now it was possible to do accurate science on islands, to observe rather than just speculate. Though earlier voyages had resulted in chance scientific discoveries, the eighteenth century initiated the scientific expedition, the prime purpose of which was not to bring back profitable goods but valuable knowledge. Scientific travel did not just bring back hard evidence; it also created the appropriate distance between the scientist and the object of his study that was to become the standard for scientific objectivity during the Age of Enlightenment. Earlier generations had relied on secondhand accounts or written texts for truth. Henceforth, nothing but first hand observation would suffice. The authority of the eye was established and the focus was now on facts.

Ships now set to sea loaded not only with the best scientists of the day, but with the most up-to-date equipment, optical and other scientific instruments capable to recording the minutest details. The new scientific explorers kept voluminous journals filled with precise, if dull, observations written in the plain style that was coming to be accepted as appropriate to science. Every effort was made to keep the observer out of the text, thus heightening the appearance of objectivity. The subjects recorded in the sea logs changed, and the fabulous, which had once been the centerpiece of travel accounts, gave way to the factual.

Science divorced itself from literature in terms of both style and content, though the travel fiction remained immensely popular among the general public.[19]

Islands held a particular attraction for the scientific travelers of the eighteenth and early nineteenth centuries. The young Charles Darwin could not wait to set foot on his first tropical island, St. Jago in the Cape Verde group. His shipmates were evidently less enthusiastic about going ashore, for he wrote in his diary: "And this Island that has given me such instruction & delight, is reckoned the most uninteresting place, that we perhaps shall touch on during our voyage." His experiences on St. Jago only whetted his appetite for the Galapagos: "I look forward to the Galapagos with more interest than any other part of the voyage." And he was not disappointed, for what he called "a little world within itself," brought him "near to that great fact—that mystery of mysteries—the first appearance of new beings on this earth."[20]

The attraction of islands lay partly in their accessibility, made possible by two centuries of commercial and strategic familiarity with the seas. By 1700 islands were much better known than continents; and it is therefore not surprising that scientific expeditions should land there first. However, it was not that science was interested in the islands for themselves. The appeal of islands lay more in the fact that, as Richard Grove has put it, "the island easily became, in practical environmental as well as mental terms, an easily conceived allegory of a whole world."[21] Islands had long served an allegorical function, symbolizing holy and hellish other worlds, representing alternative visions of society. Now, however, they would serve as easily comprehended stand-ins for the whole natural and human world. True to the Western cultural tradition, science was learning to think *with* islands.

In earlier periods islands had been so appealing precisely because they were remote and unknown, and therefore accessible to the imagination and to speculation. Their ability to function this way depended to a large degree in their belonging to *terra incognita,* beyond the edge of the known world. But now islands were positioned at the center rather than on the periphery of the known. Europe was going offshore to discover not only the secrets of nature but the truth about itself. "This periphery became central to the formulation of western environmental ideas," writes Grove. For this reason "remote islands deserve a place alongside the self-contemplation of the European past—or the history of civilizations—for their own remarkable contribution to human understanding."[22]

"The eighteenth century believed perhaps more strongly than any other that travel makes truth," one historian recently observed.[23] From the eighteenth century onward the Western natural and human sciences found it useful to travel to the ends of the earth, but more specifically to islands, to discover truths that today we find accessible closer to home. Given the superiority of water over ground transportation, islands were more accessible than interiors. Furthermore, their small scale and bounded nature made their study seem so much easier than large land masses. Another attraction lay in the very distance that separated the mainland observer from his object of inquiry, thus enhancing the appearance of objectivity. The scientific expedition became a rite of passage for young scientists and anthropologists wanting to certify their credentials. Just as the pilgrimage created the pilgrim and the voyage imitated the mariner, so scientific travel made the scientist. Much of European natural science was something that began offshore, and was created "from the outside in."[24] The same is true of Western anthropology, which also established itself on remote islands. In this respect, Europe was formed culturally as well as materially by its vast island empires. One could even say that it was the islands rather than continents which made Europe modern.[25]

The Gaze Offshore

Until the eighteenth century, the natural features of islands were sources of fear, even revulsion. Their shores were regarded as points of vulnerability and contamination for islanders; and they were no less feared by mariners, for the vast majority of wrecks occurred on or near their shores. Islands and shipwrecks were synonymous. Before there were sufficient lighthouses and rescue stations, coasts were places that sailors most feared. "Only the harbour, that scene of desire, nostalgia, and collective rejoicing, escapes the repulsive pattern," writes Alain Corbin.[26] Though it was possible to be wrecked on a continent, one could be a true castaway only on an island. It was the isolation of those marooned on islands that captured the eighteenth-century imagination. Defoe was well read in the accounts of castaways when he wrote *Robinson Crusoe*.[27] His account of Crusoe's struggle for survival and his adaptability to his environment had an impact on Charles Darwin, who encountered a real-life castaway when he visited the Galapagos and later analogized this man's experience to the other species he found there. After all, if men changed so as to adapt to nature, so too could other animals.[28]

Islands had a reputation for lawlessness and were often refuges for pirates. All coasts were considered dangerous, not only for their natural hazards but for the wreckers who dwelled on the shores. They lured ships into shallow waters and then looted them.[29] Therefore it is not surprising that people steered well clear of the coast. They were repelled by its smells and sounds, but also by its sights. Swedish travelers traditionally avoided their shores as ugly as well as dangerous, one of them reporting that on a trip to the coast "throughout the whole journey not a single beautiful place had been seen." In that region, coast dwellers built houses well away from the beach with their backs to the sea.[30] The sea was watched more out of fear than with pleasure; and when Robinson Crusoe built his fort, it was well away from the shore, an island within the island. The ocean view, so much sought after today, had little value before the nineteenth century. It was not until Sir Walter Scott wrote *The Lord of the Isles* in 1814 that anyone visited the Isle of Aran off the Scottish coast for anything but its goats milk. "The island was treated for the first time as scenery," according to Robert McLellan, as "something to be looked at . . . whose purpose was to elevate the soul."[31]

The Western world had to be taught to see the sea and its islands as natural phenomena. Before the eighteenth century the ocean was largely invisible to those onshore, for whom it was not a place in itself but a highway to other places. During the early modern period the sea was perceived by writers like Hakluyt and Ralegh, and captains like Cook and Vancouver, as "merely a space to be traversed." They did not spend much time observing it but focused on those far shores that were their points of destination. It was not until Addison and Burke attached the notion of the sublime to the sea in the first decades of the eighteenth century that it suddenly riveted Western attention and was fore-grounded in both art and literature.[32] The Dutch had invented seascapes in the seventeenth century, but it took the British to make the sea and everything that bordered it respectable subject for art and literature. The Western eye had to learn to see the oceans and their islands.[33]

In the sixteenth and seventeenth centuries, the sea had been perceived as an arena of political and economic struggle. Maps of the time filled it with ships of many flags, often doing battle with one another. Sea monsters lingered as sym-bols of watery dangers, but by the eighteenth century the oceans were becom-ing more benign. Charts now showed seas with smooth surfaces crisscrossed by lines of longitude and latitude that gave cognitive and psychological comfort to those who ventured on them. Soon the monsters and the satanic isles that had once populated the oceans would be banished forever.[34] As biblical geosophy gave way to scientific geography, the seas were emptied for the first time of reli-gious content.

It was not so much that sea travel had become safe in the course of the eigh-teenth century. The oceans remained associated with death and destruction, and seafaring continued to be the most dangerous profession until the mid-nine-teenth century when sail was replaced by steam. "The machinery, the steel, and the fire, have stepped in between man and the sea," wrote Joseph Conrad. "A modern fleet of ships do not so much make use of the sea as exploit a highway. The modern ship is not the sport of the waves."[35] In an equally nostalgic vein, Felix Riesenberg has written that "the whole process of steam and machinery and steel at sea has been negative. Passages have been shortened; these new elements have constantly taken away from the seas bad and good, until little but mediocrity remains."[36] This was, however, the culmination of a much longer process of technological and scientific mastery that had already by the eighteenth century rendered the sea a non-place, a mirror to the lands around it.

Nature's Islands and Peoples

While eighteenth- and early-nineteenth-century science was disenchanting some islands like the Las Encantadas, it was reenchanting others, particularly in the far Pacific. Even naturalists like Joseph Banks could not help but use the terminology of paradise to describe what they were encountering. But although the Galapagos would ultimately be known as Darwin's Eden, few any longer thought they had found the biblical original. The old Eden had been God's creation; the new paradise was nature's gift. Louis-Antoine de Bougainville's description of Tahiti in the 1760s displayed none of the millennialist obsession that had driven Columbus three hundred years earlier: "Nature has placed the islands in the most perfect climate in the world, had embellished it with every pleasing prospect, had endowed it with large, strong, and beautiful people. Nature herself dictated the laws. The inhabitants follow them in peace and constitute perhaps the happiest society that the world knows."[37]

Natural conditions were now seen as contributing to moral virtue, something that Christian civilization had never previously conceded. Indeed, the philosophers of the eighteenth century had come to distrust religion's capacity to produce goodness. Only nature could make amen good, for, as Diderot wrote in 1751: "The life of savages is so simple, and our societies are such complicated machines! The Tahitian is so close to the origins of the world, while the European is so close to old age."[38] Happiness and goodness had ceased to be theological issues and had become objects of environmental and anthropological study. Islands would now seem to hold the clues to understanding not only the nature of plants and animals, but the nature of mankind.

The Enlightenment replaced divine predestination with natural determinism. Montesqieu was the first of the philosophers to assign a determining role to geography, arguing that it shaped not only flora and fauna but human populations in significant ways. The plausibility of these ideas were given additional force by Charles Darwin when he affirmed the influence of the environment on the origins and the evolution of species.[39] It became common to talk about mountain people, swamp dwellers, and islanders as formed by their environments. Bodin and Montesqieu were convinced that there was something peculiar about islanders. Though the former thought they were inherently untrustworthy, the latter concluded that "island peoples are more jealous of their liberty than con-

Illustration 13   Devil's Crown, Onslaw Island, Galapagos archipelago. Photo by Eliot Porter.

tinental ones."[40] The *Encyclopaedia of Britannica* of 1797 came down solidly on
Montesqieu's side: "By the unerring and unalienable laws of nature, the people
who live in an island are or may be entirely free." Furthermore, as islands were
seen as more conducive to trade, they are bound to be more prosperous. "All

these blessings and benefits are insured by the lesson that Nature dictates."[41] The term "insularity" entered the English literature only in 1755 and carried none of the pejorative meaning that later attached to the word. In the eighteenth century insular peoples were thought to be not only among the most free, but the most cosmopolitan and progressive people in the world. In the poetry of the day the island was, according to Markham Ellis, a trope of "connection, belonging, and community."[42]

Naturalists had always found islands a happy hunting ground for new species, but in the early nineteenth century isles took on a special importance to the rapidly evolving biological sciences. It was on his visit to the Galapagos in 1835 that Charles Darwin jotted in his notebooks: "The Zoology of Archipelagos will be well worth examination."[43] He had noted a variation among the mockingbirds found there, evidence that species were not stable but changing. It would take more than twenty years for him to arrive at an explanation for this variation based on a theory of natural selection, but islands were now on the scientific map. Alfred Russel Wallace, the great self-taught naturalist whose observations in the Indonesian archipelagos brought him to same conclusions about natural selection, was equally convinced of the centrality of islands to science. "Islands possess many advantages for the study of the laws and phenomenon of distribution," he later wrote in *Island Life*. "As compared with continents they have a restricted area and definite boundaries, and in most cases their geographical and biological limits coincide."[44]

What appealed to scientists about thinking *with* islands was the same thing that had made them attractive to monks and utopians, namely their apparent isolation, seeming boundedness, and the fact that so much about them was still a mystery.[45] That islands were only partly isolated, only imperfectly bounded, and well known to their own inhabitants was sometimes conceded but then immediately ignored by a Western academic establishment heavily invested in its island sciences. Over the course of the late eighteenth and early nineteenth centuries the idea of "insularity," the notion that there was something peculiar about islands and island populations, gained momentum. It was particularly strong among the naturalists, who began to notice the difference in the number and character of island species as opposed to those found on the mainlands. Noting that island animals tended to be smaller, some naturalists attributed this dwarfing effect to scale of the places they found themselves in. Others noted the prevalence of gigantism and attributed this to the same source. Science also attributed the scarcity of populations, persistent archaism, and endemism to islands.

Ultimately all these observations were synthesized in the various works of Wallace and Darwin, the discoverers of the theory of natural selection. Henceforth islands would be the favored place for doing biological science. Most recently, genetic research has fastened on islands like Iceland and Tristan da Cunha, assuming that these will reveal the secrets of the human genome more readily than continental populations.[46] The multiplicity of islands recommends them as places for laboratory-like experiments, where theories can be tested. But what makes an island most appealing is that appears to be a "visibly discrete object" which satisfies all the requirements of modern scientific protocols.[47] Today the Galapagos is ecotourism's most important site, a place like Mecca or Jerusalem, where visitors come with the sacred text in hand to behold with awe the place where evolution was discovered. The isolation and boundedness of the place add to the aura of the science that is still being done there.[48]

The prestige of the new biology was so great by the later nineteenth century that learned circles began arguing from what was discovered about animals to humans, thereby creating secular myths about the nature of islands and islanders that have had a powerful hold on the popular imagination right to the present day. Insularity became one of those unexamined categories that nineteenth century naturalists bequeathed to twentieth-century geography. The notion that there is a natural "law of islands" gradually gained the status of conventional wisdom.[49] In this century perhaps the most persuasive exponent of geographical determinism was Ellen Churchill Semple. "Of all geographical boundaries," she wrote, "the most important is that between land and sea." Noting that all landmasses are islands, she declared that "consequently, the human species, like this form of terrestrial life, bears a deeply ingrained insular character." While acknowledging that islands have often been the crossroads of human migration, she insisted that the "other tendency of islands [is] to segregate their people, and in this aloofness to give them a peculiar and indelible natural stamp."[50]

Semple combined geographical determinism with theories of inherited traits to formulate a notion of island races, the two most prominent being the English and the Japanese. "Consider the pronounced insular mind of the globe-trotting Englishman," she wrote, "the deep-seated local conservatism characterizing that world-colonizing nature, at once the most provincial and cosmopolitan on earth."[51] By her time it was becoming common to refer to the British as an "island race," a theme that was to come to the fore in the world wars of the twentieth century. It was simply assumed that island peoples would be more conservative, accounting for the greater number of archaisms supposed found there. Semple was convinced that islands preserved old forms, even to the point of extinction. The idea that "the sea selects and then protects its island folk" expressed perfectly her Social Darwinist assumptions. She believed Ireland exemplified insular atavism, and she described the Faerøes and Iceland as "museums of Norse antiquities."[52]

Today it is easier to see that the case for insularity was flawed with racialist essentialism from the very beginning. It turns out that small scale just as frequently leads to contact with the outside world, and that islanders have been among the world's most inveterate travelers and migrants. We have seen how in the early modern period islanders were among the most cosmopolitan of all the world's people, isolated perhaps but hardly insular in their habits and attitudes, confirming Lucien Febvre's point that "isolation is a human fact, but not a geographical one. In the case of islands, it depends on navigation, which is certainly not a natural fact."[53]

Island Races and Other Modern Mythologies

As Simon Schama reminds us, the modern world has its own myths "alive and well and all about us if only we know where to look for them."[54] Science, which was supposed to put an end to such things, came to be one of the chief sources of modern mythologies. As had been the case in previous centuries, modern Western cultures have tended to locate their mythic places at a distance. In the late eighteenth century the South Seas were the location of many. Today the Galapagos could be said to have a mythic status in modern science. But modernity's mythical geographies are all around us, and we need look no further than the ideas of blood and soil associated with our ideas about nations. The modern territorial state constructed for itself imagined communities called nations coextensive with the borders they designed for themselves or imposed on other polities. By the nineteenth century the maps of the world were drawn according to the territorial imperatives of the nation-state. Boundaries were indelibly marked and interiors uniformly colored to suggest the homogeneity of populations.[55] Nothing seemed to objectify the existence of territories better than so-called natural boundaries—rivers, seas, and mountains—so it is not surprising that islands would emerge as the most clearly marked territories of all, with island nations like Britain making the strongest claims to being internally cohesive and racially pure.

While the idea of England as "sceptred isle," as "this other Eden, demy paradise, This Fortress built by Nature for her selfe, Against infection, and the hand of warre," had long been present in English consciousness, it was less geography than religion that set the English apart in the early modern period.[56] The English Channel had not been seen as a natural boundary when England still had continental possessions, and not until the era of the French Revolution and Napoleon did the English came to see their boundaries as fixed by the sea and their character as distinctly insular. The idea of the island nation or the island race became ever stronger in the course of the nineteenth century, often to the obliteration of the distinct multiethnic character of Britain itself. And it is worth noting that it was preeminently the English, particularly English males, who thought of themselves in insular terms. Other inhabitants, women and the Scots and the Welsh, did not think of themselves in this way.

In the nineteenth century, when the perceived difference between land and sea was at its greatest, naval force seemed sufficient to protect the sceptred isle against all enemies. But with the invention of the airplane, this confidence was shattered. The erasure of physical barriers only intensified the fiction of English insularity. In the Second World War, it was Churchill's rallying cry: "We shall defend our island whatever the cost may be."[57] When the Channel Tunnel, an idea that had been around for almost two hundred years, came under serious consideration again in the 1980s, the mythology of insularity was invoked once again. Fearing that it would open the way for disease, immigrant hordes, and terrorists, the English living closest to the channel grounded their resistance in geographical terms, portraying their land to be a garden of delights about to be destroyed.[58]

The modern tendency has been to essentialize and totalize space, turning relative differences into absolute ones. From the nineteenth century onward boundaries became much more strongly marked and the cohesion of interiors exaggerated. And this was particularly true of islands and islanders.[59] One consequence of seeing islands as bounded, internally consistent wholes is to attribute to them a spacial unity and temporal synchronicity they rarely have in reality. Though it is common to think of continents as harboring regional diversity and sheltering peoples at various stages of development within their bounds, this has been consistently denied to islands, which are normally seen as culturally and temporally homogeneous. Islands were thought of as the least complex of territories, the easiest to grasp intellectually and to categorize geographically and historically. As a consequence, they were also the most frequently mythologized, the least likely to be understood in all their complexity.

Beginning in the eighteenth century, smaller islands were increasing relegated to the past, losing their contemporaneity to become associated with bygone eras, with prehistory itself. This began with the encounters with the island peoples of the Pacific, who came to be seen not only as more natural but as belonging to an earlier time. Joseph-Marie Degerando, writing in 1797, wrote of the "philosophical traveller, sailing to the ends of this earth, [who] is in fact travelling in time; he is exploring the past; every step he makes is the passage of an age."[60] To the admirers of remote island peoples, their displacement from history was a precious gift, protecting them from the corruptions of modern civilization. But this innocence made them seem, like the children to which they were so frequently compared, vulnerable to the point of extinction. When consigned to a prehistorical condition island peoples were sometimes identified with nature it-self. But even when they were recognized as peoples having a history, they were assigned to the earliest—usually the savage—stage of human evolution. In the emerging Western understanding of history, island peoples were normally un-derstood to be less developed than mainlanders, which provided further rein-forcement of the continents' view of themselves as the vanguard of civilization.[61]

Islanding Anthropology

As biblical history lost credibility and deep time was opened to Western con-templation, islanders were much more likely than continentals to be assigned to the newly discovered category of prehistory or simply to be regarded as peoples without history.[62] This was the condition that the new cultural anthropology of the Enlightenment initially assigned them and in which they remained incar-cerated for most of the nineteenth and twentieth centuries. The nascent study of human cultures, another of the progeny of the eighteenth-century human sci-ences, found islands attractive from the very beginning. The concept of culture as a bounded object capable of being studied in isolation was one of the found-ing fictions of anthropology as a science. In the nineteenth century, culture came to be understood as an internally coherent, clearly differentiated thing, a unique bundle of ideas and practices tied to particular peoples living in partic-ular places.[63] It followed that cultures were best preserved in places that were bounded and insulated, like the rural village rather than the metropolis, on is-lands rather than somewhere in the vastness of continents. Following the labo-ratory rationale of the natural sciences, anthropologists were convinced that "because of their wide diversities, small-scale dimensions, and relatively isola-tion, the Pacific Islands can provide excellent—in some ways unique—labora-tory-like opportunities for gaining deeper understandings in Human Biology, Political Science, etc."[64]

As the profession of anthropology developed, the field trip to an island be-came a crucial rite of initiation. The standard was set by A. Haddon, a Cam-bridge scholar who set out for the islands of the Torres Strait in the 1880s. Since that time the great landmarks of the field have been associated with islands: Radcliffe-Brown's study of the Andaman islanders of the Indian Ocean was begun in 1908; Firth's work on the Soloman Island of Tikopia and Malinowski's observations of the Trobriands of Papua, New Guinea, were both published in the 1930s, followed by Margaret Mead's studies of Samoa, which appeared just after the Second World War. These are only a few examples of what Jonathan Skinner calls anthropology's "unnatural focus of attention" on islands. What all had in common was the tendency to project the qualities of smallness, remote-

Illustration 14   Margaret Mead at Manus, Admiralty Islands, 1928–29

ness, and unknownness on islands, regardless of their actual size, history, or real relationship to the outside world.[65]

Despite Raymond Firth's own evidence that the Tikopia islanders had been extensively exposed to western religion and technology since the early nineteenth century, when foreign plant and animal species were also introduced, he insisted on describing the islands as "altogether outside the orbit of European culture" and "almost untouched by the outside world." He used the term "primitive" even while observing that "most of these islanders have taken to farming, to cricket, to politics, and a few even to anthropology, from which they cast a quizzical eye on the solemnity of European values and institutions." The locals' intense curiosity about the world at large was acknowledged and their wanderings across the Pacific documented, but they remained for Firth an profoundly insular people, essentially unchanged over the centuries.[66]

As late as the 1990s the more distant and isolated the place, the greater the prestige it bestowed on its anthropologists. As had been the case with pilgrims, locations that could be reached only with great difficulty offered the greatest rewards of all. As long as communications remained slow and sporadic, island research retained its privileged position. For novice anthropologists, the voyage was their rite of passage, certifying their credentials and offering access to prestigious positions back home. But, as with research in the natural sciences, distance from the subject was also vital. Those who "went native" or did not return from the field were suspected of being less objective. And, of course, those locals who had turned themselves into anthropologists could never be trusted with their own ethnography. The only ticket to the anthropological profession was a round trip.

Anthropology had come to depend, as did biology, on the metaphor of the island to sustain itself as an intellectual enterprise. It constructed a vision of the world as a mosaic of cultures seen as timeless and bounded things that could be objectively studied from a distance. It arranged cultures along spatial and temporal scales that privileged mainlands over islands. Islands and mainlands had come to be mutually defining, with the one taking on characteristics opposite of the other.[67] Mainlands are invariably near, while islands are always far or remote. Mainlands are always at the center and known, islands always on the periphery and unknown. In terms of history, mainlands occupy the present, while islands are associated with the past. Continents stand for progress, while islands exemplify backwardness. Always the "other" to mainlanders, islands serve to sustain continents' view of themselves as being at the center of the world order. Until very recently the "quizzical eye" of islanders was unable to deflect the all-powerful gaze of visitors from the continents.

No Island Is Really an Island

Today it is easier to see the constructedness, the mythological status of the island/mainland dichotomy. It is now clear that, to paraphrase John Donne, no island is an island entire to itself. There is no such thing as total isolation. Goods, people, and ideas have always moved across boundaries, even so-called natural ones; and there is no culture in the world that can be said to be fixed and bounded, separate from other cultures. The distinction between islands and mainlands is, as we have seen, an arbitrary one, good to think with but difficult to demonstrate from physical geography itself. Islands and mainlands belong to the same geological, biological, and cultural continuum. "In a literal sense, there is nothing specific to island societies as a category," notes Thomas Eriksen. "Nor are islands necessarily more isolated than other places."[68] Isolation is not something that is given, but created. It is at least as common on continents as on islands. When groups isolate themselves, making "cultural islands" of themselves by either declaring themselves remote or identifying with the past rather than the present, they do so quite self-consciously.

This kind of islanding has gone hand in hand with cultural contact for centuries, but became more widespread in the nineteenth and twentieth centuries as the process that we now call globalization intensified. Young men from the Faerøe Islands living in Copenhagen in the nineteenth century first learned to think of themselves as islanders there. Danish nationalists made clear to them that they were strangers on the mainland, so they created a Faerøese culture, complete with a newly invented written language, which they then brought back to the islands. By the 1890s they had established their insularity, which resulted in semiindependence from Denmark after the Second World War.[69] Because of its involvement with imperial economies since the seventeenth century, Mauritius has one of the most diverse populations in the world, but it nevertheless has seen the rise of a revitalization movement intent on maintaining a spurious Mauritian purity by cutting itself off not only from the world but its neighbors.[70]

Iceland is another example of a place that, while fully engaged with the world on every level and by no sense remote except in terms of physical distance, has developed an image of itself as a cultural island, pure and uncontaminated by the outside world, true to its origins and therefore more Nordic than the Nordic mainlands. None of this has anything to do with the nature of the island itself. Iceland's cultural insularity was in fact born on the mainland. Its sense of its own uniqueness was initially shaped by eighteenth- and nineteenth-century visitors who romanticized Icelanders in much the same way that peoples of the South Seas were idealized as especially virtuous and uncorrupted. William Morris, the English socialist, saw Iceland as a model for his kind of utopian society, while Theodore Roosevelt declared Iceland the true home of democracy.[71] The first indigenous Icelandic identity was forged on the mainland, born among Icelandic students in Copenhagen, who were affected by romantic nationalism that was current there in the early nineteenth century. Once brought back to the island it developed a momentum of its own, culminating ultimately in national independence from Denmark.

Today's Icelanders play with the world's view of them as remote and exotic while maintaining a view of themselves as being at the very center of the world. The idea that they are the "last surviving Vikings" is a powerful magnet for tourists, but this strong identification with the deep past also serves Icelanders as psychological protection against the traumas that engagement with modernity and encounters with the world at large have brought to the island. Iceland today is perhaps the most dynamic but also most rooted country in the world. Its constructed insularity and aboriginality has served it well.[72] But not all islands have profited from the totalizing and essentializing notions that have been thrust upon them by continental science and anthropology. In the modern age, the myth of insularity cuts both ways.

CHAPTER 7

WORLDS OF LOSS

Islands in the Nineteenth Century

> The whole concept of the island, which until recently was implicit with all manner of promise, is now redolent with loss.
>
> —James Hamilton-Paterson,
> *The Great Deep: The Sea and Its Thresholds*

IT IS DIFFICULT TO IMAGINE LOSING A MOUNTAIN or a continent, but islands are forever going astray. According to Henry Strommel there were at least two hundred "lost" islands on maritime charts in the nineteenth century. Many were there after centuries of fruitless searching, others were of more recent vintage, but all were testimony to the way that "remote or uncharted islands have exercised a peculiar fascination over the imagination."[1] Today, despite the fact that the world is now mapped in the minutest detail, searches for "unknown" islands continue. Using the Landsat satellite, even the minutest isles are now locatable. In 1976 one the size of an average house lot was found and was named Landsat after its discoverer. As in the past, each new find enlarges the realm of *terrae incognitae* and stimulates further imagining. Three years after Landsat Island was put on the map, an American admiral of an aircraft carrier was so certain that he had located an undiscovered reef off Diego Garcia that two extensive searches were authorized, called off only after much waste of time and expense.[2]

Even as we map the globe with ever greater precision, islands remain chimerical. "One seldom looks at an island without also imagining it disappearing behind a bank of fog or storm clouds which at length clear to reveal an empty ocean," writes James Hamilton-Paterson.[3] But even when they are not lost in any geographical sense, islands remain our most poignant symbols of temporal absence, the locus of longings peculiar to the modern era. In earlier periods, islands could be lost in space but were always present in time. Paradisical and utopian is-lands occupied a distant present. As long as time and space constituted a closed system, everything was to one degree or another contemporary. "Up to the nine-teenth century those who gave any thought to the historical past supposed it much like the present, " writes David Lowenthal. "And chroniclers portrayed by-gone times with an immediacy and intimacy that reflected the supposed like-ness."[4] In the biblical understanding of history that prevailed until then, nothing was beyond resurrection. As symbols of decay rather than extinction, even ruins bore the promise of regeneration.[5]

Our modern sense of loss is quite different. The lost islands of today are not just misplaced but gone forever because time's arrow now points in only one di-rection, away from the past, toward the future. The past is unrecoverable except through memory or some form of deliberate historical reconstruction. The boundary between past and present may be variously located, but it is deeply etched in our psyches. Even as our sense of time has deepened, from a few thou-sand years to billions, it no longer takes centuries to make something historical. Yesterday's throwaways are today's antiques; and golden ages, previously set in some distant time, now belong to our lifetimes, usually to our childhoods, which now constitute a secular substitute for paradise lost.

Redolent with Loss

Our obsession with getting on, with moving ahead, prompts us to draw up the bridges to our past. The measure of an "advanced" society is the degree to which it has left the past behind; modern maturity is equally dependent on the metaphor of growth, leaving behind a series of extinguished earlier selves.[6] Yet precisely because the modern collective and individual sense of self is so reliant on distancing the past, both have become wholly dependent on tangible evi-dences of what has been lost to validate themselves. Never before has so much been memorialized, reconstructed, and preserved. Modern Western culture haunts its dead and cultivates its losses. Peter Fritzsche describes our "well-articulated despair over the disappearance of the past [which] is constantly, even obsessively, represented in reflection and mourning."[7]

The story modern Western civilization has told itself about progress requires that it distance itself from the past in order to reassure itself of its forward move-ment. As Fritzsche puts it: "While nostalgia takes the past as its mournful sub-ject, it holds it at arm's length. Nostalgia constitutes what it cannot possess and defines itself by its inability to approach its subject, a paradox that is the essense of nostalgia's melancholia."[8] Over the last two hundred years we have invented all kinds of ways to accomplish this extraordinary mental feat. We collect the past within the walls of museums and preserve it in special historical districts. We cultivate, even create, ruins for the same purpose. We not only store useless bygones in our attics, but turn our homes into memory palaces. Never have the dead been better provided for than in the modern cemetery; never has childhood been so carefully protected and its memories more tenaciously preserved

The modern sense of the passing of time depends on a series of bounded, discrete locations—home, school, workplace, retirement communities, cemeteries— which keep each age and era separate from another. In effect, the modern sense of self depends on the spatialization of the past, islanding it by keeping it neatly bounded and distant. Not all spaces are amenable to this function. Open, contiguous spaces do not readily maintain the aura of historicity. Urban life offers few refuges for the past. The period styles of suburbs offer only the illusion of tradition, propelling our quest for the bygone ever farther afield. Remote places seem so much better suited to the preservation of the past, and none better than islands, which have become, often despite themselves, a prime repository of pastness.

Ever since the eighteenth century, continents have been wresting from islands their previous status as destinations, temporal as well as spatial. As time's arrow pointed toward the mainland, islands came to be seen as backwaters, places of origins or points of return, the ultimate symbols of worlds transcended and eventually lost altogether. Places that had once been seen as full of promise became emblems of loss. Island economies, previously the leading edge of capitalist development, were now termed traditional and preindustrial. Island societies, once among the most cosmopolitan and dynamic in the world, came to be seen as static and aboriginal. Community, something that modernity had torn apart, seems to have survived only on islands.

Once again islands were becoming symbols of something that had little to do with their own realities. Some islands did lose their economic base and populations, but many remained fully engaged with the world economy, intensely affected by its repeated ruptures and adapting to these in a most innovative fashion. Indeed, over the course of the nineteenth century, the pace of change on most islands was as great, if not greater, than that in many parts of the mainlands. But this did not prevent them from being viewed as anachronisms, mired in the past, appearing, as was the fate of the Hebrides, "as if in a rear-view mirror."[9] By the end of the nineteenth century it was Atlantic islands' destiny to become emblems of pastness for mainlands held prisoner by their myth of progress.

Modern nostalgia is the product of the profound sense of historical rupture that came with the revolutions of the late eighteenth and early nineteenth centuries. At this critical moment, the past became a foreign country, all the more precious because it seemed so remote and inaccessible. The nineteenth century began by ruthlessly destroying all it deemed anachronistic. It ended, however, cultivating anachronisms, preserving bygones but also inventing them. Islands became important sites for the appreciation of the quaint and the primitive. If islands no longer provided a vision of the future, they were nevertheless ideal venues for time travel to bygone eras. They came to be associated with the infancy of mankind and with childhood itself. Reconfigured as places of origin, islands were no longer treated as gateways to the future but as access to a mythic past. Once the favored destination of male adventurers who left women and children at home, islands became the resort of families, identified with domestic pursuits and with home itself. What had once provided space for masculinist dreams of escape now nurtured fantasies of return to the womb.

Illusions of Insularity

It has been said that "the Portuguese caraval opened the Atlantic world, and the railway closed it."[10] In the nineteenth century, Western civilization came decisively onshore, turning its back on the oceans. The great age of islands was giving way to a new age of continents, an era that brings us to the brink of our own times. Though we cannot attribute this shift to any one factor, two developments were clearly central: the rise of the territorially bounded nation-state and the triumph of industrial capitalism. The oceans, which had previously connected, now divided. As destiny became continental, the boundary between land and sea took on a new meaning. Now that time's arrow pointed inland, all that lay offshore suddenly seemed archaic.

In the nineteenth century, nations drew their boundaries tighter, making ever greater distinctions between themselves and their neighbors. At the same moment, capital, which had previously been content to control access to markets, embarked on its own territorialism. The new industrial capitalism was based on possession not just of commodities, but of the means of production. Merchants previously content to buy product from independent producers began to concentrate manufacturing under their own direct control in growing cities. The importance of controlling production utterly transformed attitudes toward both time and space, making both industrial capital's most valuable assets. Access was no longer sufficient; control on a national scale became essential. By the middle of the nineteenth century, national economies of scale clearly constituted the desired future. In the early twentieth century, it seemed evident that continental nations, what Halford J. Mackinder called "heartlands," would rule the world.[11]

Islands that previously constituted their own worlds and had been only loosely connected to mainlands now found themselves in an anomalous situation. They were either yoked so tightly to powerful mainlands as to become almost indistinguishable from them or were suddenly remote temporally as well as spatially. Islands that previously had been the favored location as ports and trading places became part of mainlands through massive bridge and tunnel projects. Manhattan had already ceased to think of itself as an island when the Brooklyn Bridge was opened in 1883. That event symbolized the triumph of the continental over the insular. "The continent is entirely spanned," noted one celebrant, "and one may visit, dryshod and without the use of ferry boats, every city from the Atlantic to the Golden Gate."[12] Other islands, like Ellis and Angel Islands, took on new functions as continental gateways, regulating the vast flows of people that now moved directly from continent to continent through vast empty oceans.

Water, previously the passage, now became the barrier. With railway tracks laid coast to coast, travel by land was for the first time in human history faster and more efficient. This changed the strategic equation, creating the basis for land-based military and political power. It coincided with the emergence of territorially based national identities, reinforced by the essentializing, increasingly racialist, ideologies of "blood and soil" so popular by the end of the nineteenth century. In this new world, islands retained something of their economic and strategic value, but as steam displaced sail, the old functions of islands as watering oases, resupply stations, and drydocks was bound to fade. St. Helena, one of the vital stopovers for ships heading for the Cape of Good Hope, began its rapid decline with the opening of the Suez Canal. The Panama Canal had a similar effect on Bermuda and the Falklands. Searoutes between continents were now nonstop. Oriented mainly to the continents, offshore islands lost contact with one another and became truly isolated for the first time in centuries. Island insularity grew in direct proportion to continental inwardness, for the degree to which islands were now regarded as both isolated and distant was as much a consequence to the growing boundedness and cohesiveness of mainlands as any real change in the islands themselves.

Despite their newly perceived remoteness, offshore islands were actually more closely tied to the mainlands both economically and politically. The grasp of the territorial nation-state proved far firmer than the old empires, for it extended not only legal but cultural control to its island possessions. In the wake of the missionary came the schoolteacher. As the nationalizing replaced the Christianizing project, island peoples came ever more firmly within the orbit of national cultures, which used them as anchorage for their own past. Icelanders came to be imagined as more like the original Norse than those living in Norway. The people of the Blaskets and Hebrides were seen as authentically Gaelic in ways that those living on the Irish and Scottish mainlands could never be. True Yankees may have disappeared from Boston and Portland, but they were still to be found on Mt. Desert or Nantucket. Mainlanders were intent on finding on islands peoples who were untouched by the rapid changes that they themselves were experiencing. Yet islands were anything but exempt from modernity's ceaseless creative/destructive forces, arising first from commercial expansion and later from the industrial revolution. Indeed, island peoples were even more exposed than many mainland populations to modernity's structural as well as cyclical ruptures, proving themselves at least as innovative and adaptable. Islands had long since ceased to be subsistence economies. Those devoted to a single export crop like sugar had traditionally imported food, but even islands that mixed farming with fishing rarely produced enough of what they needed. Wage work had a long history on islands, with men leaving their farms for months during the offshore fishing seasons. Whaling sometimes meant years at sea for Nantucket men. Islanders also staffed the merchant marine and navy, but increasingly it was employments on the mainland that drew young islanders, women often going into domestic service, men into fishing and industrial employment. Nowhere were islands self-sufficient.

In the early nineteenth century, islanders were probably the most traveled and cosmopolitan people in the world. Fishing and whaling took island men far from home, and captains of merchant ships were often accompanied by their families to the Far East and other exotic destinations. "In the old days, a good part of the best men here knew a hundred ports and something of the way people lived in them," relates the old Captain Littlepage in Sarah Orne Jewett's novel *The Country of the Pointed Firs*. "They saw the world for themselves, and like's not their wives and children saw it with them. Shipping's a terrible loss to this part of New England from the social point o'view, ma'am." By the end of the century both men and their families were more closely tied to their nearest mainlands with the consequence, according to the old salt, that "a community narrows down and grows dreadful ignorant when it is shut up in its own affairs and gets no knowledge from the outside world."[13]

Migration to mainlands had become a rite of passage for young islanders everywhere in the Atlantic. Their remittances home kept many islands going. A Blasket man commented to Robin Flower: "Weren't it a great thought Columbus had, to find America? For, if it wasn't for America, the Island wouldn't stand a week."[14] Some would return with their savings to marry and settle, but for others "working away" became a way of life.[15] The Blaskets became so dependent on the nearby mainlands not only for economic infusions of support but for women to marry that there was already a saying: "The islander has to repay the man on the mainland."[16]

But economic change was also happening on as well as off island. Until replaced by other sources of alkali, the kelp industry transformed the life on many Scottish and Irish islands in the eighteenth and nineteenth centuries.[17] Lumbering and quarrying came to Maine islands. The men of Swans Island had always alternated between fishing and farming; in the nineteenth century they proved extremely resourceful first with cod and mackerel fishing, and, when these gave out, with herring and lobster, each time adapting to new technologies.[18] Successful adaptation often required bigger boats and processing plants, necessitating higher levels of capitalization and bringing islands even more into the orbit of the mainlands. While Lewis men spent a good part of the year off island, their daughters also migrated to mainland ports to work in the curing and packing houses.

Migration transformed the demographics of many islands, leaving behind aging and feminized populations. During the fishing season, Swans became an "island of women."[19] By and large, island women became more dependent on the earnings of husbands and sons. Like the new suburbs ringing mainland cities, men went off to work, leaving women to toil at home. Women's work became disguised as a labor of love, making islands appear more leisured than they actually were. Hidden behind the domesticated appearance of many islands was a world of child and female labor as intense as anything to be found in the big cities. But because they were seen as belonging to an earlier era, islands readily took on the coloration of hominess, especially for the visitors who found only women and children there.

In the nineteenth century, islands were every bit as connected to continental economies as any of the remoter interior parts of mainlands, and in many cases even more so. Political and economic change had oriented the once semiautonomous archipelagos exclusively to the ports of their mainlands in such a way that left them far more dependent. The steamship had reduced their isolation but underlined their insularity. Regular ferry services anchored islands more firmly to the nearest coast, orienting them away from the wider multicultural Atlantic worlds to which they had once belonged. These new connections did not so much narrow as widen the perceived distance between the islands and the mainlands however. Of the Orkneys it has been said that regular ferry service created "that degree of remoteness which lent a certain romantic charm without the stifling isolation which made contact with polite society impossible."[20] As genteel mainlanders came to be more frequent visitors to islands, the result was not a diminution but a magnification of differences between them and islanders. Even as physical isolation was being overcome, the illusion of insularity was being cultivated for the benefit of the newly developed tourist industry.

How Islands Became Remote

Remoteness was not something associated with islands until the late eighteenth and early nineteenth centuries. It arrived at the western isles of Scotland by the

Illustration 15 "Rocks at Porcupine Island near Mt. Desert," painting by Sanford Gifford, 1864

middle of the eighteenth century, even as these became involved for the first time in wider commercial activity. The population of the Shiant Islands increased and then, quite suddenly, collapsed, leaving only one family to shepherd the flocks of sheep kept there. The number of inhabited islands in the Outer Hebrides dropped from forty-two to sixteen. "Life on the Shiants, which for centuries might have felt like a blessing, could not have been more like a prison," writes Adam Nicolson, the Shiants' current owner.[21]

But even as one phase of island life was ending, another was beginning. "Just as isolation and loneliness were making the Shiants a kind of hell, the first dreamy-eyed travelers from the south were coming to see the islands as a vision of earthly beauty. As the place became difficult and empty for the Hebrideans, it became beautiful and empty for outsiders."[22] Among the first to arrive were the poets and artists, who found there the ultimate expression of the sublime that became the prime aesthetic of the late eighteenth and early nineteenth centuries. In their wake came the educated elites, eager to experience that which they had read about or seen in urban galleries.

Even islands that were neither deserted or yet entirely deindustrialized were often portrayed as wilderness. In the 1840s and 1850s artists from New York City discovered Maine and its islands, casting them into the role of the eastern United States' nature preserve. The paintings of Thomas Cole, Sanford Gifford, and Frederic Church depicting the rugged features of Mount Desert Island created a mythic place and made it one of the first great tourist attractions in America. The fact that the journey took considerable time and effort heightened the sense of wilderness and remoteness. Toward the end of the century, when Mount Desert itself became ever more accessible to steamboat and rail, these qualities were transferred to a succession of other isles—Monhegan, Isle of Shoals, Deer Isle—with the result that, despite rapidly improving communications, the sense of distance was enhanced rather than diminished. Still later, when the motor car brought Maine within easier reach of urban populations, its islands were enveloped in an even greater sense of remoteness.

From the beginning, the journey to Maine's islands was described as a "pilgrimage," but one that involved travel in time as well as space, a return to nature and a more natural way of life. By the 1880s a powerful impulse to nature conservancy was evident among visitors intent on holding back the very forces of progress that they themselves had brought Down East. The locals, who had always viewed the land and the sea from a utilitarian perspective, found metropolitan enthusiasms for pristine scenery and simple living odd, even bizarre. "Yes, I know it's what them artist men come here fur," one old Mainer told a reporter. "But what it amount ter, after all their squattin' and fussin', I don't know."[23]

Summer visitors to Mount Desert were in the vanguard of the effort to ban automobiles from the island. The Rockefellers used a fortune built on oil to build carriage trails, while other sophisticated rusticators indulged in a fantasy of returning to a simple life in the bosom of nature, insisting on calling their coastal mansions "cottages." In pursuit of their conservationist agenda, the leaders of the summer community systematically ignored the island's ongoing history of industrial activities, including quarrying, lumbering, and shipbuilding, focusing instead on a much more distant past, the heroic age of exploration and prehistory. Charles W. Eliot's 1904 development plan even went as far as to declare that "the greater part of the island has never been inhabited or cultivated."[24]

The orgy of renaming that followed reflected the visitors' desire to live in a natural, archaic environment. The town of East Eden was renamed Bar Harbor and prosaic Green Mountain gained historical depth when it became majestic Mount Cadillac. When Rockefeller generosity made possible the creation of a national park, its nomination in 1929 as Acadia completed a process of temporal displacement that severed the island's connection to its own immediate history by associating it with a mythic past. In the competition to attract a generation of tourists more interested in nature than presidential history, the little port of McKinley changed back to its original designation as Bass Harbor in 1966.[25]

Europe's islands were also becoming a favored destination of romantic time-travelers seeking connection with what was imagined to be a simpler and more virtuous past.[26] Iceland shed its earlier reputation for barbarism to become in the eighteenth century a favored place to find the last of nature's noblemen living in harmony with the land as well as with one another. Images of primal innocence had been attached to St. Kilda since Martin Martin's visits there in the late seventeenth century. He described the people as possessing "true primitive honour and simplicity," they "being the only people in the world who feel the sweetness of true liberty."[27] In the eighteenth century, St. Kilda faced stiff competition with the newly discovered isles of the South Pacific, but sustained its reputation as a blessed isle despite the utter impoverishment of its people. "If this island is not the Utopia so long sought, where is it to be found?" asked one of its early nineteenth century devotees, ignoring entirely the isle's utter dependency.[28] The population had long since abandoned fishing and lived largely off birds and their eggs. The first steamer arrived in 1838 and by the 1870s there was summer tourist season in which the St. Kildans played out their assigned historical role as ancient Celts, allowing themselves to be photographed for a price, manufacturing bogus relics to meet their needs in what had become for them, as for every other island, a cash economy.[29] By the end of the century they were acutely "aware to what extent their lives were an anachronism."[30] When the government finally decided it could not provide further subsidies, the St. Kildans were ready, even eager to go. The evacuation of 1930 went off without incident.[31]

Islands had come to be seen by mainlanders as living museums where what had been sacrificed to modernity elsewhere miraculously survived in a purer, more authentic form. First came the antiquarians, then the folklorists, and finally the linguists, all bent on finding and collecting what was believed to have disappeared on mainlands. Many islanders were pleased to find the houses, furniture, and implements that previously had nothing but use value suddenly priced as antiques. They were equally impressed when their songs, dances, and languages were recorded by strangers with fancy university degrees.[32] The attention lavished by Irish nationalists at first astonished and then inspired the Blasket Islanders, many of whom were prompted for the first time to learn how to write in their spoken tongue. The remarkable series of books produced by the islanders in the early twentieth century are evidence of the survival of a vital island culture, but they are masterpieces of realism that stand in sharp contrast to the romances written about the Blaskets by outsiders. The islanders bemoaned their isolation rather than celebrating it. Peig Sayers, the bard of the island, was a mainland woman who had married into an island family for whom the island was "this lonely rock in the middle of the great sea."[33]

By this time the islanders' worlds had narrowed considerably, but this new cultural insularity was reinforced by frequent contact with outsiders who gloried in what they believed to be the uniqueness of the islands and sought to preserve the folk cultures that supposedly survived on the Blaskets, Iona, and other remote islands. However, the insularity that mainlanders so admired was for the islanders themselves a burden, even a danger. As they became more aware of themselves as anachronisms their response mixed pride with embarrassment.[34] The older generation remained cosmopolitan and steadfastly bilingual, conscious of the utility of English and refusing the cultural islanding that the mainland purists advocated. It was generally the younger folk, those most exposed to modern education, who were the readiest to insulate themselves from English culture in the name of Celtic ethnicity or Irish or Scottish nationalism.

It proved hard to ignore the expectations that visitors brought with them. From Boswell and Johnson onward, they came looking for the primitive and ignoring all contrary evidence of modernity. In the 1890s John Millington Synge visited the Aran Islands expecting to find a life reputed to be "perhaps the most primitive that is left in Europe."[35] In time he came to see that what stood for primitivism was in fact a reflection of desperate poverty. But this did not deter several generations of mainland romantic nationalists from holding tight to false stereotypes and foisting these onto the islanders. John Messenger found that many inhabitants of Ireland's Inis Beag behaved in tourist season "according to

the nativist and primitivist expections of outsiders: attire becomes more traditional, canoes are rowed with greater vigor, conversation becomes more boastful
and the like." The men passed themselves off as able seamen, though the seafaring tradition had already faded. Like many Atlantic islanders, they had also
lost the ability to swim, but, intent on demonstrating a certain kind of archaic
Irishness, they hid their affiliations with modernity from the visitors.[36] Messenger's book was bitterly attacked by Irish nationalists who persisted in viewing the
islanders as repositories of antique values but those familiar with the islands conceded that he was not so far wrong. "All those Gaelic peasant buffs, they deify
the islanders far too much," wrote one close observer of the isle of Inishmurray,
abandoned in 1948. "They were just ordinary people who lived on the coast,
and when it got too bleak for them they just left, no fuss about it, it didn't matter to anyone."[37]

The tale of the evacuations of Maine islands in the early twentieth century
tells much the same story. Once an island became firmly established within the
orbit of the mainlands, the pressure to move onshore became ever more powerful. For some fishermen access to mainland markets proved irresistible; the re-
placement of sail by motored boats ended the advantage of being offshore. But
often it was the children who occasioned the move. Islanders everywhere wor-
ried that their children could not get an education because they were living "in
a grave." Maine mothers were often behind the move onshore.[38] Families with
children were among the first to go, leaving behind single folk and older persons, who left when life became untenable. Mrs. Babbage, who left Great Gott
Island in the 1920s, later said that she had "always hoped the island would
sink."[39] By and large islanders went voluntarily, even eagerly. They left the
mourning for "lost" island life to the mainlanders, who soon began to buy up
island properties and turn them into summer places.

The Necessity for Ruins

Before summer people arrived, they had already mythologized the islands, making the islanders icons of the rootedness and community thought to be disappearing in mainland Europe and America. The image of the Hebridean small
farmer, known as a "crofter," already established in the 1870s, represented for
mainlanders "a free and independent way of life which in a civilization pre-
dominantly urban and industrial in character is worth preserving for its own in-
trinsic quality."[40] Though crofting had never provided a sufficient living and
usually was supplemented by other employments or government subsidies, it
was portrayed by its advocates on and off the islands as a simpler, purer existence, always on the brink of extinction and therefore in need of perpetual res-

cue. Already crofting was surviving because of the political support it got from mainlanders. And many crofts were sustained by exiles, who returned only during the summer.

Islanders had come to live in a time warp not of their own making. They saw themselves through the eyes of outsiders who were bent on preserving crofting as tradition no matter how recent its origins. In many instances it was the visitors who stood in the way of sensible changes, conserving outmoded ways that the islanders themselves would rather have turned their backs on. When Lord Leverhulme attempted to modernize the economy of Lewis and Harris in the 1920s he met more resistance from the mainland government than from the islanders themselves. It wanted to keep things the same, regardless of the islanders' desire for economic change.[41] Despite their association with tradition, islands had in fact "moved with the times, albeit it awkwardly."[42] Often the very things that seemed old were in fact quite recent innovations. On Colonsay it was visitors who wore the tartan, itself the invention of an eighteenth-century entrepreneur, and who improved on island lore. It seemed to John McPhee that as far as they were concerned the power of tradition had "grown, not atrophied across the centuries."[43]

The crofting system in the Hebrides was not regularized until 1911. Many of the crafts associated with the islands were also of recent vintage, including the Harris tweed industry, which is a thoroughly modern phenomenon, as much the product of changing urban tastes as indigenous clothing traditions. Like the Highland tartan, the Harris tweed jacket was a relatively recent invention. Scots nationalism contributed to the popularity of the tartan, but demand for tweed can be credited largely to the late Victorian English taste for sports clothes and the clever urban advertisers who seized upon the "homespun" and "hand woven" labels to maintain market share. Weaving was not indigenous to the islands until nineteenth century enclosures evicted many smallholders, replacing them with sheep and driving the poorest of them to work at home for low wages at looms owned by urban merchants. Weaving remained low-skilled wage work even as it underwent its makeover as an "ancient craft" in the early twentieth century.[44] Despite the fact that only the final parts of the weaving process was done in homes and most looms were highly mechanized, the association of tweed with a bygone way of life remained fixed in the minds of contemporaries. "The tweed is more than a cloth," writes Susan Parman, "it is peat smoke and windswept moorland and an image of free individuals who have escaped city life and machines and are masters of their own destinies, an image that fits very well with the complex meanings of crofting."[45]

Today the western isles of Scotland and Ireland all promise the visitor a return to the past, a glimpse of life as it once was less frenzied, more communal. Note has been taken of "the tendency to mythologize these islands, to use them to conceptualize notions of community, peasantry, and preindustrial history."[46] This is no less true of many of America's Atlantic islands, which went through similar transformations in precisely the same period. Though Martha's Vineyard's career as a summer island began as a religious resort, Nantucket appealed to more secular yearnings, generated from the 1870s onward in the great eastern cities, which initially focused on the remoter parts of the New England countryside but came to rest on islands. Despite its semi-industrial history as a major cosmopolitan whaling port, the collapse of Nantucket's maritime economy at mid-century presented a challenge to local businessmen looking for a way to capitalize on its crumbling wharfs and rapidly deteriorating building stock. After failing to attract investors in shorefront properties, island entrepreneurs seized on history as a commodity. They discovered that not only could antiques be "manufactured for the trade," but so too could the look of quaintness.[47] This began in 1870 when one of the abandoned houses was designated the island's "Oldest House." By the 1880s other buildings received similar historical designation, some of them restored to look older than they actually were. With the founding of the Nantucket Historical Association in 1894 this traditionalizing project went forward with even greater vigor. The island's urban, industrial past was so carefully hidden behind this genteel facade that visitors could be forgiven for thinking "history [had] stopped nearly a half century ago."[48]

Few perceived the rich and dynamic protoindustrial history documented by the decaying wharfs and rotting sailing ships grounded in the harbors. The islands' engagement with the wider Atlantic world, their willingness to accept and master change, was missed entirely by those who saw only wreckage.[49] What on the mainlands would have been celebrated as evidence of progress was interpreted here as lethargy and backwardness. And all that had gone before was subsumed under the blurry vision of the Good Old Days, that original state of bliss from which industrial society had fallen. Dilapidated houses and cellar holes were visible signs of that decay, marking the boundary between now and then, but also holding out the possibility of renewal for those who would invest in restoration. "Ruins provide an incentive for restoration, for a return to origins," John Brinckerhoff Jackson has noted.[50] It was the old houses (few of them older than the eighteenth century) that attracted the mainland buyers, for they seemed to them to represent the original Nantucket regardless of their actual age or condition.

In the modern aesthetic ruins add to the romance of a place, distancing it from its own history, covering up an industrial or otherwise unappealing legacy.[51] What Jackson has called the modern "necessity for ruins" can also be seen operating on Irish and Scottish islands, where roofless houses and empty foundations standing next door to new houses are ubiquitous. There too ruins

Illustration 16   Ruins of Black House, Isle of Lewis, Scotland

symbolize the gap between past and present, while at the same time offering a bridge for a kind of fanciful time travel. In the Hebrides, the turf houses, called Black Houses, were often perceived as belonging to a timeless golden age despite the fact that they are no older than the seventeenth century. What on the mainland would have been cleared away is allowed to remain as a marker of an impassible temporal boundary between then and now, a treasured reminder of the world that had been lost but could someday be redeemed.

Perceiving the good old days to be a timeless time erased not only the islands' economic history but their cosmopolitan past. The memory of Nantucket's earlier racial and social diversity fell victim to a process of Americanization that was not unlike the nativizing projects in Ireland and Scotland. Seeking to celebrate the essence of Yankee values at a time of increased immigration from eastern and southern Europe, the elites of the eastern seaboard seized upon the islands as the last preserve of pure Yankee stock, somehow insulated from the erosions of interbreeding by their isolation and remoteness. The multiethnic and multiracial history of the littoral and its islands was suppressed in an era obsessed with racial purity. Whites were so busy distancing themselves from African and Native Americans that they ignored the mixed nature of island communities all up and down the Atlantic seaboard. Forgetting the fact that island populations had been the most widely traveled and most heterogeneous people up the middle of the nineteenth century, Nantucketers were stereotyped and described, as were islanders everywhere, as "natives," a patronizing term that mainlanders would never have applied to themselves.[52]

Retreating into the Past

The " native" is assumed to be untouched by outside influences, more rooted to place, less affected by change. Just as anthropologists naturalized and essentialized the cultures of Pacific islands, the antiquarians and folklorists exaggerated the integrity and coherence of the Atlantic isles they visited. Ignoring the degree to which these had been affected by frequent in- and outmigrations, transformed by religious conversions and schisms, and riven by class, racial, and ethnic differences, they claimed to have found there clearly bounded, homogeneous cultures more authentic than anything to be found on the continents. Henceforth islanders would play the locals to mainland cosmopolitans, representing for them a stasis, purity, and depth no longer to be found in modern life.

Visitors to the isles saw themselves as returning to the source, refreshing themselves at the well of aboriginality. Islands provided unique access to an undisturbed past. At the same time, islanders imagined the visitors to possess the magic of modernity which they were so desperate to acquire. The residents of late-nineteenth-century Iona were so eager to appear up to date that they risked disappointing the tourists seeking to connect with Celtic roots. The *Oban Times* reported in 1889 that "many strangers visiting the island during the summer months are surprised to find it a nineteenth century place" with many modern amenities.[53] By this time many of the isles had become quite dependent on imports, every bit as contemporary in tastes in goods and clothing as mainlanders. The Hebrides exported its tweed to the fashionable London markets, but Hebrideans would not wear it. On Inishbofen, where the craft of weaving had long since died, nothing but modern fabrics would do. According to Deborah Tall, returning islanders "wear their country suits as a point of status and take pride in having trouble readapting to island ways." Islanders preferred canned food to fresh, ignoring the harvest of berries and shellfish that so delighted the tourists. For the people of Inishbofen "the industriousness of years past is now a symbol of poverty, humiliation." They told Tall that they would not eat mussels because it reminded them of famine times when shellfish was all that was to be had on the island.[54]

Islanders of the Atlantic tended to internalize the image of backwardness while struggling to keep up with the latest trends onshore. Invariably better informed about the mainland than it was about them, they felt vulnerable and insecure, genuinely puzzled as to why anyone would turn his back on modernity. "I move backward as they move forward," remembered Tall.[55] For her, island life meant a new beginning, but for those born there time seemed to be running out. Islanders were particularly aware of disasters, not only in their own pasts but those happening contemporaneously. Their history did not move smoothly toward some predictable future but seemed to teeter precariously. The inhabitants of little Colonsay were keenly aware of other island evacuations.[56] The talk on Inishbofen was also about the past and impending catastrophes.[57] Even when islands held their own, islanders had great difficulty perceiving themselves as belonging to and surviving the modern world. They had turned fatalistic about their personal as well as their collective chances in the tides of change that were rising higher by the year. Many islands had turned away from the sea and lost the capacity to harvest its riches. In the process, islanders often lost the survival skill of swimming, saying it was better to drown quickly than to try to save oneself in icy waters.[58]

Yet this very sense of insecurity provides a clue to why insularity thrived in an otherwise tightly integrated world. Even as they become less isolated physically, islands maintained their cultural boundaries, defining themselves not only through language, music, and dance but through selective memory of their own pasts. In the case of the Shetland isle of Whalsay, the society and economy have been successfully modernized through fishing. Still, the people there like to think of themselves as traditional crofters, for it is said that "a man likes to have some land to walk over." Though houses have central heating, the past is conjured up in rituals of peat cutting and open fires in the hearth. "Whalsay people have become intensely modern, but have managed to do so without denigrating the past or deserting it," writes Anthony Cohen. "They use history to orient themselves in the volatile present."[59] The same was true of the Icelanders, who learned to harvest the fruits of the sea by industrial means, yet strongly identified themselves with their farming past. The historically unspecified golden age of old Norse had become not only the chief source of their sense of uniqueness but also an important attraction to tourists seeking authentic Vikings.[60] Like the people of Whalsay, "Icelanders feel the need to define themselves more closely than ever before, because the island is getting more involved with the international scene and moving out of the periphery."[61] There, as elsewhere, connection produced cultural insularity.

That Happy Prelapsarian Place

In the course of the late eighteenth and early nineteenth century the antithesis between land and sea was redrawn, though the differences were etched even more deeply than before. The land, especially its settled parts, was now identified with civilization, while the sea was understood as untamed pure nature. Though the Americas still had vast unexplored interiors containing huge tracts of wilderness, Europe had only the sea to call by that name. By the middle of the nineteenth century, Britain had lost nearly all the original wild places that the first generations of romantics had so gloried in. The Lake District had become, according to Jonathan Raban, its original theme park.[62] Lacking wild lands, the British chose this moment to make the sea their wilderness. It was then that Englishmen began to return to the sea, not as an occupation, but as avocation. It became for them their last frontier, the place where, in small sailing boats, they would test themselves against the elements, proving their manhood to themselves and to the women waiting on shore. "England's only untamed wilderness, where men might still be small and alone in the vastness of Creation, was the sea," writes Raban. "To go to sea was to escape from the city and the machine."[63]

In art as well as in life, the sea became the "sublime environment of Nature, beyond History, against which Man could test his physical strength and moral courage, far from the influence of land based society."[64] The sea had become the "other," an alterity through which Europeans could know themselves as individuals and as a civilization. The shore was the place where for, Europeans and Europeanized Americans, history and time stopped. "People who live on continents get into the habit of regarding the ocean as journey's end, full stop at the end of the trek. When North Americans reached the Pacific, there was nothing to do except build the end-of-the-world state of California," according to Raban.[65]

Existing beyond the reaches of civilization and entirely outside history, the oceans were once again associated with the primordial. Their shores came to be seen as the prime place to explore origins, personal and collective. "People came here to wonder about the earth's past and the origins of life," notes Alain Corbin.[66] At the edge of the sea they looked for fossils revealing the earliest stages of evolution. But they also came to seek traces of their earliest selves, for the beach had come by that time to be associated with childhood and thus with a psychological depth associated with no other landscape. As the prime location of earthly and human memory, the seashore took on a whole new meaning in the modern age.[67]

As the perceived differences between sea and land widened, the island reemerged, as it had so many times in the past, as a kind of liminal place with features of both land and sea.[68] As W. H. Auden perceived them, islands were third places, hovering somewhere between the wild sea and civilized land, "where there is no conflict between natural desire and moral duty."[69] Though the sea offered the ultimate escape from stifling civilization, the great adventure

for Victorian men seeking to prove their masculinity in an increasingly effem-
inized domesticated world, the island was a retreat where they could preserve
something of their innocence in an otherwise cruel and unforgiving world.
There were still plenty of Crusoes, men who viewed islands as their own private kingdoms and a projection of their own inflated egos, but there were also
males like Pastor Wyss, the author of *Swiss Family Robinson*, for whom the island was the setting for family romance, where the instinct for adventure gave
way to that yearning for security and comfort that was also a feature of the Victorian era. On land, time moved relentlessly forward, but on the island it
moved backward to a more innocent age, toward the beginnings of the human
species or to the childhood of the individual. As the fantasy of returning to the
innocence of childhood became more powerful among middle-class men in the
nineteenth century, the appeal of Crusoe's island gave way to that of Swiss Family Robinson and finally to that of Peter Pan. And as islands grew less valuable
politically and economically, their reputation for happy domesticity grew pro-
portionally. Islands became ever more associated with the kind of virtuous life
that was becoming harder to come by on the mainlands. Occupying a place between the overcivilized land and the wildness of sea, islands were increasingly
attractive to a Western middle class yearning for personal freedom but not at
the expense of moral respectability. Islands came to be seen as the preeminent
"happy Prelapsarian Place."[70]

By the twentieth century, islands ceased to be thought of as destinations and
became places of return, fixed points where an increasingly mobile mainland
urban population eager for seasonal respite could savor a sense of stability and
continuity. Nineteenth-century summer visitors to the islands of Maine first
boarded in the houses of farmers and fishermen, helping them extend the island
way of life for a few more decades. Later, wealthy "rusticators" built a few cottages on shore frontage, but it was not until the 1930s and 1940s, when fishermen and farmers removed to the mainland, that the old houses came on the
market for the first time and island ownership shifted to the summer people. Yet
descendants of the original islanders retain a strong presence on many islands.
They return to bury their dead in the old family cemeteries. Some hold onto island properties, leaving them vacant for most of the year and returning on occasion to visit the old "homeplace" even when it has become a tumbledown ruin.[71]

Island Retreats

Already in the nineteenth century, people on the mainland were experiencing
the erasure of place produced by increased mobility and speed of communication. The resulting sense of rootlessness triggered the uniquely modern quest for

place in a placeless world, for home in the vast, featureless landscapes of urban industrial society. The search was not just for residence but for that elusive sense being at home in the world, as much a mental as a physical endeavor, more likely to be achieved at a distance in the absence of that which was called home. In a world of temporal and spatial movement, where for many there was no longer a place to return to, home became a state of mind, "something to be taken along wherever one decamps."[72]

In the nineteenth century, residence and sense of place were already becoming two different things. Being resident in a place for a long time did not automatically produce a sense of being at home. On the contrary, it was often exiles and people "from away" who developed the strongest attachments to a place, for, as Yi-Fu Tuan tells us, "It is distance between self and place that allows the self to appreciate a place."[73] Indeed, distance had become so essential to the contemporary sense of place that the greater the perceived distance the stronger the attraction. It was not among resident islanders, but among exiles and visitors that islands first took on mythical aura of the ultimate homeplace, more honored in its absence than presence.

"Under conditions of modernity, place becomes increasingly *phantasmagoric,*" writes Anthony Giddens.[74] Home became detached from residence, less a physical location than a mental construct, a thing of dreams as well as memories, no less real even if it is rarely, sometimes never, actually inhabited.[75] This separation began in the nineteenth century when Victorian architecture began to provide for certain domestic spaces, the parlor and the nursery, to serve as the mental space of home, leaving the rest of house for the mundane purposes of everyday living. In the twentieth century, modern architecture left few places for fantasy and memory to dwell within the house. Over time the dream house and memory palace moved out, transferring ever farther afield to weekend and summer places. These became locations of "the lost origin and the future dream, both vanishing points where we imagine ourselves at peace, surrounded by comfort and harmony."[76] It proved easier to animate meaningful, habitable worlds at a distance, with the result that for those who can afford them, the dearest homeplaces are often those they visited only occasionally, sometimes never returned to, however frequently they are visited mentally. Island houses, rarely occupied year-round, were already becoming in the late nineteenth century the quintessential family places where generations, scattered throughout the mainlands, could share time and space, if only occasionally. In Amy Cross's view, the summer place is "not real estate, it is more a state of mind that can be packed and moved to any woods or seaside. And many of us travel through life with a memory of a perfect place waiting for our return."[77]

WORLDS OF LOSS / 141

By the late nineteenth century, islands and other remote islanded places had become the favorite locus of middle-class family holidays. Summer had become the season for time as well as geographical travel, especially to retreat to the good old days associated with childhood.[78] By then childhood had come to be a primary source of selfhood, the thing adults most frequently used to explain themselves to themselves and to others. Modern maturity has been particularly demanding on men, requiring that they distance themselves from domestic, childish things, producing in them a yearning for childhood that has characterized middle-class male culture ever since. In the resulting quest for childhood lost, summer islands became the favored place for retrospection and recuperation. The isles allowed a brief sojourn in childishness that did not threaten the adulthood associated with mainland existence. Islands thus gained the reputation for being good places for "creating and preserving memories, particularly youthful ones."[79] There adults could reconnect not only to their children and grandchildren, but to their own childhoods. Of Swans Island it is said that "the island has become associated with a brother, a son, but more often with mother, with whom they spent their summer here. The retreat is not only away from the world but into a safer, happier period of time of their lives, youth or childhood when someone shared their cares or assumed the full burden of them."[80] There, and only there, was paradise lost fully recoverable.

CHAPTER 8

ISLANDS LOOMING

The Imagined Isles of Global Tourism

It is not down on any map, true places never are.

—Herman Melville, *Moby Dick*

"LOOK, IT'S LOOMIN'," SAID THE BOATMAN in a quiet voice. We turned to see the island that was our destination levitate and high white cliffs appear where only a shoreline had been visible before. Astonished, I shouted for the others to look. For several minutes we stared until the island descended, becoming once again a line on the horizon. I later learned that looming is something known to virtually all sailors, accounting for the boatman's lack of excitement. It is a kind of mirage, like the kind seen in deserts, produced by certain light and atmospheric conditions. Yet, even now that I know what it is, looming never ceases to fascinate me.

Today islands are looming all around us. If you did not know that they constitute only 6.7 percent of the world's land surface and 10.5 percent of its population, you might think the globe was nothing but a vast archipelago because islands take up such a disproportionate part of the contemporary mindscape.[1] Islands occupy a great deal of mental space; and though this is consistent with their prominence in Western mythical geography, this latest looming is different from earlier ones. Islands today rarely serve a religious purpose; they are seldom the location for utopian projects; nor are they the platforms for science and anthropology they once were. Today the voyage to the islands serves more personal ends. Islands have become a source of personal and social identity for millions of people who never have been or ever will be resident islanders.

Populations are everywhere encroaching on coasts. Today one half of the world's population lives within thirty-seven miles of a sea. Movement toward the shores has its seasonal and generational variations, but the pressure increases despite warnings of coastal fragility and vulnerability to flooding in an era of global warming.[2] Some people are more fond of their shores than others. Almost three quarters of the English population used to take their vacations at Britain's seasides before they discovered even more attractive beaches elsewhere.[3] The seaside remains the favored resort, particularly for families with children; and the appeal of islands is much more dependent on their beaches than their interiors.[4] There is a strong element of nostalgia, of time-travel back to childhood evident in island tourism, but some would also say that as a culture we are recapitulating the history of early humans, who moved from the center of Africa to the shores because these afforded an easier life. As Carl Sauer observed, we now repeat that journey, though our quest is no longer for subsistence. "When all the lands will be filled with people and machines, perhaps the last need and observance of man will still be, as it was at his beginning, to come down to experience the sea."[5]

The surge to the shore has now moved onto the nearest continental islands. When the barrier islands on the East Coast of America were bridged, a human tsunami surged from the mainland, driving up land prices and displacing long-time islanders, most of whom are poor and, in the case of the Sea Islands, people of color. Although the general trend has been toward the depopulation of year-round residents, those islands that are most accessible to urban areas are now more densely populated than at any time in their history. The resort island of Hilton Head has become like Manhattan, so accessible that it loses all semblance of both remoteness and islandness. As Gunnar Hansen observes: "This island was hardly an island anymore, but rather an extension of some middle American fantasy."[6]

Hardly Islands Any More

There was a time not so very long ago when islands were physically isolated, truly remote from mainlands. Today distance is not a barrier for those who can afford modern means of travel and communication. No place exists in isolation, and everything belongs to the world at large. Nothing is physically remote for the world's elites, but for the vast majority of the world's inhabitants who are fated by their poverty either to remain fixed in place or forced to move in search of livelihood, distance remains a curse. Much of the world is now on the move, becoming more nomadic. Still, we need to make a distinction, as does Zygmunt Bauman, between the tourists, who can afford to go anywhere, and the vagabonds, who have little choice in the matter. For the tourists, isolation, remoteness, and smallness are things that are prized and increasing sought after. Because these qualities are in short supply, their value is now enormously inflated. But for the vagabonds of this world, being from a small place and far from the center of the big world holds no allure. On the contrary, a small place, like Jamaica Kincaid's island of Antigua, is a badge of shame and a source of despair.[7]

Islands have played a crucial, if unwitting, role in the modern triumph of time over distance. They were key sites in the electronic communications revolution that has drawn the world into ever closer contact over the past two centuries, first as bases for undersea cable networks and later as nodes for wireless communications. Marconi used Cape Breton Island as his first transatlantic transmission station, and today islands are often international telemarketing centers because their inhabitants' exceptional language abilities make them an ideal and relatively cheap labor force.[8]

Islands were also key to the mechanization of sea travel in the nineteenth century, with places like the Cape Verdes serving as coaling stations for steamships. The switch to oil-fired marine engines in the early twentieth century eliminated that function, but other islands acquired a new role in the early phases of aviation, when Newfoundland and Azores became essential to transatlantic air routes. During the Second World War, the strategic importance of islands in both the Atlantic and Pacific was so great that they were often the first places to be occupied by belligerents.

But air travel also hastened the eclipse of physical borders. Even before the First World War it was apparent to the British that they were no longer protected by their fabled islandness. In 1906, when the French aviator Santos-Dumont managed to stay aloft for all of 722 feet, the *Daily Mail* was ready to concede: "England is no longer an island. . . . It means the aerial chariots of a foe descending on British soil if war comes."[9] H. G. Wells's 1908 novel, *The War in the Air,* declared that "the little island in the silver seas was at the end of its immunity," and, while it took some time for this truth to sink in, islands would never be the same in the age of intercontinental bombers and missiles.[10]

On the other hand, the erosion of physical barriers in no way diminished the appeal of the idea of the island. As World War II approached, British politicians became ever more attached to the idea of the "island race," a term that had caught on in the nineteenth century. The evacuation of Dunkirk was treated as a victory for insularity, and the white cliffs of Dover became celebrated ramparts of what came to be seen as a "tiny island nation."[11] Although the postwar era made physical distance even more irrelevant, the cultural and political appeal of islandness remained undiminished. The building of the Chunnel in 1994 did not so much diminish as enhance insularity among the English living closest to the continent. As physical proximity increased, psychological and cognitive distance expanded.[12] The idea of the island grew stronger even as its reality eroded.

Illustration 17   Bridging of a small Norwegian island

The last thirty years has seen more islands connected by bridges, tunnels, and high-speed ferries than in all of previous history. Not only is Britain now attached, but the main Danish islands of Fyn and Sjaelland were bridged, the latter linked to Sweden by motor and rail for the first time. Skye, Prince Edward Island, and dozens of lesser known islands are now accessible by motor vehicles. The Norwegians, the world's great experts in tunneling, have invested heavily for the purpose of making even the smallest coastal islands viable and reversing migration to the mainland. More distant Scottish and Norwegian isles are now well served by frequent and efficient ferries.

This process has not been without controversy, with continentals generally keener than islanders about the creation of so-called fixed links. But there are islanders entrenched on both sides of the issue of whether this is a good or bad thing in the long run. For resident islanders, a fixed link is often seen as a positive economic step, rescuing them from isolation and backwardness, making their small places a part of the larger world. When the western isle of Achill was bridged in 1886 it lost its reputation for being Ireland's "darkest Africa."[13] But for those more recent arrivals who came seeking smallness and remoteness, bridging and tunneling appeared as threats because they seem to remove "the perfection of the island."[14]

Bridges and tunnels may alter the status of an island, but it still remains an island, reinforcing Georg Simmel's observation that in connecting two things we simultaneously underline what separates them. Noting that human beings are "connecting creatures who must always separate and cannot connect without separating," Simmel wrote that bridging two things only underlines their distinctiveness.[15] Insularity and connectedness are but two sides of the same coin, their meanings forever entangled.

Islands are now awash with seasonal sojourners. Movement has become more typical than settlement as the global economy accelerates a universal sense of homelessness.[16] In the last thirty years, long- and short-term relocation has reached levels never experienced before in human history. Leisure travel, which was once exceptional, is now the single largest industry in the world. Alongside mass tourism, and often as a consequence of it, are movements of people in search of work rather than leisure. Sex tourism to the Dominican Republic produced two-way traffic, for as European and American men arrive, many of the women with whom they become involved leave in search of better conditions on the continents.[17] Vagabonds and tourists often share the same geographies even though they do not move in the same circuits.

In this world of constant flux it is increasingly difficult to tell the visitors from the locals. Identity, once associated with location, has slipped its territorial moorings to become transnational. People no longer identify with or can be identified exclusively by their place of residence. They gain their sense of individual and collective selfhood from associations with distant places, with places that exist as much in dream and memory as in reality. In an increasingly mobile world, humanity can no longer be neatly divided into separate, rooted communities. The old link between territory and identity no longer holds, but as anthropologists Akhil Gupta and James Ferguson tell us, even as "actual places and locations become ever more blurred and indeterminate, *ideas* of culturally and ethnically distinct places become perhaps more salient."[18]

In a media environment saturated with images from all parts of the world, people have become attached to places they have never seen and pasts they have never had.[19] Although this islomania is not entirely new, it seems to be intensifying. Free-floating ideas about lands and people, sometimes described as "ethnoscapes" or "mindscapes," are all the more precious because they are safe from the depredations to which real places and peoples have been subjected. Displaced islanders carry their "islescapes" with them wherever they go. As John Connell and Russell King note, they are more attached to these islescapes when they are abroad than when they at home, leading to an unprecedented situation in which "island communities are simultaneously being united in virtual space and becoming fragmented across the globe."[20] The same images are no less precious to mainlanders who have a similar if not greater investment in creating and preserving their own islescapes.[21] And here lies the explanation of why in an age when nothing is physically inaccessible or unknowable, the dream of the small, remote, and undiscovered place has become so powerful.[22]

The Dream of Islands

Today our most significant places are not those we dwell *in* physically but those we dwell *on* mentally. They are not physical locations, but cultural constructions, often kept at a distance.[23] Roots are invariably found elsewhere; nor are house and home any longer the same. Among the world's more affluent classes, the strongest sense of home adheres not to our regular places of residence but to weekend and summer places. Even as American houses grow ever larger, they become ever emptier, in part because we no longer have time to spend there now that women as well as men are in the workforce. The house has become a space of vicarious experience rather than a place for actual living. Marjorie Garber has written that "we build exercise rooms instead of exercising, furnish libraries instead of reading, install professional kitchens instead of cooking." Space becomes a substitute for the time, "and the house becomes the unlived life . . . the place where we stage the life we wish we had time to live."[24]

Home has become a non-place, "something to be taken along whenever one decamps."[25] The separation of home from house is a relatively recent phenomenon in the Western world where only the affluent classes who can afford to have second homes. Yet the idea of maintaining a family home or a family place at a distance is by no means unknown to poor people throughout the world, especially those who have been displaced or are on the move. Natives of the Caribbean island of Nevis living in England and the United States retain a strong attachment to a piece of island land or a house that they do not regularly occupy and only rarely visit.[26] Similar homeplaces, vacant but kept up by families, dot the landscapes of rural America, confirming the notion that culturally constructed sites in the there and then have displaced the physical locations of the here and now as our primary sources of personal and collective identity.[27] On Malta old houses share space with new lavish "emigrant houses," status symbols of Maltese success in London, Sydney, and other far-flung places.[28]

It has been said that "home 'moves' us most powerfully as absence or negation."[29] And homelands are also best appreciated by the exile, one of the reasons why nationalism is so often produced outside rather than inside countries. This is no less true of islands, where the attraction is the product of distance rather than proximity. As we have already seen, Icelandic and Faerøes identities were originally forged on mainlands. What was true of the nineteenth century is evident again today. In the case of the Caribbean, "island identities were reshaped by migrants' activism at distant metropolitan shores, but rarely were migrants any less islanders after migration," write Connell and King.[30] The Nevisian identity is stronger in New Haven and Leeds than it is on the island itself.[31] The same is true of former Blasket Islanders who now reside in the neighborhood called Hungry Hill in Springfield, Massachusetts. They have a stronger sense of being Blasket people than when they actually lived on the island. The same is true of those exiled by the Second World War and Soviet occupation from the coastal islands of Estonia. They hold tight to idealized islescapes that are at odds with the islands' past.[32]

Exiles often find that there is an unbearable tension between the world they remember and the landscapes that await them. Cole Moreton writes of one Springfield man who found that "the dreams and memories he had of the [Blasket] island were more vivid and comforting than the reality of the empty and abandoned village whose life would be impossible for someone grown soft in America. Still he couldn't quite let the old place go. 'Maybe some day I'll go back and build another house there.'"[33] Like so many Nevisians who have similar dreams, his plans were never realized. Older Estonian exiles do not even like to go back to the islands, for their remembered islescapes are so at odds with the current realities. It is usually a younger generation who build second homes, because, having only the vague memories of their childhood, they are less likely to be repelled by what they find.[34]

It is said that absence makes the heart grow fonder, and it is not uncommon to find former residents holding islands at a temporal as well as a physical distance, returning only seasonally. In the case of Nevis, the newly invented August "Culturama" is aimed not at tourists, but former residents, during which, Karen Fog Olwig writes, "the entire island of Nevis is virtually being turned into one big nostalgia family home to be visited and celebrated by everybody."[35] Many of the Estonian isles have also become summer islands, as has most of the Maine archipelago, where only fourteen islands now have permanent residents. This is equally true of most of the Scandinavian and Canadian islands. The people who have the strongest attachment to these islands live elsewhere most of the year. Temporal, like physical absence, reinforces rather than diminishes the islands' appeal because remoteness in time also adds to the appreciation of a place. The favorite song of Torres Strait islanders living on the Australian mainland is Neil Murray's "My Island Home," which includes the lines: "Now I'm down here living in the city/And my island home is waiting for me." "The homes that many have not seen for many years become once again important," writes John Connell, "if not as places to return to, then as points of reference."[36]

Small Is Beautiful

It is small islands that have the greatest appeal. Tom Baum tell us that it is not uncommon for tourists visiting one island to "avail themselves of the opportunity to visit smaller neighbors."[37] D. H. Lawrence's story *The Man Who Loved Islands* is about a man who seeks but fails to find fulfillment on ever smaller islands.[38] Undeterred by this cautionary tale, the real estate market for single-owner isles is booming, raising prices sky high and all out of proportion to the real value of the properties.[39] The notion that small is beautiful is a very modern idea. In earlier periods what was small was "insignificant, despicable, and common as dust."[40] The small was simply an inferior form of the big, incomplete and transitory. Just as the child was a lesser adult, so the meaning of anything small could be best appreciated in its larger version. Educated elites had some appreciation of miniatures and models, but these were novelties until the nineteenth century. Living in physically cramped quarters, hemmed in by physical boundaries, ordinary people dreamed of something bigger rather than smaller.

As we have already seen, the old way of emphasizing the importance of something had been to exaggerate its size. Early maps invariably showed islands as much larger than they actually were. The ancients imagined Ceylon (now Sri Lanka) to be larger than the Indian subcontinent, while Renaissance *isolario* were full of outsized isles, real and imagined.[41] But in the modern period the hierarchy of size was overturned, and the small has come into its own as representing a superior version of the large. "The truth of the great is found in the small," writes Joseph Amato.[42] Today we prefer the smaller to the bigger islands. "The smaller and more enclosed they are," writes Philip Conkling, "the larger the window on the infinite, the farther they telescope into heaven."[43]

We who live on a much grander scale, knowing no physical limits, have become enamored of the diminutive and the miniature. Islands appeal to us because they are the most enclosed of all land forms, and smaller islands evoke the greatest fascination and affection. "Islands seduce us because sometimes the universe seems too big," write Bill Holm. "We want to shrink it a little so that we can examine it, see what it is made of, and what is our place in it."[44] This impulse can be traced back to the nineteenth century, when Henry David Thoreau spoke of how "an island pleases my imagination, even the smallest, as a small continent and integral part of the globe. I have a fancy for building my hut on one."[45] He did not actually do so, but Holm tells us that "Walden Pond was his desert island, his plunge into spiritual bedrock, his downsizing of the universe in order to get a better look at it."[46]

As the actual scale of things has tended to gigantism, the appreciation of the diminutive has increased enormously. There can be no such thing as the small

apart from the big. The smallness of islands is a function of the bigness of mainlands, which revealed their true vastness only when they were finally explored
and surveyed in the nineteenth century. It was also then that the big city seemed
about to overwhelm the village and the small town. But in our own times there
has been a reaction against giantism. Big cities are now filled with fenced-in
plots where people have planted small gardens and built tiny houses. These can
be found in the largest cities of Germany and Sweden but also in the poorest
sections of New York's Bronx where Puerto Ricans maintain their *casitas,* miniature versions of their island homes. It seems that people who have little control
over other dimensions of their lives are able to exercise a satisfying degree of creativity within the private urban islands they have created.[47]

The natural features of small islands provide an ideal setting for imagining
small worlds, but this does not occur spontaneously. John Fowles remarks that
a small island is a place "encompassable at a glance, walkable in a day, that relates to the human body closer than any other geographical formation of
land."[48] But such a relationship is never formed casually or immediately. It is the
product of repeated visits, deep familiarity, and many perambulations around
the shores. Fowles's own identification with his favorite Greek island developed
only slowly: "Eventually it let me feel it was mine: which is the great siren call
of islands—that they will not belong to any legal order, but offer to become part
of all who tread and love them."[49]

Islands are probably the most closely observed, thoroughly mapped and de-
nominated places in the world today. Every path is marked, every landmark
named. Even when the natural landscape is undisturbed, the symbolic landscape
is extensively cultivated. Islands are among the most photographed and painted
places on earth; they are endlessly talked about, their stories told and histories
recorded. We do our best to reduce islands to human scale regardless of their actual physical size. And because it is surrounded by water, an island is like a
framed picture, appearing to its viewer as small but at the same time all the more
comprehensible.[50] The framing allows us the illusion that we know an island
more thoroughly, lending weight to the modern notion that it is through the
small that we can understand the large. An island appears to us as a microcosm,
even when it bears no resemblance the universe as a whole.[51]

In a world of giantism, smallness has taken on unprecedented value.
Touristed islands are invariably described as small regardless of their size; and life
there is not only scaled down but slowed down, especially by the mainlanders
who have come to reside there. The houses they build are smaller, and even
when they are sizable they are described as "cottages" rather than as mansions.
The miniaturization has little to do with the space available. Rather it seems to
be a matter of choice, people preferring a "scale model of something bigger." On

the Isle of Man not only is the railway narrowgage but the roads and scenic turnouts are smaller.[52] On Martha's Vineyard and Nantucket the building of upscale houses caused a furor, with the summer people being in the vanguard of those who objected to what were regarded as monstrosities.

Downsizing is one of the ways we regain control of our lives. In the past twenty years, it has been accompanied by what Juliet Schor calls "downshifting," an effort to cope with a pervasive sense of time famine.[53] The cottage cultures that have proliferated throughout the Western world all show the same characteristics: a desire for the simpler, slower life.[54] Living at a smaller scale slows and even stops time, for, as Susan Stewart suggests, "the miniature offers a world clearly limited in space but frozen and thereby both particularized and generalized in time." Model ships and railways enable the fantasy of returning to an earlier era. So too does the cottage, particularity when it is on an island. "As in the case of all models, it is absolutely necessary that the Lilliput be an island. The miniature world remains perfect and uncontaminated by the grotesque so long as its absolute boundaries are maintained."[55] To produce the desired effects, smallness requires remoteness.

Return of the Remote

It is one of the great paradoxes of our times that the value of remoteness increases even as modern communications make all parts of the world more accessible. Pockets of remoteness are appearing everywhere in and outside the Western world, sometimes quite close to major urban centers where the greatest demand for remoteness is generated. Though peninsular Brittany is only a couple of hours from Paris and Vermont is within reach of New York, they are now regarded as almost as remote as the Hebrides or the islands of Down East Maine. The remote has drawn ever closer, with the result that its value, as measured in property sales and in the profits made by the tourist industry, has increased many fold. The price of country cottages has shot up, and the value of island real estate has not been far behind. Both have outpaced the rise in prices of many city properties over the past twenty years. Remoteness sells, as Gunnar Hansen found out when he visited the Sea Islands on the Carolina coast and spotted a sign reading "Lost Island. Residential lots for sale."[56]

The scarcity of physical remoteness has driven up its value and encouraged a kind of cultural counterfeiting. Because remoteness is nowhere, it can be anywhere. We have learned to produce what we can no longer find, often quite close to home. While some locations like the Himalayan Mountains and the polar regions remain truly distant, most places regarded as remote, including islands, are much closer at hand. Remoteness is not a matter of physical distance because remoteness is not something measured in miles or kilometers. No island is too near or too far to seem remote, for remoteness is in the eye of the beholder.[57] Toronto Island, almost within the shadow of the Canadian city's skyscrapers, is a world apart.[58] Hen Island is other example of place, within sight of New York City, that, because it is neither bridged nor wired to the mainland, seems far away. Never was this more apparent than on August 15, 2003, when a massive electrical failure blacked out the entire metropolitan region, leaving the Hen Islanders, with their solar power and propane tanks, to appear as a small world of light in a sea of darkness.[59] Most locations which now qualify as remote exist within a certain zone of accessibility, within reach of modern transportation and communications but beyond the range of the easy commute. Places that are inaccessible are disqualified, but so too are those reached too quickly and easily. In this modern age, remoteness is constituted of just the right mixture of time and space. While only twelve miles off Long Island, the trip to Fishers Island requires a change of ferries and four hours each way, enough to sustain its remoteness.

Neither physical distance nor natural features automatically bestow remoteness. Instead, it is the product of social processes, of autobiography and history, of economics and politics as well as a sociology, of which islands are a prime illustration. We have seen that the association of remoteness with islands is a quite recent phenomenon, something that is culturally constituted and maintained. "Space is given by the ability to move," Yi-Fu Tuan tells us. "We acquire the feel of distance by moving from one place to another."[60] But a sense of remoteness is the product of a certain mode of movement. Any place, however far, which is arrived at too quickly is automatically disqualified. Travel to the remote is invariably ritualized, a series of passages, each stretching the sense of temporal and spatial distance between the place of origin and the place of destination. Starting, stopping, and waiting are all part of the construction of remoteness. Getting there must be something of an adventure, a test, amounting often to a trial that transports the traveler mentally as well as physically to a different world.

Transportation that is too direct erases remoteness. The road must not be too straight or the journey uninterrupted. The feeling of remoteness is enhanced when the journey is compounded of several different modes of transportation: a plane ride, then a bus or a boat, and the last bit on foot, pushing a heavily laden wheelbarrow. Attaining remoteness must involve effort and an investment of time, though not measured only in hours or minutes. The kind of time required to reach a remote place differs not so much in quantity as in quality. The time to a nonremote place is, like the route that takes us there, direct and linear. The time to a remote place is full of starts and stops, looping back on itself through a series of repetitions. The more and longer the waits, the more frequent the returns, the remoter a destination feels whatever the actual distance traversed. Climbing mountains and crossing waters virtually guarantees remoteness, but this is as much a product of the uncertainty and degree of difficulty as of physical distance. The rites of passage involved in our constructions of remoteness vary from place to place, from island to island, and are passed on, like an old family recipe, from generation to generation, becoming so habitual that it is easy to forget that they are a product of history rather than geography.

Islands have become the contemporary world's favorite location for remoteness not because they are distant but because they necessitate the spatial practices that create a sense of remoteness. Most densely populated areas of Europe and North America have islands within reach. They are more accessible than mountains, but, in contrast to the trip to parks or rural villages, the journey to islands is never direct or easy. It is not so much the land but the water that gives islands the desired qualities of remoteness. The remoteness of islands fluctuates with the tides. A place like Mont St. Michel becomes remote only at high tide, when the causeway connecting it to the mainland is inundated. At low tide, it loses this quality entirely. Because tourists imagine Mont St. Michel only at high tide, any proposed changes, such as elevating the causeway, that would deprive it of its appearance of islandness stir intense controversy.[61]

Those who value remoteness must constantly be on guard against bridge and tunnel builders who would connect islands with mainlands. In recent years, intense conflicts have developed, not just between islanders and mainlanders, but between factions of islanders. Those who object to bridging and tunneling are usually newcomers who have come seeking remoteness. The proponents are likely to be locals who regard direct transportation and communications as highly desirable. In the case of the newcomers, water provides a valuable barrier, but for the locals it is a reminder of what lies beyond. While those "from away" glory in being cut off, the locals become increasingly anxious about their isolation. It is they who demand better roads, more telephone lines, and regular ferry service.

Remoteness is inseparable from movement, but it is created through a special kind of movement that separates at the same time it connects. This is best described as a rite of passage that removes the traveler mentally from one place before incorporating him or her into another. The creation of remoteness is rarely the product of a one-time journey, but is usually constructed over a number of years. The remote can never be a final destination, for it is through circular, repetitive sojourns that both the contemporary sense of remoteness and sense of home are created. And in an age when distance is so easily transcended, simply going far is insufficient. It is now necessary to travel through time as well as space, for contemporary remoteness is as much associated with a sense of pastness as with physical distance. It has that quality of being there rather than here, but also of being then rather than now.

Remoteness is the product of a relationship between two places, but these places are unequal to one another. Today, powerful mainlands bestow remoteness on relatively powerless islands. This imbalance explains the paradox that those who live yearround in places defined as remote feel open and unprotected, drawn ever closer and more vulnerable to the continental land masses that now define the terms of distance.[62] When strangers have the power to impose their image of there and then on a place, the locals' sense of living in the here and now is noticeably heightened. This is what John McPhee experienced during his sojourn on the small Scottish island of Colonsay, where the visitors dressed in store-bought tartans and were full of book-learned lore. They were the ones steeped in Colonsay's history.[63] For the resident islanders, it was not the past but the future that carried the greater weight. The mainland was forever on their minds, and they talked constantly of other islands that had lost population and had eventually been evacuated entirely. They imagined Colonsay not as a place of eternal return, but as somewhere at the end of time, living its last days.

What is meant by roots today has little to do with physical rootedness. In our mobile society, it is connection to the past rather than to place that is most sought after. People now travel to remote places they would never think of living in to seek their roots. They are often confounded by the locals' lack of interest in the past, for the physically rooted are quite content to live in the present, and are indifferent or even hostile to historical preservation. In many places the recent wave of interest in genealogy and local history is generated largely by people "from away" as they are called in Maine, from "come-overs" as they known in Man, or from "blow-ins" as the Irish like to call them.[64] Their appreciation of place is constituted through a temporal distance, making them oblivious to the presentist concerns of the locals.

If the absence of marked roads and straight paths is a sure sign of remoteness, the lack of wires is another. Remoteness requires that communications be not too easy or too direct, for the remote must be one step behind technologically. Remote islands have long had postal but rarely telegraph or telephone services. Today, some summer people have civilian band radios, but cell phones are often resisted. Where simplicity still trumps convenience, instant communication is regarded as a threat to the treasured sense of solitude. These sentiments are rare among full-time residents. They are often quite forthright about their isolation, boredom, and sense of being trapped. "If I was an artist, I'm sure I'd never leave," writes a young Vinalhaven woman eager to move on to college. "The bad point of the island is that being so small it is very restrictive." Another writes: "I yearn to escape my island so that I can escape from the provincialism while expanding my life and my future. Islesboro will always be my home and place that I will love to come home to and visit, but it is time to build some bridges."[65]

To the locals remoteness is like a one-way street. It allows the outside world to flood in but does not allow access to what that world takes for granted. It heightens island residents' sense of backwardness, and they overcompensate by acquiring the modern conveniences that the newcomers are trying to escape from. While those "from away" glory in the simple life, the locals purchase faster boats, bigger cars, and all the modern conveniences money will buy, including the latest communications technology. It is the locals, not the strangers, who watch television and use cell phones. Those who seek out remote places insist on keeping modernity at bay, roughing it or living in ways they imagine earlier generations to have done. Not surprisingly, they tend to be preservationists, restorers, and reenactors. Newcomers to remote areas are often the ones to resurrect the old crafts and folk arts long after the locals have abandoned them.

Retirees on places like the Isle of Man, Majorca, Malta, and Corfu become staunch conservationists of the islescapes that they first came to love as tourists and that brought them back as permanent residents. They often resist developments favored by less affluent locals, resulting in simmering conflicts.[66] Exiles from the islands also tend to want to keep things the way they imagine they always were; much of the pressure to keep old, sometimes outmoded ways comes from the mainlands. On the Hebridean island of Harris, small farming known locally as crofting must be kept alive by subsidies. The Swedish island of Gotland is known for its homebrewing, but the initiative came not from the old-timers but from a younger generation. And it was led not by the farm women, who traditionally did the brewing, but by men living in the island's largest town, Visby. These same men spend much of their year working on the Swedish mainland, where they have clubs at which they drink island home brew and dream of the place they have left behind.[67]

Summer Islands

Apart from uplands, where animals are brought for summer pasturage, summer islands are probably the most seasonal of all land forms, fully occupied, according to climate, for only part of the year. The fact that the houses there stand empty for nine or more months of the year makes them all the more attractive as places for mainlanders to discover themselves individually and collectively.[68] The circular journey, reinforced by the circularity of the calendar year, has a way of erasing intervals of time. Though we may be a year older, now out of college or retired, we do not feel that different upon return to a place we love. A firm sense of identity, so dependent on a sense of sameness over time and space, is thereby reinforced rather than disrupted. The fact that the house appears just the same as when we left it bridges time and abrogates history. A woman in an Ursula Le Guin novel inspecting the kitchen after a year's absence feels that "everything is circular, or anyhow spiral. It was no time at all, certainly not twelve months" since she was last there.[69] Eliot Porter remembers vividly the moment of return to his family's summer island in Maine. "At last, unbelievably, I was on the island. It had not changed; everything was the same."[70]

Summer's association with leisure began only in the nineteenth century; winter's link with play in the sun is even more recent. The European and North American middle classes were the first to take summer vacations as we now know them. The removal of bourgeois women from work and the vacation times of their schooled children made this possible, though initially the men stayed behind in the city as demanded by their role as full-time breadwinners. In the early nineteenth century the symbolic association of women and children with the seashore was already well established. As the terrors of the shore receded, the sea took on a nurturing quality. "Roused by the proximity of the mothering sea," writes Alain Corbin, "feminine instincts blossom there which, in the wife, help protect virtue when it is threatened by a husband's prolonged absence." Surrounded by water, islands were the safest places of all, often compared to a mother's bosom, where the "scene of regression can be freely played out" for months on end.[71] It was not until the twentieth century that men joined in the family vacation, and this only intensified in their minds the association of islands with childishness and playfulness.[72] "There is a perpetual mystery and excitement in living on the seashore, which is in part a return to childhood," notes Gavin Maxwell. When an adult stands at the edge of the sea, "he stands at the brink of his own consciousness."[73]

It was middle-class men who first came to see the summer vacation through rosy lenses. For them the summer island came to represent escape, though for women it had a different significance; because of the lack of modern conveniences, the move to the summer place was not for women a break from normal household tasks but an intensification of chores.[74] No wonder women came to think of the summer less nostalgically, unless, of course, they had servants to help with the ongoing work of housekeeping and child care. As for the people who live year-round in resort communities, the summer is anything but playful. It is the time of the year when they work even harder to earn a good part of their annual income. Local women and children are often heavily involved in the seasonal economy, leaving them little time for themselves. Local families make money by renting out their houses, so they have no summer house to call their own. Ruth Moore, the Maine author brought up on Great Gott Island, bitterly remembered giving up her bedroom to lodgers. Her memory of an island childhood was decidedly less glowing than that of the mainland children who spent their summers in her mother's boarding house.[75] The summer world of the sojourner could not have been more different from that of the full-time resident.[76]

The image of summer as paradise is, like the concept of childhood with which it is associated, a product of modern urban culture. It has been said that today childhood is "a mythological country continuously mapped by grownups in search of their subjectivity in another time and place."[77] We can trace this quest back to the later nineteenth century when middle-class male writers and artists made childhood, like islands, a repository of all that seemed threatened by a rapidly changing industrial world, the ultimate symbols of worlds that were being lost and thus the focus of intense nostalgia. This longing was the product of a masculine life course that demanded that men put all things associated with femininity and childhood behind them. Women's lives were more continuous and their sense of loss less acute, but for men the end of childhood was like the expulsion from the original garden of earthly delights, producing an unrequited yearning.[78]

A newly invented set of child-centered holidays, the most important of which were Christmas and summer vacation, provided men with a symbolic connection to childhood. The middleclass festive calendar came to revolve increasingly around children, times of renewal when adults grown weary of the urban industrial world could return to simpler, happier times of their own pasts. Childhood became the most photographed of all life's phases. "We fend off death's terrors snapshot by snapshot," observes Anne Higonnet, "pretending to save the moment, halt time, preserve childhood intact."[79] Certain times of year came to be seen as conducive to this recovery project. Memory abhors vast spaces, so bounded sites—the garden, the cottage, the island—came to be regarded as mnemonically powerful. "Islands are better at creating and preserving memories, particularly youthful ones," writes Thurston Clarke, "and the best islands for doing this are the simple and uncluttered ones."[80]

Islanded places are now seen as ideal places not only to bring up children but to create and preserve a pristine, enduring image of childhood, the bedrock of adults' sense of who they are. People who have grown up on or summered on islands invariably want to return to them with their children or grandchildren. It has been said that "islands infantilize people," perhaps because they divest adults of their routines and encourage playfulness, but also because in the case of summer islands occupied over several generations, they allow them to connect to their own childhoods and thus to what they perceive as their true selves.[81] In a culture in which identity has become so deeply dependent on a sense of the personal and collective past, the search for "lost" childhoods tends to turn again and again to summer islands.

Island Sojourns and the Quest for Self

In the ancient world, travel was often undertaken in a quest for something greater than the self. Christian pilgrimage was also a way of connecting with something transcendent. Travel today moves in the opposite direction. According to Camus it "brings us back to ourselves." For Michael Crichton travel is essential to identity: "Often I feel I go to some distant region of the world to be reminded of who I really am."[82] It seems that it is easier to find ourselves at a distance than closer to home. The same thing applies to modern time travel, which opens up the foreign country of the past to our quest for identity. Our origins are always placed at some distance from the present; and roots are all the more impressive and pedigrees more prestigious when they run deep.[83]

We now live in what some have called a "world of movement," and others have described as "plurilocal" or "multicentered." Migration has been described by John Berger as the "quintessential experience of the age." It is the paradox of our times that "it is perhaps only by way of transience and displacement that one achieves an intimate sense of belonging."[84] Even when we cannot travel far in time and space, even when past and place have vanished, the modern quest for self at a distance is undeterred. Knowing that we cannot go home again, we who reside in the developed world search for it in the most unlikely places.

Today you do not have to travel far to find the foreign and the exotic. You can join an "African safari" in Florida or visit a Danish village in California. In what have been called staged authenticity, distant places and times are evoked with great success and profit. The little Iowa town of Amana has put itself on the tourist map by staging a Bavarian Oktoberfest and Cajun Mardi Gras. Historic Williamsburg and Mystic Seaport have set the standards for historical re-creation, formulae is now followed around the world. Sturbridge Village never existed in colonial times, but it seems older than many of the true colonial towns in Massachusetts. All that is needed to create the appropriate sense of temporal and spacial distance is an islanded site where the outside world is made invisible. The modern imagination does the rest.[85]

Islands are particularly attractive to time travelers. In his novel, *England, England,* Julian Barnes tells the story of a project that turns the Isle of Wight a bite-size version of old England so perfect that even the English can't tell the difference.[86] Islands are now the sites of staged authenticity so convincing that tourists are fooled into thinking that they have access to life as it really was. Elements of island life have been packaged and commodified to profit from tourist dreams. This "conscious insularism" is particularly widespread in the Caribbean, but is also evident in Mauritius and many other places. It has become common to create a cultural island within the physical island to meet the tourists' expectations.[87] When real isles do not fit the image of what an island should be, they can be remade. In a similar way, fenced-off tourist enslaves of Haiti and Jamaica produce versions of authentic island life while keeping the visitors from encountering the less savory side of those impoverished places.[88] When real islands will no longer do, artificial islands are created. The Holland American line has created one in the Caribbean where its cruise ships stop to shop and enjoy the flavor of a perfect paradise. The locals encountered there are daytime employees of the company who commute to work from nearby islands. In the evening, paradise is deserted except for security guards.

But the construction of these spaces of self-discovery is by no means dependent only on commercial providers. People are quite capable of constructing for themselves that desired sense of temporal and spatial distance. Great Gott Island is not very remote as far as physical distance is concerned. It is about a mile off Mount Desert Island (its mainland) and within sight and sound of the Bass Harbor Head lighthouse but much closer at the lowest tides, when a hidden bar brings it within a few hundred yards. In severe winters an ice bridge has been known to form between Gotts and the Head, but on a foggy day the island seems wholly cut off from its mainland and from the world itself. Families have been coming to Great Gott for more than a century, always in the summer, rarely more than once a year, slavishly following the same route and schedule to get there. In the case of my own family, the journey began in the 1960s *en famille* in a Volkswagen bus with just enough space for my wife and myself, two boys, a dog, an occasional passenger, luggage, and nonperishable supplies. Today, a midsize sedan is sufficient to get two of us to Maine, yet the trip still follows the same pattern, taking the same highways, making the same stops, a ritual as strictly observed as that of any pilgrimage. It is perfectly possible to fly to Maine and to reach the island comfortably and speedily in a few hours, yet the process of getting there has meaning inseparable from the destination. To get there in any other way is simply unthinkable.[89]

No matter how much additional time we have promised ourselves, the trip is never without anxiety. We approach the coast with one eye on the clock, the other on the skies. There is always the concern that the boatman has not gotten our message about time of arrival, that the seas will be too rough, or that the tide, which affects when and where we land on the island, will be too low. The last few miles are always passed in the kind of tense silence that precedes any significant rite of passage. We feel some relief when we are in sight of the town dock and spy the boat waiting on reasonably high tide in a calm sea, but we still know that the most arduous part of passage lies ahead.

Exchanging one form of transportation for another adds nothing to ease the trip but is an essential part of the passage. "Somehow, a ferry crossing is the most

Illustration 18   Cemetery on Great Gott Island, Maine

thrilling trip, possessing the size and ceremony of a seagoing voyage, but ruthlessly edited so that only the pleasures of embarking and disembarking remain," writes Amy Willard Cross.[90] Taking an unscheduled boat magnifies this effect, focusing one's attention on the process of arrival and departure without erasing the experience of the water itself. There is the ordeal of moving ourselves from car to dock and then to boat, an effort that we know must be repeated at the island itself.

Even then, however, the journey is not complete. The house, closed tight and surrounded by grass grown high by early summer, is still some way from the landing, a distance made greater by the island's old-fashioned modes of transportation. It takes several trips by wheelbarrow and backpack before we are ready to unlock the door and step across the threshold to assess the effects of eleven months of storms, mice, insects, and the occasional human intruder. Even if there are no unanticipated problems, it will take two or three days for us to feel fully at home. The water system must be resurrected, refrigerator and stove restarted, the curtains hung and beds made. The grass must be conquered, screens and shutters fitted, the wood supply replenished. And all this is accomplished in the full knowledge that what is done must be undone in a month or so when it is time for the rites of closing and departing to be scrupulously enacted.

A place remote and islanded does not come cheap, in terms of time, effort, or expense. Even if the old house was a bargain when we bought it thirty-five years ago, the amount of money spent on keeping it in repair, quite apart from major improvements, would have paid for many "carefree" vacations. As the owner of any summer place will testify, it is not a place of leisure but of labor of a physical kind that eleven months of urban and suburban living leave one quite unprepared for. Furthermore, such a remote and islanded place brings one into conflict with nature. On Gotts Island there are none of the protections from tempests, fogs, and, in wet summers, mosquitoes that we can count on at home in the city or suburb.

At the end of our month or so on Gotts, there is the equally ritualized act of saying goodbye to neighbors, closing up the house, and wheelbarrowing to the shore where the boat is waiting. Our last stop on the island is the cemetery, where we visit for one last time the grave marker of our youngest son, Ben, killed more than a decade ago in an air accident in Kenya. The ultimate symbol of absence, the cemetery, has taken on enormous significance, not just for us but for the many families whose members are memorialized there. Once largely neglected and overgrown, the graves at Gotts are now meticulously tended, as are similar island cemeteries all over the world.[91] It is the summer people who have invested their time and money in this effort, and many wish to be buried there rather than in the places they normally reside. The fact that the cemetery, like the island itself, goes unvisited for most of the year only adds to its appeal, for, as with so much in modern life, death is best contemplated at a distance.

It is the deserted island that has always stirred the Western imagination. The very emptiness of the place allows free rein to thoughts and feelings that are otherwise inhibited and confused by the clutter of everyday existence. Great writers have turned again and again to the desert island as their space of creativity. Caliban and Crusoe would never have been credible as continentals. And it is not just artists who find island amenable to those imaginative processes that set mankind apart from all other species. As we have seen, islands, especially the small and remote, domesticate and simplify, allowing all of us to dwell on issues that seem too large when confronted on the mainlands of our existence. They are places to which we can turn to recover our individual and collective sense of self, for, as Diana Loxley put it, islands provide the "uninhabited territory upon which the conditions for a rebirth or genesis are made possible."[92] We do so as much in absence as presence, always maintaining that precious quality of separation associated with the sacred.

Eternal Return

The appeal of remote and islanded places cannot be explained in terms of economy or convenience. "Fundamentally, summering at the cottage is a symbolic

Illustration 19   Boats of the Outward Bound School at Hurricane Island, Maine

act," observes the Canadian writer Roy Wolfe.[93] To travel so far, using means of transportation that are by contemporary standards slow and uncomfortable, sets the summer islander as far apart from the tourist as the pilgrim is removed from the Sunday worshiper. But it is precisely the ritualized coming and going that differentiates places remote and islanded from the ordinary tourist site. Islands have always had those qualities of "non-places," described by Marc Auge as locations "promoted to the status of 'places of memory,' and assigned to circumscribed and specific position" which is neither here nor there, neither now or then, but always betwixt and between.[94]

Defined by both earth and water, islands have long been ambiguous liminal locales, the favored places for rites of passage.[95] Once reserved for religious rituals, islands now host a wide range of secular rites, including weddings and anniversaries. People seeking to transform themselves mentally and physically will even pay large sums to endure ordeals such as those provided on Maine's Hurricane Island by a program called Outward Bound.[96] In a pattern typical of all rites of passage, those who sign on are first divested of their mainland habits and then subjected to spartan training, which in this case prepares them for the ultimate test of surviving in an open boat for several days. Having proved that they can make it on their own, these modern Brendans then leave the island to return to civilization, convinced they are now in possession of their better selves.

Like a pilgrimage, contemporary outdoor rites of passage always involve a three-part process of separation, transition, and reincorporation. As it was in the past, the island journey is circular, a cultural practice dependent as much on departure as arrival, on the possibility of eternal return. The sacredness of any island, its perceived distance from the profane everyday world, is a product of ritualized repetitions, producing a sense of time as recoverable and repeatable.[97] The intensity of the island experience depends on the certain knowledge that one must leave. A summer cottage loses its meaning when it becomes a permanent residence, for seasonality is fundamental to achieving remoteness. It is in absence rather than in residence that islands exercise their strongest hold over our imaginations.

In a society that dotes so much on linear progress, what is astonishing is, as Orvar Löfgren alerts us, the "the centrality of returns, of motion backward in both physical and mental terms."[98] We feel compelled to go back so that we can move forward; and though we no longer obey the cyclical rhythms of nature, culture has created a plethora of seasonal cycles to which we are slavishly devoted. We may live on linear time, but we live *by* daily, weekly, and annual cycles that endow existence with existential meaning.[99] Our modern lives are traced in the circuits we have created and adhere to with all the devotion of a medieval pilgrim. And just as the sacredness of a religious mecca depends on its distance from everyday existence, so the meaning of the summer or winter island is produced by the fact that it is a place of perpetual return, not of permanent destination. Ironically, the very meaning of the island depends on our transience. We come and go so it can remain the island in our mind that never changes, the fixed pivot of our turning world, our secular proof of eternity.[100]

We leave home in order to feel at home; we travel far to get closer to our real selves. But the voyage remains, as it was in the time Odysseus and of Brendan, a round trip. As T. S. Eliot put it:

We shall not cease from exploration
And the end of all our exploring
Will be to arrive where we started
And know the place for the first time.[101]

For islands to serve the mainlands' latest cultural imperatives, they must be kept at a certain spatial and temporal distance. When he visited the Sea Islands off the coast of the Carolinas, Gunnar Hansen found that city folk who were purchasing land had no real intention of living there: "They just wanted the idea. They want the word ISLAND emblazoned on their stationery."[102] Even as physical islands retreat to the margins of history and geography, islands of the mind loom large in our consciousness of ourselves and the world around us. The less they are occupied, the more they preoccupy the modern imagination.

RETURNING HOME TO EARTH ISLAND

> Once a photograph of the Earth, taken from the outside, is available—once the sheer isolation of the Earth becomes known—a new idea as powerful as any in history will be let loose.
>
> —Sir Fred Hoyle

FOR MOST OF HUMAN HISTORY MUCH OF MANKIND has believed itself to occupy one great earth island. Not until quite recently did Western civilization divide humanity into mainlanders and islanders. Now, having seen our planet from the perspective of outer space, we are reassessing that distinction. This book has shown that no island is any longer really an island. It is equally true that continents have lost their distinctiveness. From a distance we can see what our ancestors sensed but could not prove, namely that the earth itself is one great island in a sea of space.

As early as 1951 Rachel Carson was convinced that the ancients had been right about our insularity. Wherever she looked she saw only the sea around us.[1] Now, however, it is outer space which gives meaning to the idea of human insularity. In 1968 David Brower, the radical environmentalist, declared that "man needs an Earth National Park, to protect on this planet what he has not destroyed and what need not be destroyed."[2] By then Margaret Mead and others were beginning to talk of "earth island," and in 1982 Brower established the Earth Island Institute in San Francisco, devoted to what he called CPR for the earth—conservation, preservation, and restoration—giving new life and real momentum to this ancient metaphor.

The consciousness of ourselves as inhabitants of one vast island or, as the Polynesians understood it, one great sea of islands, is absolutely vital to our common political, economic, and ecological survival. And if the realization of global society still seems far off, we nevertheless need to concentrate on this ultimate island of the mind, on what connects us not only as a human species but as part of an ecological system that embraces plants and animals, the sea and the air as well as the earth. From outer space it is easier to see that the lines which have been drawn on maps and the distinctions made between different life forms are artificial and do not represent the world as it actually functions.

John Fowles has written that he loves islands so much because "they make us stop and think a little: why am I here, what am I about, what is it all about, what has gone wrong."[3] Only when we leave a place do we come to fully appreci-

Illustration 20   View of Earth from 1.32 million miles, 6:07 A.M., December 11, 1990

ate it; and our journey into outer space has made us stop and think again about our island home. This latest phase of the human journey has brought us full circle, and the recovery of the ancient notion of earth island puts us in touch with the positive aspects of our shared insularity. We need to remind ourselves that before the nineteenth century insularity was understood as liberating and energizing, creating a vital sense of common purpose and direction. Islands compelled early modern people to stop and think a little. Now we are recuperating that original meaning because, without a sense of belonging to the same earth island, sharing resources and goals, globalization is but an empty promise, more a danger than a solution to the ecological, political, and economic problems that face rich and poor nations alike. The metaphor of earth island offers a framework within which we can stop and think about the challenges that we must confront collectively. It is true that thinking with islands comes with risks. As we have seen, Western islomania has not always been a positive force in the world. But because the island remains such a powerful metaphor, it must be reclaimed. Were it to be focused on our precious earth island, and not just on particular islands, it could make an enormous difference in the struggle to save the planet.

NOTES

Introduction

1. Lawrence Durrell, *Reflections on a Marine Venus: A Companion to the Landscape of Rhodes* (London: Faber & Faber, 1953), pp. 15–16.
2. Yi-Fu Tuan, *Topophilia: A Study of Environmental Perception, Attitudes, and Values* (Englewood Cliffs, N.J.: Prentice Hall, 1974), p. 118.
3. Rod Edmond and Vanessa Smith, introduction to *Islands in History and Representation,* ed. Rod Edmond and Vanessa Smith (London: Routledge, 2003), p. 4.
4. Bill Holm, *Eccentric Islands: Islands Real and Imaginary* (Minneapolis: Milkwood, 2000), p. 4; Gretel Ehrlich, *Islands, the Universe, Home* (New York: Viking, 1991), p. 65.
5. According to Eviatar Zerubavel we typically think with "islands of meaning." See his *The Fine Line: Making Distinctions in Everyday Life* (Chicago: University of Chicago Press, 1993), chapter 1: On this Western tendency to think of the world as consisting of isolated objects and essences, ignoring that which connects, see Richard E. Nisbett, *The Geography of Thought: How Asians and Westerners Think Differently . . . and Why* (New York: Free Press, 2003), chapter 1.
6. Epile Hau'ofa, "Our Sea of Islands," *The Contemporary Pacific: A Journal of Island Affairs* 6, no. 1 (spring 1994): 153.
7. Ian Watson, "The Challenge of Maintaining Parity for Offshore Islands," *Middle States Geographer* 31 (1998): 133.
8. Eric Wolf, *Europe and the People without History* (Berkeley: University of California Press, 1982), pp. 3–7.
9. See, for instance, Martin W. Lewis and Karen Wigan, *The Myth of Continents: A Critique of Metageography* (Berkeley: University of California Press, 1997); Philip E. Steinberg, *The Social Construction of the Oceans* (Cambridge: Cambridge University Press, 2001); Alain Corbin, *The Lure of the Sea: The Discovery of the Seaside in the Western World, 1750–1840* (Berkeley: University of California Press, 1994); Edwin Bernbaum, *Sacred Mountains of the World* (Berkeley: University of California Press, 1997); Stephen J. Pyne, *How the Canyon Became Grand* (New York: Viking, 1998); and Simon Schama, *Landscape and Memory* (New York: Vintage, 1996).

Chapter 1

1. Rhys Carpenter, *Beyond the Pillars of Heracles: The Classical World Seen through the Eyes of Its Explorers* (New York: Delacourte, 1966), pp. 24–32; Bernard Knox, introduction and notes to *The Odyssey,* by Homer, trans. Robert Fagles (New York: Penguin, 1996), pp. 25–36; and Fernand Braudel, *The Mediterranean in the Ancient World,* trans. Sian Reynolds (London: Allen Lane, 2001), pp. 22–25.

2. *The Dictionary of Imaginary Places,* ed. Alberto Manguel and Gianni Guadalupi (New York: Harcourt Brace, 1980).
3. James S. Romm, *The Edges of the Earth in Ancient Thought, Geography, Exploration, and Fiction* (Princeton, N.J: Princeton University Press, 1992), pp. 10–13; Peregrine Horden and Nicholas Purcell, *The Corrupting Sea: A Study of Mediterranean History* (Oxford: Blackwell, 2000), chapter 1.
4. Romm, *Edges of the Earth,* p. 32.
5. Mary W. Helms, *Ulysses' Sail: An Ethnographic Odyssey of Power, Knowledge, and Geographical Distance* (Princeton, N.J.: Princeton University Press, 1988), chapter 1.
6. John R. Gillis, *A World of Their Own Making: Myth, Ritual, and the Quest for Family Values* (New York: Basic Books, 1995), chapter 6.
7. Helms, *Ulysses' Sail,* chapters 1 and 2.
8. Romm, *Edges of the Earth,* pp. 24–26.
9. Robert Kunzig, *The Restless Sea: Exploring the World Beneath the Sea* (New York: W.W. Norton, 1999), p. 7; and David Konstan, "Ocean," in *The Encyclopedia of Religion,* Vol. 11 (New York: Macmillan, 1987), p. 56.
10. See Richard Carrington, *A Biography of the Sea* (New York: Basic Books, 1960), pp. 243ff.
11. Romm, *Edges of the Earth,* pp. 16–17.
12. Alain Corbin, *The Lure of the Sea: The Discovery of the Seaside in the Western World, 1750–1840* (Berkeley: University of California Press, 1994), p. 12.
13. See Eric Leed, *The Mind of the Traveler: From Gilgamesh to Global Tourism* (New York: Basic Books, 1991), pp. 7–11, 25–27.
14. Homer, *Odyssey,* 1:1–2; see also Samuel Eliot Morison, *The European Discovery of America: The Northern Voyages, A.D. 500–1600,* Vol. 2 (New York: Oxford University Press, 1992), p. 26.
15. See Leed, *Mind of the Traveler,* pp. 2–12.
16. James Hamilton-Paterson, *The Great Deep: The Sea and Its Thresholds* (New York: Random House, 1992), p. 67.
17. Romm, *Edges of the Earth,* p. 26.
18. Braudel, *Mediterranean in the Ancient World,* pp. 260–61.
19. See Jonathan Raban, *The Oxford Book of the Sea* (New York: Oxford University Press, 1992), pp. 3–4.
20. Ibid., p. 3.
21. Romm, *Edges of the Earth,* pp. 23–26.
22. Corbin, *Lure of the Sea,* p. 6.
23. Leed, *Mind of the Traveler,* p. 33.
24. See Gordon J. Davies, *The Earth in Decay: A History of British Geomorphology, 1578–1878* (New York: Elsevier, 1969), pp. 5–6.
25. Ibid., p. 38.
26. Ibid., pp. 38, 41, 56.
27. Thomas Burnet quoted in Davies, *Earth in Decay,* p. 71.
28. See Casey Fredericks, "Plato's Atlantis: A Mythologist Looks at Myth," in *Atlantis: Fact or Fiction?,* ed. Edwin Ramage (Bloomington: Indiana University Press, 1978), pp. 86–96.
29. Edmundo O'Gorman, *The Invention of America: An Inquiry into the Historical Nature of the New World and the Meaning of Its History* (Bloomington: Indiana University Press, 1961), p. 68.
30. Ibid.
31. See Romm, chapters 1 and 3; and Sprague L. de Camp, *Lost Continents: The Atlantis Theme in History, Science, and Literature* (New York: Gnome, 1954), pp. 15, 221–24.
32. de Camp, *Lost Continents,* p. 225.

33. Carol Zaleski, *Otherworld Journeys: Accounts of Near-Death Experiences in Medieval and Modern Times* (New York: Oxford University Press, 1987), p. 65.

34. Corbin, *Lure of the Sea,* pp.17–18.

35. Barry Cunliffe, *Facing the Atlantic: The Atlantic and Its Peoples, 8000 B.C.-A.D. 1500* (New York: Oxford University Press, 2001), chapters 7–11.

36. Helms, *Ulysses' Sail,* pp. 26–27.

37. Quote from Hesiod in Morison, *Northern Voyages,* p. 4; Geoffrey Ashe, *Atlantis: Lost Lands, Ancient Wisdom* (London: Thames & Hudson, 1992), pp. 23–25.

38. J. V. Luce, "Ancient Explorers," *The Quest for America* (London: Pall Mall, 1971), p. 87.

39. Cunliffe, *Facing the Atlantic,* p. 10.

40. de Camp, *Lost Continents,* p. 218.

41. Ibid., p. 33.

42. See Leed, *Mind of the Traveler,* p. 179.

43. See Yi-Fu Tuan, *Segmented Worlds and Self: Group Life and Individual Consciousness* (Minneapolis: University of Minnesota Press, 1982), p. 52.

44. See Yi-Fu Tuan, *Topophilia; A Study of Environmental Perception, Attitudes, and Values* (Englewood Cliffs, N.J.: Prentice Hall, 1974), p. 17.

45. See Jean Gottmann, *The Significance of Territory* (Charlottesville: University of Virginia Press, 1973), pp. 19–27.

46. Robert Bartlett, *The Making of Europe: Conquest, Colonization, and Cultural Change, 950–1350* (London: Penguin, 1994), pp. 5–23, 306–309.

47. Ibid., pp. 126–38: Patricia Seed, *Ceremonies of Possession in Europe's Conquest of the New World* (Cambridge: Cambridge University Press, 1999).

48. O'Gorman, *Invention of America,* p. 68.

49. Daniel Lord Smail, *Imagining Cartographies: Possession and Identity in Late Medieval Marseille* (Ithaca, N.Y.: Cornell University Press, 1999), pp. 115–39.

50. See Robert L. Reynolds, "The Mediterranean Frontiers, 1000–1300," in *The Frontier in Perspective,* ed. W. D. Wyman and C. Kroeber (Madison: University of Wisconsin Press, 1957), pp. 21–34.

51. See James Muldoon, introduction to *The Expansion of Europe: The First Phase* (Philadelphia: University of Pennsylvania Press, 1971), pp. 20–21.

52. See Davies, *Earth in Decay.* 19.

53. See Tuan, *Topophilia,* p. 134.

54. See Aaron J. Gurevich, *Categories of Medieval Culture,* trans. G. L. Campbell (London: Routledge, 1985), pp. 42–43.

55. As quoted in Gurevich, *Categories of Medieval Culture,* p. 69.

56. Sir Thomas Browne quoted in Donald Gifford, *The Farthest Shore: A Natural History of Perception* (New York: Vintage, 1991), pp 71–72.

57. See Gillis, *World of Their Own Making,* pp. 41–47.

58. Craig Koslofsky, "From Presence to Remembrance: The Transformation of Memory in the German Reformation," in *The Work of Memory: New Directions in the Study of German Society and Culture,* ed. A. Confino and P. Fritzsche (Champlain/Urbana: University of Illinois Press, 2002), pp. 30–31.

59. Gurevich, *Categories of Medieval Culture,* p. 107.

60. Wilcomb Washburn, "The Meaning of 'Discovery' in the Fifteenth and Sixteenth Centuries," *American Historical Review* 67, no. 1 (October 1962): 3.

61. Raymond R. Ramsay, *No Longer on the Map: Discovering Places That Never Were* (New York: Viking, 1972), p. 111.

62. John Mandeville, *The Travels of Sir John Mandeville* (London: Penguin, 1983), p. 193.

63. See Gurevich, *Categories of Medieval Culture,* p. 85

64. Ibid., p. 79.
65. See Denis E. Cosgrove, *Social Formation and Symbolic Landscape* (London: Croom Helm, 1984), pp. 18–19.
66. John Kirtland Wright, "Terrae Incognitae: The Place of Imagination in Geography, *"Human Nature in Geography* (Cambridge: Harvard University Press, 1966), pp. 68–88.
67. Mandeville, *Travels,* pp. 183–4.
68. Davies, *Earth in Decay,* pp. 19–23.
69. For a discussion of the ways time and space were understood, see Alessandro Scafi, "Mapping Eden: Cartographies of Earthly Paradise," in *Mappings,* ed. Denis Cosgrove (London: Reaktion, 1999), pp. 60–64; also David Woodward, "Reality, Symbolism, Time and Space in Medieval World Maps," *Annals of the Association of American Geographers* 75 (1985): 510–21.
70. David Woodward, "Medieval Mappaemundi," *The History of Cartography,* Vol. 1, ed. J. E. Harley and D. Woodward (Chicago: University of Chicago Press, 1987), p. 286.
71. See Romm, *Edges of the Earth,* 24–26.
72. See Scafi, *Mapping Eden,* pp. 59–60.
73. Hamilton-Paterson, *Great Deep,* p. 64.
74. See Richard Ellis, *Imagining Atlantis* (New York: Knopf, 1998), chapter 1; Edwin S. Ramage, "Perspectives Ancient and Modern," in *Atlantis: Fact or Fiction?,* ed. Edwin S. Ramage (Bloomington: Indiana University Press, 1978), pp. 21–26; Fredericks, "Plato's Atlantis," pp. 86–99.
75. See Barry Cunliffe, *The Extraordinary Voyage of Pytheas the Greek* (New York: Penguin, 2002).
76. Ibid., p. 116.
77. See Kirsten Hastrup, "Nature as Historical Space," *Folk* 31 (1989), p. 10.
78. See Romm, *Edges of the Earth,* chapter 4. On Scandinavia as an island, see Lief Sondergaard, "At the Edge of the World: Early Medieval Ideas of the Nordic Countries," in *Medieval Spirituality in Scandinavia and Europe,* ed. Lars Bisgaard et al. (Odense, Denmark: Odense Press, 2001), pp. 53–56.
79. Helms, *Ulysses' Sail,* p. 220.
80. Claude Kappler, quoted in Jean Delumeau, *History of Paradise: The Garden of Eden in Myth and Tradition,* trans. M. O'Connell (New York: Continuum, 1995),p. 98; Helms, *Ulysses' Sail,* p. 24.

Chapter 2

1. Paul Shepard, *Nature and Madness* (San Francisco: Sierra Club, 1982), p. 47.
2. Simon Schama, *Landscape and Memory* (New York: Vintage, 1996), p. 7.
3. *Oxford English Dictionary*
4. See Shepard, *Nature and Madness,* p. 51.
5. See Paul Carter, *The Road to Botany Bay: An Exploration of Landscape and History* (New York: Knopf, 1988), chapter 9.
6. See George Williams, *Wilderness and Paradise in Christian Thought* (New York: Harper & Row, 1962), chapters 1 and 2.
7. Ibid., p. 131.
8. Diana Loxley, *Problematic Shores: The Literature of Islands* (New York: St. Martin's, 1990), p. 3.
9. Mircea Eliade and Lawrence Sullivan, "Center of the World," in *The Encyclopedia of Religion,* Vol. 33 (New York: Macmillan, 1987), pp. 166–70; Mirceas Eliade, *Patterns in Comparative Religion* (New York: New American Library, 1964), chapter 11; Yi-Fu Tuan, *Topophilia: A Study of Environmental Perceptions, Attitudes, and Values* (Englewood Cliffs, N.J.: Prentice Hall, 1974), pp. 16, 36.

10. Eliade, *Patterns of Comparative Religion*, p. 433.
11. Yi-Fu Tuan, "Sacred Space: Exploration of an Idea," *Dimensions of Human Geography*, ed. Karl Butzer (Chicago: University of Chicago Department of Geography, Research Paper 186, 1978), p. 84.
12. See Gordon J. Davies, *The Earth in Decay: A History of British Geomorphology, 1578–1878* (New York: Elsevier, 1969), pp. 38–47.
13. See Barry Cunliffe, *Facing the Ocean: The Atlantic and Its Peoples, 8000 B.C.–A.D. 1500* (Oxford: Oxford University Press, 2001), p. 155; also V. Gordon Childe, *The Dawn of European Civilization* (New York: Knopf, 1958).
14. Barry Cunliffe, *The Extraordinary Voyage of Pytheas the Greek* (New York: Penguin 2003), chapter 4.
15. Peregrine Horden and Nicholas Purcell, *The Corrupting Sea: A Study of the Mediterranean History* (Oxford: Blackwell, 2000), pp. 440–460.
16. Cunliffe, *Facing the Ocean*, p. 362.
17. Pierre-Roland Giot, "The Attractions for Coasts and Islands from Later Prehistory to the Dark Ages," *Atlantic Visions*, ed. John de Couray Ireland and David C. Sheely (Dublin: Boole, 1989), p. 128.
18. Cunliffe, *Facing the Atlantic*, p. 31.
19. On the contrast with Eastern cultures, where the desire to impose order on nature is less pronounced, see John Prest, "Garden" in *The Encyclopedia of Religion*, Vol. 5 (New York: Macmillan, 1987), pp. 487–88.
20. Eric Leed, *The Mind of the Traveler: From Gilgamesh to Modern Tourism* (New York: Basic Books, 1991), p. 210; on the view that the myth of Eden is the product of environmental loss, see Paul Shepard, *Man in the Landscape: A Historic View of the Esthetic of Nature* (New York: Alfred J. Knopf, 1967), chapter 3.
21. Edwin Bernbaum, *Sacred Mountains of the World*, new edition (Berkeley: University of California Press, 1997), pp. 108–112.
22. On ancient notions of the sacred, see Tuan, "Sacred Space," pp. 84–85.
23. See James S. Romm, *The Edge of the Earth in Ancient Thought: Geography, Exploration, and Fiction* (Princeton, N.J.: Princeton University Press, 1992), chapter 4.
24. See Shepard, *Nature and Madness*, p. 51.
25. See Garry Trompf, introduction to *Islands and Enclaves: Nationalism and Separatist Pressures in Island and Littoral Contexts* (New Delhi: Sterling, 1999), p. xiii.
26. See Robert Bartlett, *The Making of Europe: Conquest, Colonization, and Cultural Change, 950–1350* (London: Penguin, 1994), pp. 5–23.
27. See Richard Townsend, "Geography," *The Encyclopedia of Religion*, Vol. 5 (New York: Macmillan, 1987), p. 512.
28. Ibid., pp. 510–511.
29. See Mary W. Helms, *Ulysses' Sail: An Ethnographic Odyssey in Power, Knowledge, and Geographical Distance* (Princeton, N.J.: Princeton University Press, 1988), chapters 1 and 2.
30. See James Lydon, *The Making of Ireland* (London: Routledge, 1998), pp. 7–8.
31. Eric Hirsch, introduction to *The Anthropology of the Landscape*, ed. Eric Hirsch and M. O'Hanlon (Oxford: Clarendon, 1995), p. 4.
32. Lydon, *Making of Ireland*, pp. 27–28.
33. Ibid., pp. 55–56.
34. On this process, see Simon Schama, *Landscape and Memory* (New York: Vintage, 1995), chapters 7 and 8.
35. See Jacques LeGoff, "The Wilderness in the Medieval West," *The Medieval Imagination*, trans. A. Goldhammer (Chicago: University of Chicago Press, 1988), pp. 48–52.
36. See Cunliffe, *Facing the Ocean*, pp. 472–75.
37. I owe my insights on this point to Dr. Stefan Brink of Uppsala University, Sweden.

38. E. G. Bowen, *Britain and the Western Seaways* (London: Thames & Hudson, 1972), pp. 108–110.

39. See E.G. Bowen, *Saints, Seaways, and Settlements in the Celtic Lands* (Cardiff: University of Wales Press, 1969), pp. 192–5.

40. Ibid., pp. 209–20.

41. Bowen, *Saints, Seaways, and Settlements*, p. 208.

42. See John Thomas McNeill, *The Celtic Penitentials and Their Influence on Continental Christianity* (Paris: Librarie Ancienne Homme, 1923), pp. 135–36.

43. Bowen, *Saints, Seaways, and Settlements*, p. 196.

44. J. M. MacKinlay, "'In Oceano Desertum'—Celtic Anchorites and Their Island Retreats," *Proceedings of the Society of Antiquaries of Scotland* 33 (1889–99), pp. 130–32.

45. Ibid., pp. 130–31.

46. See Des Lavelle, *Skellig: Island Outpost of Europe* (Montreal: McGill & Queens University Press, 1976), pp. 8–20.

47. See Kathleen Hughes, "The Changing Theory and Practice of Irish Pilgrimage," *Journal of Ecclesiastical History* 11, no. 2 (October 1960), pp. 143–51.

48. Peter Harbison, *Pilgrimage in Ireland: The Monuments and the People* (London: Barrie & Jenkins, 1991), p. 35.

49. Ibid., chapter 8.

50. Ibid., p. 182.

51. See Thomas Cahill, *How the Irish Saved Civilization* (New York: Doubleday, 1995), pp. 151–206.

52. MacKinlay, "In Oceano Desertum," p. 130.

53. See Alfred P. Smyth, *Warlords and Holy Men* (London: Edward Arnold, 1984), pp. 166–174.

54. MacKinlay, "In Oceano Desertum," pp. 129–33.

55. Harbison, *Pilgrimage in Ireland*, pp. 62–67.

56. Quoted in Jean Delumeau, *History of Paradise: The Garden of Eden in Myth and Tradition*, trans. M. O'Connell (New York: Continuum, 1995), p. 98.

57. Harbison, *Pilgrimage in Ireland*, pp. 37–41.

58. Ibid., pp. 42–48.

59. See K. Hughes, "Theory and Practice," p. 151.

60. John J. O'Meara, introduction to *The Voyage of Saint Brendan*, trans. John J. O'Meara (Gerrards Cross, England: Colin Smythe, 1991), p. xvii.

61. See Harbison, *Pilgrimage in Ireland*, p. 237.

62. See O'Meara, introduction to *Voyage*, p. xv.

63. See Kent Mathewson, "St. Brendon: Mythical Isle and Topographical Drift: From Iceland to Ecuador," *Atlantic Visions*, ed. J de Courcy Ireland and David C. Sheehy (Dublin: Books Press, 1989), pp. 53–57.

64. Aaron J. Gurevich, *Categories of Medieval Culture*, trans. G. L. Campbell (London: Routledge, 1985), p. 56.

65. See David Woodward, "Medieval *Mappaemundi*," in *The History of Cartography*, Vol. 1, ed. J. B. Harley and D. Woodward (Chicago: University of Chicago Press, 1987), p. 286.

66. See Richard Panek, *Seeing and Believing: How the Telescope Opened Our Eyes and Minds to the Heavens* (New York: Viking, 1998), pp. 15, 22–23.

67. Mary B. Campbell, "'The Object of One's Gaze': Landscape, Writing, and Early Medieval Pilgrimage," in *Discovering New Worlds: Essays in Medieval Exploration and Imagination* (New York: Garland, 1991), p. 10

68. K. Hughes, "Theory and Practice," p. 151.

69. See Geoffrey Ashe, "Analysis of the Legends," *Quest for America* (London: Pall Mall, 1971), pp. 39–49; Cunliffe, *Facing the Ocean*, p. 13.

70. See Vincent H. Cassidy, *The Sea Around Them: the Atlantic Ocean, A.D. 1200* (Baton Rouge: Louisiana State University Press, 1968), p. 61.

71. Ibid., pp. 166–69.

72. David Beers Quinn, "New Geographical Horizons: Literature," in *First Images of America: The Impact of the New World on the Old,* ed. Fredi Chiapelli, Vol. 2 (Berkeley: University of California Press, 1976), pp. 635–36.

73. See Leonardo Olschki, *Storia Litteraria della Scoperte Geograpfice* (Florence: Leo S. Olschki, 1937). The chapter on "Insular Romanticism," as translated by Christopher DeRosa of the University of California at Berkeley. I wish to thank Mr. DeRosa for his fine translation.

74. Ibid.

75. Ibid.

76. Robert H. Fuson, *Legendary Islands of the Ocean Sea* (Sarasota: Pineapple Press, 1995), p. 130.

77. See Frank Lestringant, *Mapping the Renaissance World: The Geographical Imagination in the Age of Discovery* (Cambridge: Polity, 1994).

78. Denis Cosgrove, *Apollo's Eye: A Cartographic Genealogy of the Earth in the Western Imagination* (Baltimore: Johns Hopkins University Press, 2001), pp 88–94: P.D.A. Harvey, "Local and Regional Cartography in Medieval Europe," *The History of Cartography,* Vol. 1, ed. J. B. Harley and D. Woodward (Chicago: University of Chicago Press, 1987), pp. 483–84.

79. P.D.A. Harvey, "Local and Regional Geography," p. 482.

80. See Frank Lestringant, "Isles," *Geographie du Monde au Moyen Age et la Renaissance,* ed. Monique Pelletier (Paris: Editions du C.T.H.S., 1989), pp. 165–67.

81. See Tom Conley, *The Self-Made Map: Cartographic Writing in Early Modern France* (Minneapolis: University of Minnesota Press, 1996), pp. 168–69.

82. See Roland Greene, "Island Logic," in *'The Tempest' and Its Travels,* ed. Peter Hulme and William H. Sherman (Philadelphia: University of Pennsylvania Press, 2000), pp. 138–45.

83. See Cosgrove, *Apollo's Eye,* pp. 95–101.

84. See Valerie Flint, *The Imaginative Landscape of Christopher Columbus* (Princeton, N.J.: Princeton University Press, 1992), chapter 6.

Chapter 3

1. John L. Allen, "Lands of Myth, Waters of Wonder: The Place of Imagination in the History of Geographical Exploration," *Geographies of the Mind: Essays in Historical Geosophy,* ed. David Lowenthal and Marilyn Bowden (New York: Oxford University Press, 1976), p. 43.

2. Valerie I. J. Flint, *The Imaginative Landscape of Christopher Columbus* (Princeton, N.J.: Princeton University Press, 1992), p. xiv.

3. Allen, "Lands of Myth," p. 45.

4. See Samuel Eliot Morison, *Portuguese Voyages to America in the Fifteenth Century* (Cambridge: Harvard University Press, 1940), p. 6; on the ancients, see Eric Leed, *The Mind of the Traveler: From Gilgamesh to Global Tourism* (New York: Basic Books, 1991), p. 180; also Edmundo O'Gorman, *The Invention of America: An Inquiry into the Historical Nature of the New World and the Meaning of Its History* (Bloomington: Indiana University Press, 1961), chapter 3.

5. David Beers Quinn, "New Geographical Horizons: Literature," in *First Images of America: The Impact of the New World on the Old,* ed. F. Chiapelli, Vol. 2 (Berkeley: University of California Press, 1976), pp. 635–58.

6. O'Gorman, *Invention of America,* p. 4; Karin E. Wigen and Martin W. Lewis, *The Myth of Continents: A Critique of Metageography* (Berkeley: University of California Press,

1997), chapter 1. See also William W. Fitzhugh and Elisabeth I. Ward, *Vikings: The North Atlantic Saga* (Washington, D.C.: Smithsonian Press, 2000).

7. Leed, *Mind of the Traveler,* p. 7.

8. Geoffrey Ashe, *The Quest for America* (London: Pall Mall, 1971), p. 270.

9. David Leeming, "Quest," *The Encyclopedia of Religion,* Vol. 12 (New York: Macmillan, 1987), p. 148.

10. Pauline Moffatt Watts, "Prophecy and Discovery: On the Spiritual Origins of Christopher Columbus's Enterprise of the Indies," *American Historical Review* 90, no. 1 (February 1985): 79.

11. See J. H. Parry, *The Discovery of South America* (London: Paul Elek, 1979), p. 52.

12. Frank Lestringant, *Mapping the Renaissance World: The Geographical Imagination in the Age of Discovery* (Cambridge: Polity, 1994), p. 7.

13. James Hamilton-Paterson, *The Great Deep: The Sea and Its Thresholds* (New York: Random House, 1992), p. 67.

14. Paul Carter, *The Road to Botany Bay: An Essay in Spatial History* (London Faber & Faber, 1987), pp. 146–48.

15. Quoted in the introduction to *The Vinland Sagas: The Norse Discovery of America* (London: Penguin, 1965), p. 15.

16. See Philip E. Steinberg, *The Social Construction of the Oceans* (Cambridge: Cambridge University Press, 2001), p. 70; Paul Butel, *The Atlantic* (New York: Routledge, 1999), pp. 20–28; and Michel Jourdin du Mollat, *Europe and the Sea* (Oxford: Blackwell, 1993), chapter 3.

17. See Lief Sondergaard, "At the Edge of the World: Early Medieval Ideas of the Nordic Countries," in *Medieval Spirituality in Scandinavia and Europe,* ed. Lars Bisgaard et al. (Odense, Denmark: Odense Press, 2001), pp. 67–68.

18. *The Vinland Sagas.,* pp. 101–102.

19. Ibid.

20. As reported by Adam of Bremen around 1075; cited in Ibid., p. 24.

21. See John Brotton, "Terrestrial Globalism: Mapping the Globe in Early Modern Europe," in *Mappings,* ed. Denis Cosgrove (London: Reaktion, 1999), pp. 71–89.

22. Hamilton-Paterson, *Great Deep,* p. 68.

23. Vincent H. Cassidy, *The Sea around Them: The Atlantic Ocean, A.D. 1250,* (Baton Rouge: Louisiana State University Press, 1968), p. 7.

24. Robert H. Fuson, *Legendary Islands of the Ocean Sea* (Sarasota: Pineapple, 1995), pp. 7, 86.

25. Quinn, "New Geographical Horizons," pp. 635–36.

26. See Anthony Pagden, *The Fall of Natural Man: The American Indian and the Origins of Comparative Ethnology* (Cambridge: Cambridge University Press, 1982), chapters 1 and 2.

27. See Yi-Fu Tuan, *Space and Place: The Perspective of Experience* (Minneapolis: University of Minnesota Press, 1977), pp. 86–87.

28. See Donald S. Johnson, *Phantom Islands of the Atlantic: The Legends of Seven Lands That Never Were* (New York: Walker, 1994), pp. 176–180; and Samuel Eliot Morison, *The European Discovery of America: The Northern Voyages, A.D. 500–1600,* Vol. 2 (New York: Oxford University Press, 1971), pp. 13–25.

29. Cassidy, *Sea around Them,* p. 167.

30. On the wanderings of Saint Brendan's Isle, see Johnson, *Phantom Islands,* chapter viii.

31. Quinn, "New Geographical Horizons," p. 636.

32. From Seneca's *Medea,* quoted in Vincent Cassidy, "The Voyage of an Island," *Speculum* 38 (October 1963), p. 595.

33. Fuson, *Legendary Islands,* pp. 14, 28; Cassidy, *Sea around Them,* p. 168.

34. See Cassidy, *Sea around Them,* p. 602.

35. Johnson, *Phantom Islands,* pp. 114–16; William H. Babcock, *Legendary Islands of the Atlantic* (New York: American Geographical Society, 1922), pp. 53–61.

36. T. J, Westropp, "Brasil and the Legendary Islands of the North Atlantic," *Proceedings of the Royal Irish Academy,* 3rd ser., 30 (1912), p. 257; Barry Cunliffe, *Facing the Ocean: The Atlantic and Its Peoples 8000 B.C.-A.D. 1500* (Oxford: Oxford University Press, 2001), p. 15.

37. See Johnson, *Phantom Islands,* p. 97.

38. See ibid., chapter 5; Fuson, *Legendary Islands,* chapter 8.

39. See Fuson, *Legendary Islands,* pp. 130–32.

40. Dora Beale Polk, *The Island of California: A History of the Myth* (Spokane, WA: Arthur H. Clarke, 1991), chapters 22–29.

41. Johnson, *Phantom Islands,* p. 2.

42. John Kirtland Wright, "Terrae Incognitae: The Place of Imagination in Geography," in John Kirtland Wright, *Human Nature in Geography* (Cambridge: Harvard University Press, 1966), p. 68.

43. José Saramago, *The Tale of the Unknown Island* (New York: Harcourt, Brace, 1988).

44. John Kirtland Wright, "Terrae Incognitae: The Place of Imagination in Geography," *Human Nature in Geography* (Cambridge: Harvard University Press, 1966), p. 68.

45. Morison, *Portuguese Voyages,* p. 83.

46. Ibid., p. 101.

47. Herman Melville quoted in Edward J. Larson, *Evolution's Workshop: God and Science on the Galapagos Islands* (New York: Basic Books, 2001), p. 7.

48. On these two cases, see Johnson, *Phantom Islands,* chapters 2 and 4.

49. See Henry Strommel, *Lost Islands: The Story of Islands That Have Vanished from the Nautical Charts* (Vancouver: University of British Columbia Press,1984), p. 79.

50. Johnson, *Phantom Islands,* chapter 8.

51. Kent Mathewson, "St. Brendon: Mythical Isle and Topographic Drift: From Iceland to Ecuador," in *Atlantic Visions,* ed. John de Courcy Ireland and David C. Sheehy (Dublin: Boole, 1989), pp. 53–56.

52. Strommel, *Lost Islands,* p. xv.

53. See Flint, *Imaginative Landscape,* p. 39.

54. Loren Baritz, "The Idea of the West," *American Historical Review,* 66, no. 3 (April 1961): 625.

55. Ibid., pp. 625–27.

56. O'Gorman, *Invention of America,* chapter 4.

57. St. Augustine, quoted in Watts, "Prophecy and Discovery," p. 94.

58. Ibid., p. 102.

59. Ibid., pp. 93–94.

60. Columbus quoted in Mary B. Campbell, "'The Object of One's Gaze': Landscape, Writing, and Earlky Medieval Pilgrimage," *Discovering New Worlds: Essays in Medieval Exploration and Imagination* (New York: Garland, 1991), p. 178.

61. Leonardo Olschki, "What Columbus Saw on Landing in the West Indies," *Proceedings of the American Philosophical Society* 84, no. 5 (July 1948): 648.

62. Las Casas quoted in O'Gorman, *Invention of America,* p. 178.

63. See Quinn, "New Geographical Horizons," p. 636.

64. See Watts, "Prophecy and Discovery," p. 102.

65. See Pagden, *Fall of Natural Man,* chapters 2–4; and Eric Wolf, *Europe and the People without History* (Berkeley: University of California Press, 1982).

66. Annette Kolodny, *The Lay of the Land: Metaphor as Experience and History in American Life and Letters* (Chapel Hill: University of North Carolina Press, 1975); Louis Montrose, "The Work of Gender in the Discourse of Discovery," *Representations* 33 (winter 1991): 1–41; and Flint, *Imaginative Landscape,* p. 67.

67. See Alain Corbin, *The Lure of the Sea: The Discovery of the Seaside in the Western World, 1750–1840* (Berkeley: University of California Press, 1994), chapter 1.

68. Jean Baudriard quoted in Gregory Nobles, "Straight Lines and Stability: Mapping the Political Order of the Anglo-American Frontier," *Journal of American History* 80, no. 1 (June 1993), p. 11.

69. See Michael Zuckerman, "Identity in British America: Unease in Eden," in *Colonial Identity in the Atlantic World, 1500–1800,* ed. N. Canny and A. Pagden (Princeton, N.J.: Princeton University Press, 1987), p. 133.

70. See Robert Garfield, *A History of São Tomé Island, 1470–1655* (San Francisco: Mellen Research University Press, 1992), maps in appendix.

71. See Lestringant, *Mapping the Renaissance World,* chapters 1 and 5.

72. O'Gorman, *Invention of America,* p. 132.

73. The words of an Englishman, Cunningham, 1559. See Justin Stagl, *A History of Curiosity: The Theory of Travel* (Chur, Switzerland: Harwood, 1995), p. 168.

74. O'Gorman, *Invention of America,* p. 132.

75. See Raymond H. Ramsay, *No Longer on the Map: Discovering Places That Never Existed* (New York: Viking, 1972), p. 111.

76. See O'Gorman, *Invention of America,* pp. 131–32.

77. This epistemological shift is explored by Michel Foucault, *The Order of Things: An Archeology of the Human Sciences* (New York: Pantheon, 1980), pp. 51–55; and by Donald Lowe, *The History of Bourgeois Perception* (Chicago: University of Chicago Press, 1982), pp. 10–11.

78. J. H. Elliott, *The Old World and the New, 1492–1650* (Cambridge: Cambridge University Press, 1970), p. 53.

79. See Denis Hay, *Europe: The Emergence of an Idea,* rev. ed. (Edinburgh: University of Edinburgh Press, 1968), pp. 99ff; Seymour Phillips, "The Outer World of the European Middle Ages," in *Implicit Understandings,* ed. Stuart Schwartz (Cambridge: Cambridge University Press, 1994), p. 62.

80. See Baritz, "The Idea of the West," pp. 625–27.

Chapter 4

1. John Allen, "Lands of Myth, Waters of Wonder: The Place of Imagination in the History of Geographical Exploration," in *Geographies of the Mind: Essays in Historical Geosophy,* ed. David. Lowenthal and Marilyn Bowden (New York: Oxford University Press, 1976), pp. 43–57.

2. John Kirtland Wright, "Terrae Incognitae: The Place of Imagination in Geography," in his *Human Nature in Geography* (Cambridge: Harvard University Press, 1966), p. 88.

3. Henri Baudet, *Paradise on Earth: Some Thoughts on European Images of Non-European Man,* trans. Elizabeth Wenholt (Middletown, CT: Wesleyan University Press, 1988), pp. 34–40.

4. Jean Delumeau, *History of Paradise: The Garden of Eden in Myth and Tradition,* trans. M. O'Connell (New York: Continuum, 1995), p. 97.

5. Ibid., p. 84.

6. Yi-Fu Tuan, "Sacred Space: The Exploration of an Idea," *Dimensions of Human Geography,* ed. Karl Butzer (Chicago: University of Chicago Department of Geography. Research Paper 186, 1987), p. 85.

7. Harry B. Partin, "Paradise," *The Encyclopedia of Religion,* Vol. 11 (New York: Macmillan, 1987), p. 186.

8. Alexandro Scafi, "Mapping Eden: Cartographies of Earthly Paradise," in *Mappings,* ed. Denis Cosgrove (London: Reaktion, 1999), p. 56; Delumeau, *History of Paradise,* pp. 95–98.

9. J. Donald Hughes, *Pan's Travail: Environmental Problems of the Ancient Greeks and Romans* (Baltimore: Johns Hopkins University Press, 1994), p. 178.

10. Ibid., chapter 10.
11. Richard Grove, *Green Imperialism: Colonial Expansion, Tropical Island Edens, and the Origins of Environmentalism* (Cambridge: Cambridge University Press, 1995), p. 21.
12. Ernst Bloch, *The Principle of Hope*, Vol. 2 (Cambridge: MIT Press, 1986), p. 756.
13. See Partin, "Paradise," p. 186, Delumeau, *History of Paradise*, pp. 5–9.
14. Delumeau, *History of Paradise*, p. 15.
15. Ibid., pp. 38–40.
16. Jacques LeGoff, "The Wilderness in the Medieval West," *The Medieval Imagination*, trans. A. Goldhammer (Chicago: University of Chicago Press, 1988), pp. 4, 230–31.
17. Carol Zalesky, *Otherworld Journeys: Accounts of Near Death Experiences in Medieval and Modern Times* (New York: Oxford University Press, 1987), chapters 1–3.
18. Bloch, *Principle of Hope*, p. 760.
19. John Mandeville, *The Travels of Sir John Mandeville* (London: Penguin, 1983), p.
20. See Valerie Flint, *The Imaginative Landscape of Christopher Columbus* (Princeton, N.J.: Princeton University Press, 1992), chapters 5 and 6.
21. See Grove, *Green Imperialism*, p. 32.
22. See John Prest, *The Garden of Eden: The Botanic Garden and the Re-creation of Paradise* (New Haven, CT: Yale University Press, 1981), p. 31.
23. See Delumeau, *History of Paradise*, pp. 104–5: Flint, *Imaginative Landscape*, chapter 5.
24. Baudet, *Paradise on Earth*, p. 33.
25. Grove, *Green Imperialism*, p. 4.
26. Ibid., pp. 18–20.
27. Eric Leed, *The Mind of the Traveler: From Gilgamesh to Modern Tourism* (New York: Basic Books, 1991), p. 116.
28. Annette Kolodny, *The Lay of the Land: Metaphor as Experience and History in American Life and Letters* (Chapel Hill: University of North Carolina Press, 1975), chapter 1; Louis Montrose, "The Work of Gender in the Discourse of Discovery," *Representations* 33 (winter 1991): 1–41.
29. On islands as female, see Grove, *Green Imperialism*. p. 32; on ambivalence toward the abundance of islands, see T. J. Jackson Lears, *Fables of Abundance: A Cultural History of Advertising in America* (New York: Basic Books, 1994), pp. 26–37.
30. Lears, *Fables of Abundance*, pp. 28–29.
31. John Smith quoted in Kolodny, *Lay of the Land*, pp. 19–20.
32. See Lears, *Fables of Abundance*, p. 37.
33. Charles L. Sanford, *The Quest for Paradise: Europe and the American Moral Imagination* (Urbana: University of Illinois Press, 1961), p. 53.
34. See Alfred Crosby, *Ecological Imperialism* (Cambridge: Cambridge University Press, 1986), chapter 4; Grove, *Green Imperialism*, pp. 29–31
35. See Leo Marx, *The Machine in the Garden: Technology and the Pastoral Ideal in America* (New York: Oxford University Press, 1964), pp. 41–66.
36. Quoted in Marx, *Machine in the Garden*, p. 45.
37. Grove, *Green Imperialism*, p. 35.
38. See Alain Corbin, *The Lure of the Sea: The Discovery of the Seaside in the Western World, 1750–1840*, trans. Jocelyn Phelps (Berkeley: University of California Press, 1994), p. 15.
39. Ibid., p. 44.
40. John R. Stilgoe, *Common Landscape of America, 1580–1845* (New Haven: Yale University Press, 1982), p. 27.
41. Michael Zuckerman, "Identity in British America: Unease in Eden," in *Colonial Identity in the Atlantic World, 1500–1800*, ed. N. Canny and A. Pagden (Princeton: Princeton, N.J.: University Press, 1987), p. 126.

42. On the emergence of European botanical gardens, see Prest, *Garden of Eden,* p. 17: Richard Drayton, *Nature's Government: Science, Imperial Britain, and the 'Improvement' of the World* (New Haven, CT: Yale University Press, 2000), p. 24.

43. Max F. Schulz, *Paradise Preserved: Recreations of Eden in Eighteenth- and Nineteenth-Century England* (Cambridge: Cambridge University Press, 1985), p. 37; Delumeau, *History of Paradise,* p. 133.

44. Tuan, "Sacred Space," p. 59.

45. See Schulz, *Paradise Preserved,* chapters 8, 9, and 12.

46. See Frank E. Manuel, "Toward a Psychological History of Utopia," in *Utopias and Utopian Thought,* ed. Frank E. Manuel (Boston: Houghton Mifflin, 1965), p. 75.

47. Frank E. Manuel and Fritzie F. Manuel, *Utopian Thought in the Modern World* (Cambridge: Harvard University Press, 1979), p. 29.

48. Ibid., p. 15.

49. Ibid., p. 21.

50. Lewis Mumford, *The Story of Utopias* (Gloucester: Peter Smith, 1954), p. 16.

51. Bruce Chatwin, *The Songlines* (London: Jonathan Cape, 1987).

52. F. and F. Manuel, *Utopian Thought,* p. 21.

53. Lears, *Fables of Abundance,* p. 26.

54. Northrop Frye, "Varieties of Literary Utopia," *Utopias and Utopian Thought,* ed. F. Manuel (Boston: Houghton Mifflin, 1965), p. 48.

55. Aaron J. Gurevich, *Categories of Medieval Culture,* trans. G. L. Campbell (London: Routledge, 1985), p. 74.

56. See Garry W. Trompf, "Utopia," in *The Encyclopedia of Religions,* Vol. 15 (New York: Macmillan, 1987), pp. 159–60.

57. Louis Marin, "The Frontiers of Utopia," *Utopias and the Millennium,* ed. Krishan Kumar and Stephen Bann (London: Reaktion, 1993), p. 15; also Manuel, "Psychological History of Utopias," p. 72.

58. See Peter Harbison, *Pilgrimage in Ireland: The Monuments and the People* (London: Barrie & Jenkins, 1991), p. 53; Mary Lee Nolan and Sidney Nolan, *Christian Pilgrimage in Modern Western Europe* (Chapel Hill: University of North Carolina Press, 1989), pp. 323, 327.

59. Leed, *Mind of the Traveler,* p. 27.

60. Victor Turner quoted in Simon Coleman and Jake Elsner, *Pilgrimage Past and Present: Sacred Travel and Sacred Space in World Religions* (London: British Museum Press, 1995), p. 206.

61. Frye, "Varieties of Literary Utopia," p. 26.

62. Victor Turner, "The Center Out There: Pilgrim's Goal," *History of Religions* 12, no. 3 (February 1973): 213.

63. See Marin, "Frontiers of Utopia," p. 14

64. See Mary B. Campbell, "'The Object of One's Gaze': Landscape, Writing, and Early Medieval Pilgrimage," in *Discovering New Worlds: Essays in Medieval Exploration and Imagination* (New York: Garland, 1991), p. 2.

65. Ibid., pp. 12–13.

66. See F. and F. Manuel, *Utopian Thought,* p. 29.

67. See Partin, "Paradise," p. 188.

68. See Francoise Choay, "Utopia and the Philosophical Status of Constructed Space," *Utopia,* ed. R. Schaer, G. Claeys, L. T. Sargeant (New York: Oxford University Press, 2000), p. 347.

69. David Harvey, *Spaces of Hope* (Edinburgh: Edinburgh University Press, 2000), p. 160.

70. See Manuel, "Toward a Psychological History of Utopias," pp. 78–79.

71. See Philip W. Porter and Fred E. Luckerman, "The Geography of Utopia," in *Geographies of the Mind: Essays in Historical Geosophy,* ed. David Lowenthal and Marilyn Bowden (New York: Oxford University Press, 1976), pp. 204–11.

72. Manuel, "Toward a Psychological History of Utopias," p. 79.

73. John Fowles, *Islands* (Boston: Little, Brown, 1978), p. 17.

74. Cynthia Bourgeault, "Living There," *Island Journal* 14 (1997): 8–18.

Chapter 5

1. Felipe Fernandez-Armesto, *Civilizations: Culture, Ambition, and the Transformation of Nature* (New York: Free Press, 2001), p. 430.

2. Epile Hau'ofa, "Our Sea of Islands," *The Contemporary Pacific: A Journal of Island Affairs* 6, no. 1 (spring 1994): 152.

3. Edmundo O'Gorman, *The Invention of America* (Bloomington: Indiana University Press, 1961), p. 132.

4. See Raymond H. Ramsay, *No Longer on the Map: Discovering Places That Never Were* (New York: Viking, 1972), p. 111.

5. See Justin Stagl, *A History of Curiosity: The Theory of Travel, 1550–1800* (Chur, Switzerland: Harwood, 1995), pp. 167–68.

6. See Elizabeth MacMahon, "The gilded cage: From Utopia to Monad in Australia's Island Imaginary," in *Islands in History and Representation,* ed. Rod Edmond and Vanessa Smith (London: Routledge, 2003), p. 190

7. See J.S.R. Phillips, *The Medieval Expansion of Europe* (Oxford: Oxford University Press, 1988), p. 255.

8. See Ian K. Steele, *The English Atlantic, 1675–1740: An Exploration of Communications and Community* (New York: Oxford University Press, 1986), p. vi.

9. Eviatar Zerubavel, *Terra Cognita: The Mental Discovery of America* (New Brunswick, N.J.: Rutgers University Press, 1992), chapter 1

10. See E.G.R. Taylor, *Late Tudor and Early Stuart Geography, 1583–1650* (London: Methuen, 1934), p. 158.

11. J. H. Parry, *The Discovery of the Sea* (New York: Dial, 1974), p. xii.

12. Daniel Boorstin, *The Discoverers* (New York: Random House, 1983), p. 154.

13. Michael Biggs, "Putting the State on the Map," *Comparatives Studies in Society and History* 41, no. 2 (1999), pp. 376–77.

14. See Charles Maier, "Consigning the Twentieth Century to History: Alternative Narratives for the Modern Era," *American Historical Review* 115, no. 3 (June 2000):808.

15. American contributions are usefully summarized in John H. Kemble, "Maritime History in the Age of Albion," in *The Atlantic World of Robert G. Albion,* ed. Benjamin W. Labaree (Middletown, CT: Wesleyan University Press, 1975), pp. 3–17. Also see Labaree, "The Atlantic Paradox," in *The Atlantic World of Robert G. Albion,* pp. 195–217; and Benjamin Labaree et al., eds. *America and the Sea: A Maritime History* (Mystic, CT: Mystic Seaport Museum, 1998).

16. See J.G.A. Pocock, "The Atlantic Archipelago and the War of the Three Kingdoms," in *The British Problem, 1524–1707,* ed. Brendan Bradshaw and John Morrill (New York: St. Martin's, 1996), p. 174.

17. See J. H. Elliott, *The Old World and the New, 1492–1650* (Cambridge: Cambridge University Press, 1970), p.104.

18. Robert S. Lopez, epilogue in *First Images of America: The Impact of the New World on the Old,* Vol. 2, ed. Fredi Chiapelli (Berkeley: University of California Press, 1976), p. 888.

19. Ibid., p. 889.

20. See David Beers Quinn, *North America from Earliest Discovery to First Settlement* (New York: Harper & Row, 1975), pp. 472–73.

21. Ibid., chapter 18.

22. See Stephen Royle, *A Geography of Islands: Small Island Insularity* (New York: Routledge, 2001), p. 59.

23. See Lopez, epilogue, p. 889.
24. Fernand Braudel, *The Mediterranean and the Mediterranean World in the Age of Philip II* (New York: Harper & Row, 1972), p. 103.
25. See Philip E. Steinberg, *The Social Construction of the Oceans* (Cambridge: Cambridge University Press, 2001), p. 69.
26. See Charles Verlinden, "The Transfer of Colonial Techniques from the Mediterranean to the Atlantic," in *The European Opportunity*, ed. Felipe Fernandez-Armesto (Aldershot: Variorum, 1995), pp. 225–48.
27. Felipe Fernandez-Armesto, *Before Columbus: Exploration and Colonization from the Mediterranean to the Atlantic, 1229–1492* (London: Macmillan, 1987), p. 137.
28. Ibid., chapters 4–9.
29. See Quinn, *North America*, pp. 64–66
30. William D. Phillips, *Medieval Origins of European Expansion* (Minneapolis: University of Minnesota Press, 1996); Valerie Flint, *The Imaginative Landscape of Christopher Columbus* (Princeton, N.J.: Princeton University Press, 1992).
31. J.S.R. Phillips, *The Medieval Expansion of Europe* (New York: Oxford University Press, 1988), p. 255.
32. Andrew Fletcher quoted in Anthony Pagden, *Peoples and Empires: Europeans and the Rest of the World from Antiquity to the Present* (London: Weidenfeld & Nicolson, 2001), p. 94.
33. C. R. Boxer, *The Dutch Seaborne Empire, 1600–1800* (London: Penguin, 1973)
34. J. H. Parry, *The Discovery of the Sea* (New York: Dial Press, 1974), p. xiii.
35. Ibid., p. xii.
36. Ibid., p. vi; Quinn, *North America*, p. 472; Samuel Eliot Morison, *The European Discovery of America: The Northern Voyages*, A.D. *500–1600* (New York: Oxford University Press, 1971), p. 481.
37. Alfred W. Crosby, *Ecological Imperialism* (Cambridge: Cambridge University Press, 1986), chapter 4.
38. Elizabeth Mancke, "Early Modern Expansion and the Politicization of Oceanic Space," *Geographical Review* 89, no. 2 (April 1999): 227.
39. See Quinn, *North America*, chapter 19; and Geoffrey W. Symcox, "The Battle of the Atlantic, 1500–1700," *First Images of America: The Impact of the New World on the Old*, Vol. 1, ed. Fredi Chiapelli, (Berkeley: University of California Press, 1976), pp. 265–77.
40. See Anthony Pagden and Nicholas Canny, "Afterword: From Identity to Independence," in *Colonial Identity in the Atlantic World, 1500–1800*, ed. Anthony Pagden and Nicholas Canny (Princeton, N.J.: Princeton University Press, 1987), p. 273.
41. Pagden, *Peoples and Empires*, p. 56.
42. Parry, *Discovery of the Sea*, p. 108.
43. Ibid., p. 216.
44. It is just such an island fief that Don Quixote was seeking in Cervantes's famous novel.
45. See Marcus Rediker and Peter Linebaugh, *The Many-Headed Hydra: Sailors, Slaves, Commoners and the Hidden History of the Revolutionary Atlantic* (Boston: Beacon, 2000).
46. See Jack Greene, "Changing Identity in the British Caribbean: Barbados as a Case Study," in *Colonial Identity in the Atlantic World 1500–1800*, ed. Anthony Pagden and Nicholas Canny (Princeton, N.J.: Princeton University Press, 1987), pp. 213–65.
47. See David Ringrose, *Expansion and Global Interaction, 1200–1700* (New York: Longman, 2001), pp. 63–77.
48. Ibid.
49. T. Bentley Duncan, *Atlantic Islands: Madeira, the Azores and the Cape Verdes in Seventeenth-Century Commerce and Navigation* (Chicago: Chicago University Press, 1972), p 211.
50. Pagden, *Peoples and Empires*, pp. 67–68.

51. Ellis Markham, "'The Cane-Land Isles': Commerce and Empire in the Late Eighteenth-Century Georgic and Pastoral Poetry," in *Islands in History and Representation,* ed. Rod Edmond and Vanessa Smith (London: Routledge, 2003), p. 49

52. Pagden and Canny, afterword, p. 273; and Michael Zuckerman, "Identity in British America: Unease in Eden," in *Colonial Identity in the Atlantic World, 1500–1800,* ed. Anthony Pagden and Nicholas Canny (Princeton, N.J.: Princeton University Press, 1967, p. 136.

53. See Symcox, "Battle of the Atlantic."

54. Pagden, *Peoples and Empires,* p. 95.

55. Mancke, "Early Modern Expansion," p. 225.

56. Duncan, *Atlantic Islands,* p. 3; Wilcolm Washburn, "The Form of Islands in Fifteenth, Sixteenth and Seventeenth-Century Cartography," in *Geographie du Monde au Moyen Age et la Renaissance,* ed. Monique Pelletier (Paris: Editions du C.T.H.S.,1989), pp. 201–206.

57. Hau'ofa, "Our Sea of Islands," p. 152.

58. Duncan, *Atlantic Islands,* p. 59.

59. Jeffery Knapp, *An Empire Nowhere: England, America, and the Literature from Utopia to the Tempest* (Berkeley: University of California Press, 1992), pp. 4–13.

60. Bernhard Klein, *Maps and the Writing of Space in Early Modern England and Ireland* (New York: Palgrave, 2001), p. 135.

61. Pocock, "Atlantic Archipelagos," p. 174.

62. Markham, "The Cane-Land Isles," p. 42.

63. Stephen J. Pyne, *How The Canyon Became Grand: A Short History* (New York: Viking, 1998), p. 5.

64. Kenneth Pomeranz and Steven Topik, *The World That Trade Created: Society, Culture, and World Economy, 1400-Present* (Armonk, N.Y.: M. E. Sharpe, 1999), p. 43.

65. Duncan, *Atlantic Islands,* p. 2. On the appeal of the Caribbean, see Michael Zuckerman, "Unease in Eden," p. 136.

66. Duncan, *Atlantic Islands,* p. 247.

67. See K. G. Davies, *The North Atlantic World in the Seventeenth Century* (Minneapolis: University of Minnesota Press, 1974), pp. 86ff.

68. Duncan, *Atlantic Islands,* pp. 145–54, 250–51.

69. Crosby, *Ecological Imperialism,* p. 2.

70. Ibid., 251.

71. Ira Berlin, "From Creole to African: Atlantic Creoles and the Origins of African-American Identity," *William and Mary Quarterly,* 52, no. 2 (April 1996): 251–88.

72. See Karen Ordahl Kupperman, "International at the Creation: Early Modern American History," in *Rethinking American History in the Global Age,* ed. Thomas Bender (Berkeley: University of California Press, 2002), pp. 107–108.

73. William H. McNeill, "World History and the Rise and Fall of the West," *Journal of World History* 9, no. 2 (fall 1998): 281.

74. For example, Barbados was the jumping-off spot for the peopling of other Caribbean islands. See Davies, *North Atlantic World,* p. 138.

75. Samuel Eliot Morison, *The Maritime History of Massachusetts, 1783–1860* (Boston: Houghton Mifflin, 1921), p. 11.

76. See Duncan, *Atlantic Islands,* p. 24, 155.

77. Steele, *English Atlantic, passim.*

78. Duncan, *Atlantic Islands,* p. 188.

79. Ibid., pp. 24, 155.

80. Kupperman, "International at the Creation," pp. 109–110.

81. Davies, *North Atlantic World,* p. 140; Duncan, *Atlantic Islands,* pp. 248, 251; Steele, *English Atlantic,* p. 272.

82. Pagden, *Peoples and Empires,* p. 97.

Chapter 6

1. Peter Coates, *Nature: Western Attitudes since Ancient Times* (Berkeley: University of California Press, 1998), p. 58.
2. Eric J. Leed, *The Mind of the Traveler: From Gilgamesh to Global Tourism* (New York: Basic Books, 1991), p. 179.
3. Robert H. MacArthur and Edward O. Wilson, *The Theory of Island Biogeography* (Princeton, N.J.: Princeton University Press, 1967), p. 3. This tradition continues. See H. W. Menard, *Islands* (New York: Scientific American Library, 1986), p. 1.
4. Edward J. Larson, *Evolution's Workshop: God and Science in the Galapagos Islands* (New York: Basic Books, 2001), p. 7.
5. Gordon L. Davies, *The Earth in Decay: A History of British Geomorphology, 1578–1878* (New York: Elsevier, 1969), p. 20.
6. Gabriel Plattes, 1639, quoted in Davies, *Earth in Decay,* pp. 21–22.
7. Coates, *Nature,* p. 58.
8. Meville quoted in Larson, *Evolution's Workshop,* p. 10.
9. Alain Corbin, *The Lure of the Sea: The Discovery of the Seaside in the Western World, 1750–1840,* trans. Jocelyn Phelps (Berkeley: University of California Press, 1994), chapter 3.
10. Henry Moore quoted in Davies, *Earth in Decay,* p. 111.
11. Roy Porter, afterword to *Geography and Enlightenment,* ed. David N. Livingston and Charles W. J. Withers (Chicago: University of Chicago Press, 1999), pp. 421–24.
12. Larson, *Evolution's Workshop,* p. 7.
13. Roy Porter, *The Making of Geology: Earth Science in Britain, 1660–1815* (Cambridge: Cambridge University Press, 1977), p. 110.
14. James Hutton quoted in David Stoddard, *On Geography and History* (Oxford: Blackwell, 1986), pp. 30–31.
15. Alexander von Humboldt quoted in Leed, *Mind of the Traveler,* p. 203.
16. Porter, *Making of Geology,* p. 218.
17. Dava Sobel, *Longitude: The True Story of a Lone Genius Who Solved the Greatest Scientific Problem of His Time* (New York: Walker, 1995), p. 175.
18. See Matthew Edney, "Reconsidering Enlightenment Geography and Map Making: Reconnaissance, Mapping, and Archive," in *Geography and Enlightenment,* ed. David N. Livingston and Charles W. J. Withers (Chicago: University of Chicago, 1994), p. 178.
19. Leed, *Mind of the Traveler,* chapter 7. I want to thank Professor Harry Lieberson for his ideas on the subject of scientific expeditions.
20. Charles Darwin quoted in Janet Browne, *Charles Darwin: Voyaging: A Biography* (Princeton, N.J.: Princeton University Press, 1996), pp. 190, 296–97.
21. Richard Grove, *Green Imperialism: Colonial Expansion, Tropical Island Edens, and the Origins of Environmentalism, 1600–1800* (Cambridge: Cambridge University Press, 1995), p. 9.
22. Ibid., pp. 12–13.
23. Dorinda Outram, "On Being Perseses: New Knowledge, Dislocation and Enlightenment Exploration," in *Geography and Enlightenment,* ed. David N. Livingston and Charles W. J. Withers (Chicago: University of Chicago Press, 1999), p. 281.
24. On this process, see Leed, *Mind of the Traveler,* pp. 15–16.
25. Richard Drayton, *Nature's Government: Science, Imperial Britain, and the 'Improvement' of the World* (New Haven: Yale University Press, 2000), p. xiv.
26. Corbin, *Lure of the Sea,* p. 9.

27. For a survey of the castaway literature, see Tim Severin, *In Search of Robinson Crusoe* (New York: Basic Books, 2002).

28. See Browne, *Darwin's Voyaging*, pp. 302–3.

29. See Corbin, *Lure of the Sea*, p. 229.

30. Orvar Löfgren, *On Holiday: A History of Vacationing* (Berkeley: University of California Press, 1999), pp. 113, 123.

31. Robert McLellan, *The Isle of Arran* (New York: Praeger, 1970), p. 178.

32. Jonathan Raban, *The Oxford Book of the Sea* (New York: Oxford University Press, 1992), pp. 4–9.

33. Corbin, *Lure of the Sea*, pp. 37–39, 144.

34. Steinberg, Philip E., *The Social Construction of the Oceans* (Cambridge: Cambridge University Press, 2001), pp. 108–109.

35. Joseph Conrad, *The Mirror of the Sea* (Garden City, N.Y.: Doubleday, 1924), p. 71.

36. Felix Riesenberg, *Vignettes of the Sea* (New York: Harcourt, Brace, 1926), p. 91.

37. Louis-Antoine de Bougainville quoted in Charles Withers, "Geography, Enlightenment, and the Paradise Question," *Geography and Enlightenment*, ed. David N. Livingston and Charles W. J. Withers (Chicago: University of Chicago Press, 1999), p. 82.

38. Diderot quoted in ibid., p. 83.

39. Lucien Febvre, *A Geographical Introduction to History* (New York: Alfred J. Knopf, 1925), pp. 14–15.

40. Ibid., 207–25.

41. Quoted in Markham Ellis, "'The Cane-Land Isles': Commerce and Empire in the Late Eighteenth-Century Georgic and Pastoral Poetry," *Islands in History and Representation*, ed. Rod Edmond and Vanessa Smith (London: Routledge, 2003), p. 49.

42. Ibid.

43. Darwin quoted in MacArthur and Wilson, *Island Biogeography*, p. 3.

44. Alfred Russel Wallace, *Island Life or the Phenomena and Causes of Insular Fauna and Flora*, 2nd ed. (London: Macmillan, 1892), pp. 241–42.

45. See Kirsten Hastrup, "Nature as Historical Space," *Folk* 31 (1989): 5–20.

46. See Stephen A. Royle, *A Geography of Islands: Small Island Insularity* (New York: Routledge, 2001), pp. 20–21.

47. See MacArthur and Wilson, *Island Biogeography*, p. 3.

48. See Larson, *Evolution's Workshop*, chapters 8 and 9; on recent work, see Peter R. Grant ed. *Evolution on Islands* (New York: Oxford University Press, 1998).

49. Ibid., pp. 219–25.

50. Ellen Churchill Semple, *Influences of Geographic Environment on the Basis of Ratzel's System of Anthropo-geography* (New York: Henry Holt, 1911), pp. 242, 388, 412.

51. Ibid., pp. 413–15.

52. Ibid., pp. 434–45.

53. Ibid., p. 235.

54. Simon Schama, *Landscape and Memory* (New York: Vintage, 1996), p. 14.

55. See Benedict Anderson, *Imagined Communities: Reflections on the Origins and Spread of Nationalism* (London: Verso, 1991); and Michael Biggs, "Putting the State on the Map," *Comparative Studies in Society and History* 412 (1999): 374–405.

56. Gaunt's speech in Shakespeare's *Richard II*.

57. K. G. Robbins, *Insular Outsider? "British History" and European Integration* (Reading: Stenton Lectures, 1989), pp. 5–13.

58. See Eve Darian-Smith, *Bridging Divides: The Channel Tunnel and English Legal Identity in the New Europe* (Berkeley: University of California Press, 2001), chapters 2 and 3.

59. On the process of essentializing and totalizing space, see John Agnew, *Geopolitics: Re-visioning World Politics* (London: Routledge, 1998), chapter 2.

60. Joseph-Marie Degerando quoted in Miranda Hughes, "Tall Tales or True Stories? Baudin, Peron, and the Tasmanians," in *Nature in Its Greatest Extent: Western Science in the Pacific*, ed. Roy MacLeod and Philip Rehbock (Honolulu: University of Hawaii Press, 1988), p. 80.

61. See J.G.A. Pocock, "Nature and History, Self and Other: European Perception of World History in the Age of Encounter," in *Voyagers and Beaches: Pacific Encounters, 1769–1840*, ed. Alex Calder, Jonathan Lamb, Bridget Orr (Honolulu: University of Hawaii Press, 1999), pp. 26–43.

62. See Eric Wolf, *Europe and the People without History* (Berkeley: University of California Press, 1982), pp. 13–19.

63. Raymond Williams, *Keywords: A Vocabulary of Culture and Society* (New York: Oxford University Press, 1976), pp. 76–82.

64. Douglas Oliver, as published in 1981, quoted in Terrence Wesley-Smith, "Rethinking Pacific Island Studies," *Pacific Studies* 18, no. 2 (June 1995): 124.

65. See Jonathan Skinner, "Managing Island Life: Social, Economic, and Political Dimensions of Formality and Informality in 'Island' Communities," *Social Identities* 8, no. 2 (2002): 205.

66. Raymond Firth, *The Tikopia: A Sociological Study of Kinship in Primitive Polynesia* 2nd edition (Stanford, CA: Stanford University Press, 1983), pp. xv, 4, 34.

67. Thomas Hylland Eriksen, "In Which Sense Do Cultural Islands Exist?" *Social Anthropology* no. 1 (1993): 143; Ian Watson, "The Challenge of Maintaining Parity for Offshore Islands," *Middle States Geographer* 31 (1998): 132–34.

68. Eriksen, "In Which Sense Do Cultural Islands Exist?," p. 144.

69. See Jonathan Wylie and David Margolin, *The Ring of Dancers: Images of Faroese Culture* (Philadelphia: University of Pennsylvania Press, 1981), pp. 5–9.

70. Ibid., pp. 138–42.

71. See Magnus Einarsson, "The Wandering Semioticians: Tourism and the Image of Modern Iceland," in *Images of Contemporary Iceland: Everyday Lives and Global Contexts*, ed. Gisli. Palsson and E. Paul. Durrenberger (Iowa City: University of Iowa Press, 1996), pp. 220–22.

72. See Kirsten Hastrup, *A Place Apart: An Anthropological Study of the Icelandic World* (Oxford: Clarendon, 1998), chapter 7.

Chapter 7

1. Henry Strommel, *Lost Islands: The Story of Islands That Have Vanished from Nautical Charts* (Vancouver: University of British Columbia Press, 1984), p. xv.

2. Ibid., pp. 102–103.

3. James Hamilton-Paterson, *The Great Deep: The Sea and Its Thresholds* (New York: Random House, 1992), p. 63.

4. David Lowenthal, *The Past Is a Foreign Country* (Cambridge: Cambridge University Press, 1985), p. xvi.

5. See Peter Fritzsche, "Spectors of History: On Nostalgia, Exile, and Modernity," *American Historical Review* 106, no. 5 (December 2001): 1613.

6. See Donald Lowe, *History of Bourgeois Perception* (Chicago: University of Chicago Press, 1982); and Charles Taylor, *Sources of the Self: The Making of Modern Identity* (Cambridge: Harvard University Press, 1989).

7. Fritzsche, "Spectors of History," p. 1591.

8. Ibid., p. 1595.

9. Judith Ennow, *The Western Isles Today* (Cambridge: Cambridge University Press, 1980), p. xiii.

10. J. R. McNeill, "The End of the Old Atlantic World: America, Africa, Europe, 1770–1888," in *Atlantic American Societies: From Columbus through Abolition, 1492–1888,* ed. A. Karras and J. R. McNeill (London: Routledge, 1992), p. 249.

11. His influential paper of 1904 is reprinted in Halford J. Mackinder, *The Scope and Methods of Geography and the Geographical Pivot of History* (London: Royal Geographical Society, 1951).

12. Quoted in Alan Trachtenberg, *Brooklyn Bridge: Fact and Symbol,* 2nd ed. (Chicago: University of Chicago Press, 1979), p. 8.

13. Sarah Orne Jewett, *The Country of the Pointed Firs and other Fiction* (Oxford: Oxford University Press, 1996), pp. 20–21.

14. Robin Flower, *The Western Island or the Great Blasket* (New York: Oxford University Press, 1945), p. 8.

15. Robin Fox, "Tory Island," in *The Problem of Smaller Territories,* ed. Burton Benedict (London: Althone, 1963), p. 131; and Robin Fox, *The Tory Islanders: A People of the Celtic Fringe* (Cambridge: Cambridge University Press, 1978).

16. Sean O'Crohan, *A Day in Our Life,* trans. Tim Enright (New York: Oxford University Press, 1992), p. 147.

17. On the Aran Islands kelp industry, see Stephen Royle, *A Geography of Islands: Small Island Insularity* (New York: Routledge, 2001), pp. 79–83.

18. Perry Westbrook, *The Biography of an Island* (New York: Thomas Yoseloff, 1958), chapter 4.

19. Ibid., p. 71.

20. William P. L. Thompson, *History of Orkney* (Edinburgh: Mercot, 1987), p. 235.

21. Adam Nicolson, *Sea Room: An Island Life in the Hebrides* (New York: Northpoint, 2002), p. 299.

22. Ibid.

23. Pamela J. Berlanger, *Inventing Arcadia: Artists and Tourists at Mount Desert* (Rockland, ME: Farnsworth Museum, 1999), p. 114.

24. Ibid., p. 123. Another Rockefeller duplicated this process on the Caribbean Island of St. John, creating a nature preserve in the face of considerable local opposition.

25. John R. Gillis, "Places Remote and Islanded," *Michigan Quarterly Review* 40, no. 1 (Winter 2001): 46.

26. Alain Corbin, *The Lure of the Sea: The Discovery of the Seaside in the Western World, 1750–1846,* trans. Jocelyn Phelps (Berkeley: University of California Press, 1994), pp. 213, 227.

27. Martin Martin, *A Description of the Western Islands of Scotland, circa 1695,* ed. Donald MacLeod (Stirling, Scotland: MacKay, 1934), pp. 398, 464.

28. Charles MacLean, *Island on the Edge of the World: The Story of St. Kilda* (New York: Taplinger, 1980), p. 152.

29. Ibid., pp. 131–35.

30. Ibid., p. 144.

31. Tom Steel, *The Life and Death of St. Kilda* (Glasgow: Fontana, 1972).

32. For the account of one such visitor, see Flower, *Western Island* (New York: Oxford University Press, 1945); among the Blasket writers are Maurice O'Sullivan, *Twenty Years A-Growing* (New York: Viking, 1933); Sean O'Crohan, *A Day in Our Life* (New York: Oxford University Press, 1992); Tomas O'Crohan, *The Islandman,* trans. Robin Flower (London: Chatto & Windus, 1934); see John Wilson Foster, "Certain Set Apart: The Western Island in the Irish Renaissance," *Studies: An Irish Quarterly Review,* no. 246 (1977): 261–74; also Caitlin Lange, "Dead on Revival: The Blasket Islands of West Kerry," Rutgers honors thesis, 2004.

33. Peig Sayers, *Peig: The Autobiography of Peig Sayers of the Great Blasket Island*, trans. Bryan MacMahon (Syracuse: Syracuse University Press, 1974), p. 211.On migration, see Stephen A. Royle, "From the Periphery at the Periphery: Historical, Cultural, and Literary Perspectives on Emigrants from the Minor Islands of Ireland," in *Small Worlds, Global Lives: Ireland and Migration*, ed. R. King and J. Connell (London: Pinter, 1999), pp. 39–40.

34. Thomas Hylland Eriksen, "In Which Sense Do Cultural Islands Exist?" *Social Anthropology*, no. 1 (1993), p. 140.

35. John Millington Synge, *Aran Islands* (Boston: J.W. Luce, 1911), pp. 15, 80.

36. See John C. Messenger, *Inis Beag Revisited: An Anthropologist as Observant Participant* (Salem, W.I.: Sheffield: 1983), p. 121; and John C. Messenger, *Inis Beag: Isle of Ireland* (New York: Holt, Rinehart, & Winston, 1969), p. 41.

37. James Charles Roy, *Islands of the Storm* (Chester Springs, PA: Dufour Editions, 1991),p. 122.

38. Sean O'Crohan, *A Day in Our Life*, p. 26.

39. Fessenden S. Blanchard, *Ghost Towns of New England* (New York: Dodd, Mead, 1960), p. 141.

40. Susan Parman, *Scottish Crofters: A Historical Ethnography of a Celtic Village* (Fort Worth: Holt, Rinehart, & Winston, 1990), pp. 31–33. The quotation is from 1954.

41. See Nigel Nicolson, *Lord of the Isles: Lord Leverhulme and the Hebrides* (London: Weidenfeld & Nicolson, 1960).

42. See Ennow, *Western Isles Today*, p. xiii.

43. John McPhee, *The Crofter and the Laird* (New York: Noonday, 1969), p. 145.

44. Ibid., pp. 38–46.

45. Parman, *Scottish Crofters*, p. 80.

46. Ennow, *Western Isles Today*, p. xiii.

47. See Dona Brown, *Inventing New England: Regional Tourism in the Nineteenth Century* (Washington, D.C.: Smithsonian Institution Press, 1995), p. 127.

48. From *Quaint Nantucket* (1896), quoted in Brown, *Inventing New England*, p. 133.

49. Westbrook, *Biography of an Island*, p. 69.

50. John Brinckerhoff Jackson, *The Necessity for Ruins and Other Topics* (Amherst: University of Massachusetts Press, 1980), p. 102.

51. See Lowenthal, *Past Is a Foreign Country*, p. 168.

52. See Brown, *Inventing New England*, pp. 121–22.

53. Mairi E. MacArthur, *Iona: The Living Memory of a Crofting Community, 1750–1914* (Edinburgh: Edinburgh University Press, 1990), p. 211.

54. Deborah Tall, *The Island of the White Cow: Memories of an Irish Island* (New York: Atheneum, 1986), pp. 44, 46–47, 128.

55. Ibid., p. 199.

56. McPhee, *Crofter and the Laird*, p. 82.

57. Tall, *Island of the White Cow*, pp. 44–45.

58. Ibid., p. 128.

59. Anthony P. Cohen, *Whalsay: Symbol, Segment, and Boundary in a Shetland Island Community* (Manchester: Manchester University Press, 1987), p. 132.

60. See Kirsten Hastrup, *A Place Apart: An Anthropological Study of the Icelandic World* (Oxford: Clarendon, 1998), chapter 8.

61. Magnus Einarsson, "The Wandering Semioticians: Tourism and the Image of Modern Iceland," in *Images of Contemporary Iceland: Everyday Lives and Global Contexts*, eds. Gisli Palsson and E. Paul Durrenberger (Iowa City: University of Iowa Press, 1996), p. 231.

62. Jonathan Raban, *Coasting* (London: William Collins, 1986), p. 36.

63. Ibid., p. 35; see also Jonathan Raban, *The Oxford Book of the Sea* (New York: Oxford University Press, 1992), pp. 15–17.

64. Philip E. Steinberg, *The Social Construction of the Oceans* (Cambridge: Cambridge University Press, 2001), p. 119.
65. Raban, *Coasting*, p. 299.
66. Corbin, *Lure of the Sea*, p. 97.
67. Ibid., pp. 170–71; see also W. H. Auden, *The Enchafed Flood, or, The Romantic Iconography of the Sea* (New York: Random House, 1950), p. 32.
68. Gillian Beer, "The Island and the Aeroplane: The Case of Virginia Woolf," in *Nation and Nationalism*, ed. Homi Bhabha (London: Routledge, 1990), pp. 265–90.
69. Auden, *Enchafed Flood*, pp. 28–29.
70. Ibid., p. 31.
71. Summer people also use the old island cemeteries. See Christina Marsden Gillis, "Island Mysteries," *House Beautiful* (May 1997), pp. 25–30.
72. Introduction to *Migrants of Identity: Perceptions of Home in a World of Movement*, ed. Nigel Rapport and Andrew Dawson (Oxford: Berg, 1998), p. 7.
73. Yi-Fu Tuan, "Rootedness versus Sense of Place," *Landscape* 24, no. 1 (1980), p. 4.
74. Anthony Giddens, *The Consequences of Modernity* (Stanford, CA: Stanford University Press, 1990), p. 19.
75. See John R. Gillis, *A World of Their Own Making: Myth, Ritual, and the Quest for Family Values* (New York: Basic Books, 1996), chapter 6.
76. Marjorie Garber, *Sex and Real Estate: Why We Love Houses* (New York: Pantheon, 2000), p. 204; see also Michael Ann Williams, *Homeplace: The Social Use and Meaning of the Folk Dwellings in Southwestern North Carolina* (Athens: University of Georgia Press, 1991).
77. Amy Willard Cross, *The Summer House: A Tradition of Leisure* (Toronto: HarperCollins, 1992), p. xiii.
78. See Orvar Löfgren, "Learning to Be a Tourist," *Ethnologia Scandinavica* 24 (1994): p. 124.
79. Thurston Clarke, *Searching for Crusoe: A Journey among the Last Real Islands* (New York: Ballantine, 2001), p. 147.
80. Westbrook, *Biography of an Island*, p. 150.

Chapter 8

1. See Emilo Bagini and Brian Hoyle, "Insularity and Development on an Oceanic Planet," in *Insularity and Development: International Perspectives on Islands*, ed. E. Bagini and B. Hoyle (London: Pinter, 1999), p. 7.
2. See Will Hobson, "Trawling for Facts," *Granta* 61 (spring 1998), p. 186. On coastal erosion, see Joseph T. Kelly, Alice R. Kelly, and Orrin H. Pilkey, *Living on the Coast of Maine* (Durham, N.C.: Duke University Press, 1989).
3. See Yi-Fu Tuan, *Topophilia: A Study of Environmental Perceptions, Attitudes, and Values* (Englewood Cliffs, N.J.: Prentice Hall, 1974), p. 117.
4. See Chris Ryan, "Islands, Beaches, and Life Stage Marketing," in *Island Tourism: Management Principles and Practice*, ed. M. V. Conlin and T. Baum (New York: John Wiley, 1995), pp. 79–93.
5. Carl Sauer, "Seashore—Primitive Home of Man," in *Land and Life: A Selection of Writings of Carl Ortin Sauer* (Berkeley: University of California Press, 1963), p. 311.
6. Gunnar Hansen, *Islands at the Edge of Time: A Journey to America's Barrier Islands* (Washington, D.C.: Island Press, 1993), p. 142. See also *Islands of America* (Washington: Bureau of Outdoor Recreation: Department of Interior, 1970), p. 2.
7. Jamaica Kincaid, *A Small Place* (New York: Penguin, 1988). See also Zygmunt Bauman, *Globalization: The Human Consequences* (New York: Columbia University Press, 1998), chapter 4.

8. Stephen A. Royle, *A Geography of Islands: Small Island Insularity* (New York: Routledge, 2001), pp. 117–19.

9. Quoted in K. G. Robbins, *Insular Outsider? 'British History' and European Integration* (Reading, England: Stenton Lecture, 1990), p. 5.

10. Gillian Beer, "The Island and the Aeroplane: The Case of Virginia Woolf," *Nation and Narration,* ed. Homi K. Bhabha (New York: Routledge, 1990), p. 286.

11. Robbins, *Insular Outsider?,* p. 12; James Hamilton-Paterson, *The Great Deep: The Sea and Its Thresholds* (New York: Random House, 1992), pp. 83–84.

12. See Eve Darian-Smith, *Bridging Divides: The Channel Tunnel and English Legal Identity in the New Europe* (Berkeley: University of California Press, 2001).

13. Royle, *Geography of Islands,* p. 12.

14. Tom Baum, "The Fascination of Islands: A Tourist Perspective," in *Island Tourism,* ed. D. G. Lockhardt and D. Drakus-Smith (London: Pinter, 1997), p. 24; Royle, *Geography of Islands,* pp. 114–15.

15. Georg Simmel, "Bridge and Door," *Theory, Culture & Society* 11 (1994): 5–10.

16. See Akhil Gupta and James Ferguson, "Beyond 'Culture': Space, Identity, and the Politics of Difference," *Cultural Anthropology* 7, no. 1 (February 1992): 9.

17. See Denise Brennan, "Selling Sex for Visas: Sex Tourism as a Stepping-stone to International Migration," in *Global Woman: Nannies, Maids, and Sex Workers in the New Economy,* eds. Barbara Ehrenreich and Arlie Russell Hochschild (New York: Metropolitan, 2002), pp.154–68.

18. Gupta and Ferguson, "Beyond 'Culture,'" pp. 10–11.

19. See Orvar Löfgren, *On Holiday: A History of Vacationing* (Berkeley: California University Press, 1999), p. 148.

20. John Connell and Russell King, "Island Migration in a Changing World," in *Small World, Global Lives: Islands and Migration,* ed. R. King and J. Connell (London: Pinter, 1999), p. 22.

21. On the concept of ethnoscapes, see Arjun Appadurai, "Global Ethnoscapes: Notes and Queries in a Transnational Anthropology," in *Recapturing Anthropology,* ed. Richard G. Fox (Sante Fe: School of American Research,1991), p. 191. On mindscapes, see Orvar Löfgren, "Landscapes and Mindscapes," *Folk* 31 (1989):183–208. And for islescapes, see Tiina Peil, *Islescapes: Estonian Small Islands and Islanders through Three Centuries* (Stockholm: Almquist & Wiksell. 1999), part 3.

22. On the way the dream of the island has functioned in anthropology, see Kirsten Hastrup, "Nature as Historical Space," *Folk* 31 (1989):10–11.

23. Yi-Fu Tuan, "Rootedness versus Sense of Place," *Landscape* 24, no. 1 (1980): p. 4.

24. See Marjorie Garber, *Sex and Real Estate: Why We Love Houses* (New York: Pantheon, 2000), pp. 5, 207; and Tracie Balkin, "Be It Ever Less Humble: American Homes Get Bigger," *New York Times,* May 11, 2000.

25. Nigel Rapport and Andrew Dawson, "The Topic and the Book," in *Perception of Home in a World of Movement,* ed. Nigel Rapport and Andrew Dawson (New York: Berg, 1998), p. 7.

26. Karen Fog Olwig, "Cultural Sites: Sustaining a Home in a Deterritorialized World," *Siting Culture: The Shifting Anthropological Object,* ed. K. Olwig and K. Hastrup (London: Routledge, 1997), pp. 17–38.

27. See Michael Ann Williams, *Homeplace: The Social Use and Meaning of the Folk Dwelling in Southwestern North Carolina* (Athens: University of Georgia Press, 1991); and Kirsten Hastrup and Karen Fog Olwig, introduction to *Siting Culture: The Shifting Anthropological Object* (London: Routledge, 1997), p. 7.

28. See Russell King, "The Geographical Fascination of Islands," in *The Development Process of Small Island States,* ed. Douglas Lockhart, David Drakakis-Smith, John Shenlori (London: Routledge, 1995), pp. 26–27.

29. Eric Hobsbawm, "Exile: A Keynote Address," *Social Research* 58, no. 1 (1991): 63.

30. Connell and King, "Island Migration," p. 7.

31. See Olwig, "Cultural Sites," p. 35.

32. See Cole Moreton, *Hungry for Home: Leaving the Blaskets: A Journey to America from the Edge of Ireland* (New York: Penguin, 2001), p. 235; and Peil, *Islescapes*, pp. 193–242.

33. Moreton, *Hungry for Home*, p. 266.

34. See Peil, *Islescapes*, pp. 229–30.

35. Olwig, "Cultural Sites," p. 31.

36. John Connell, "'My Island Home': The Politics and Poetics of the Torres Strait," in *Small Worlds, Global Lives: Islands and Migration*, ed. R. King and J. Connell (London: Pinter, 1999), p. 210.

37. Baum, "Fascination with Islands," p. 21; see David Lowenthal, "Small Tropical Islands: A General Overview," in *The Political Economy of Small Tropical Islands: The Importance of Being Small*, ed. Helen M. Hintjens and Malyn D. D. Newitt (Exeter: University of Exeter Press, 1992), pp. 18–29.

38. D. H. Lawrence, "The Man Who Loved Islands," *Selected Short Stories* (London: Penguin, 1982), pp. 458–80.

39. Royle, *Geography of Islands*.

40. Joseph A. Amato, *Dust: A History of the Small and the Invisible* (Berkeley: University of California University Press, 2000), p. 37.

41. Bagini and Hoyle, "Fascination of Islands," p. 7.

42. Amato, *Dust*, p. 158.

43. Philip Conkling, quoted in Carl Little, *Art of Maine Islands* (Camden: Down East Books, 1997), p. 55.

44. Bill Holm, *Eccentric Islands: Travels Real and Imaginary* (Minneapolis: Milkwood, 2000), p. 7.

45. Henry David Thoreau quoted in Sean Manley and Robert Manley, *Islands: The Lives, Legends, and Lore* (Philadelphia: Chilton, 1970), p. 2.

46. Holm, *Eccentric Islands*, p. 7.

47. Barbro Klein, "Folk Art in the Backyards and Frontyards of the Industrial World," in *Swedish Folk Art: All Tradition Is Change*, ed. B. Klein and W. Widden (New York: Abrams, 1994), pp. 165–73.

48. John Fowles, *Islands* (Boston: Little, Brown, 1978), p. 12.

49. Ibid., p. 11.

50. See Ronald Rees, "Landscape in Art," in *Dimensions of Human Geography*, ed. Karl Butzer (Chicago: University of Chicago Department of Geography Research Paper 186, 1978), pp. 49–61.

51. See Holm, *Eccentric Islands*, p. 7.

52. See Jonathan Raban, *Coasting* (New York: William Collins, 1986), p. 62.

53. Juliet Schor, *Overworked Americans: The Unexpected Decline of Leisure* (New York: Basic Books, 1991).

54. Löfgren, *On Holiday*, pp. 136–39.

55. Susan Stewart, *On Longing: Narratives of the Miniature, the Gigantic, the Souvenir, the Collection* (Baltimore: Johns Hopkins University Press, 1984), pp. 8, 68.

56. Hansen, *Islands at the Edge*, p. 138.

57. Edwin Adener, "'Remote Areas:' Some Theoretical Considerations," in *Anthropology at Home*, ed. Anthony Jackson (London: Tavistock, 1987), pp. 38–54.

58. Sally Gibson, *More than an Island: A History of Toronto Island* (Toronto: Irwin, 1984)

59. Corey Kilgannon, "Just a Speck of an Island, With a Power of Its Own," *New York Times*, August 17, 2003, p. 21.

60. Yi-Fu Tuan, *Space and Place: The Perspective of Experience* (Minneapolis: University of Minnesota Press, 1977), pp. 15–16.

61. "Battle for the Future Swirls below Proud Towers," *New York Times*, September 4, 2002.
62. See Adener, "Remote Areas," p. 42.
63. John McPhee, *The Crofter and the Laird* (New York: Noonday, 1969), pp. 82, 123, 145.
64. On this terminology, see Connell and King, "Island Migration," pp. 19–20.
65. Comments by graduating seniors, *Working Waterfront/Interisland News* July 1999, pp. 16–17.
66. Gabriella Lazardidis, Joanna Poyano-Thetoky, and Russell King, "Islands as Havens for Retirement Migration: Finding a Place in Sunny Corfu," in *Small Worlds, Globalized Lives: Islands and Migration*, ed. R. King and J. Connell (London: Pinter, 1999), pp. 297–320.
67. Personal communication with Anders Salmonsson, Lund University, Sweden, 1999.
68. Löfgren, *On Holiday*, p. 116.
69. Ursula K. Le Guin, *Searoad: Chronicles of Klatsand* (New York: HarperCollins, 1991), p. 16, as quoted in Löfgren, *On Holiday*, p. 135.
70. Löfgren, *On Holiday*, p. 149.
71. Alain Corbin, *The Lure of the Sea: The Discovery of the Seaside in the Western World, 1750–1840*, trans. Jocelyn Phelps (Berkeley: University of California Press, 1994), pp. 174, 180.
72. Ibid., p. 124.
73. Quoted in Eliot Porter, *Summer Island* (San Francisco: Sierra Club Books, 1966), p. 127.
74. Löfgren, *On Holiday*, p. 151.
75. As told to me by Ruth Moore's sister, Eleanor Trask; and reflected in Ruth Moore's novel of island life, *The Weir* (New York: W. Morrow, 1943).
76. See Peil, *Islescapes*, p. 232.
77. Elizabeth Goodenough, "Introduction to Special Issue on the Secret Spaces of Childhood," *Michigan Quarterly Review* 29, no. 2 (spring 2000): 180.
78. See Catherine Robson, *Men in Wonderland: The Lost Childhood of the Victorian Gentleman* (Princeton, N.J.: Princeton University Press, 2001).
79. Anne Higonnet, *Pictures of Innocence. The History and Crisis of Ideal Childhood* (London: Thames & Hudson, 1998), p. 95.
80. Thurston Clarke, *Searching for Crusoe: A Journey among the Last Real Islands* (New York: Ballantine, 2001), p. 147.
81. James Hamilton-Paterson, *The Great Deep: The Sea and Its Thresholds* (New York: Random House, 1992), p. 175.
82. Both quotations from Eric Leed, *Mind of the Traveler: From Gilgamesh to Global Tourism* (New York: Basic Books, 1991), pp. 1, 5.
83. See Eviatar Zerubavel, *Time Maps: Collective Memory and the Social Shape of the Past* (Chicago: University of Chicago Press, 2003), pp. 55–63.
84. Rapport and Dawson, "Topic and the Book," p. 9; John Berger, *And Our Faces, My Heart, Brief as Photos* (London: Writers & Readers Press, 1985), p. 55; Lucy Lippard, *The Lure of the Local: Senses of Place in a Multicentered Society* (New York: New Press, 1997).
85. See Lowenthal, *Past is a Foreign Country passim*; Diane Barthel-Bouchier, *History Preservation, Collective Memory, and Historical Identity* (New Brunswick: Rutgers University Press, 1996) and *Amana: From Pietist Sect to American Community* (Lincoln: University of Nebraska Press, 1981).
86. Julian Barnes, *England, England*.
87. See Thomas Hylland Eriksen, "In Which Sense Do Cultural Islands Exist?" *Social Anthropology* 1 (1993): 139–42.
88. See Royle, *Geography of Islands*, pp. 202–203.
89. See Lucy Lippard's account of travel to her summer home on Georgetown Island, Maine, *Lure of the Local*, chapter 1.

90. Amy Willard Cross, *The Summer House: A Tradition of Leisure* (Toronto: HarperCollins, 1992), p. 203.

91. Peil, *Islescapes*, p. 227

92. Diana Loxley, *Problematic Shores: The Literature of Islands* (New York: St. Martin's, 1990), p. 3.

93. Roy Wolfe, "About Cottages and Cottagers," *Landscape*, 15, no. 1 (autumn 1965): 8.

94. Marc Auge, *Non-places: An Introduction to an Anthropology of Supermodernity*, trans. John Howe (London: Verso, 1995), p. 78; See also Rapport and Dawson, "Topic and Book," pp. 5–6.

95. Arnold van Gennep, *The Rites of Passage* (Chicago: University of Chicago Press, 1960), chapter 1.

96. Hurricane Island is the site of a quarry industry off Vinalhaven, Maine. My visit to the island took place in the summer of 1998. I want to thank the officers of Outward Bound for their hospitality on that occasion.

97. See Mircea Eliade, *The Sacred and the Profane: The Nature of Religion,* trans. Williard Trask (New York: Harcourt, Brace, 1959), pp. 29–36, 68–69.

98. Löfgren, *On Holiday*, p. 149.

99. See John Gillis, *A World of Their Own Making: Myth, Ritual, and the Quest for Family Values* (New York: Basic Books, 1996), part 2.

100. See Nigel Rapport and Andrew Dawson, "Home and Movement: A Polemic," in *Migrants of Identity: Perception of Home in a World of Movement,* ed. N. Nigel Rapport and Andrew Dawson (New York: Berg, 1998), p. 27.

101. T. S. Eliot, "Little Gidding," *Four Quartets* (New York: Harcourt, Brace, 1943), p. 39.

102. Hansen, *Islands at the Edge*, p. 163.

Epilogue

1. Rachel Carson, *The Sea around Us* (New York: Oxford University Press, 1951), p. 216.

2. David Brower, forward to *Galapagos: The Flow of Wilderness,* ed. Kenneth Brower (San Francisco: Sierra Club, 1968), pp. 18–20.

3. John Fowles, *Islands* (Boston: Little, Brown, 1978), p. 105.

BIBLIOGRAPHY

Adener, Edwin. "'Remote Areas:' Some Theoretical Considerations." In *Anthropology at Home,* ed. Anthony Jackson. London: Tavistock, 1987, pp. 38–54.

Agnew, John. *Geopolitics: Re-visioning World Politics.* London: Routledge, 1998.

Allen, John L. "Lands of Myth, Waters of Wonder: The Place of Imagination in the History of Geographical Exploration." In *Geographies of the Mind: Essays in Historical Geosophy,* ed. David Lowenthal and Marilyn Bowden. New York: Oxford University Press, 1976, pp. 41–61.

Amato, Joseph A. *Dust: A History of the Small and the Invisible.* Berkeley: University of California Press, 2000.

Anderson, Benedict. *Imagined Communities: Reflections on the Origins and Spread of Nationalism.* London: Verso, 1991.

Appadurai, Arjun. "Global Ethnoscapes: Notes and Queries in a Transnational Anthropology." In *Recapturing Anthropology,* ed. Richard G. Fox. Sante Fe, New Mexico: School of American Research, 1991), pp. 193–210.

Ashe, Geoffrey. "Analysis of the Legends." In *Quest for America.* London: Pall Mall Press, 1971, pp. 15–52.

———. *Atlantis: Lost Lands, Ancient Wisdom.* London: Thames and Hudson, 1992.

———. *Quest for America.* London: Pall Mall, 1971.

Auden, W. H. *The Echafed Flood, or, The Romantic Iconography of the Sea.* New York: Random House, 1950.

Auge, Marc. *Non-places: An Introduction to an Anthropology of Supermodernity.* trans. John Howe. London: Verso, 1995.

Babcock, William H. *Legendary Islands of the Atlantic.* New York: American Geographical Society, 1922.

Bagini, Emilo, and Brian Hoyle. "Insularity and Development on an Oceanic Planet." In *Insularity and Development: International Perspectives on Islands.* Ed. E. Bagini and Brian Hoyle. London: Pinter, 1999, pp. 358–70.

Baldacchino, Godfrey. "The Challenge of Hypothermia: A Six-Proposition Manifesto for Small Island Territories." *Round Table* 353 (2000): 65–79.

Balkin, Tracie. "Be It Ever Less Humble: American Homes Get Bigger." *New York Times,* May 11, 2000.

Baritz, Loren. "The Idea of the West." *American Historical Review.* 66. no. 3 (April 1961): 618–40.

Barnes, Julian. *England, England.* London: Cape, 1998.

Barthel-Bouchier, Diane. *Amana: From Pietist Sect to American Community.* Lincoln: University of Nebraska Press, 1981.

———. *History Preservation, Collective Memory, and Historical Identity.* New Brunswick, N.J.: Rutgers University Press, 1996.

Bartlett, Robert. *The Making of Europe: Conquest, Colonization, and Cultural Change, 950–1350.* London: Penguin, 1994.

Baudet, Henri. *Paradise on Earth: Some Thoughts on European Images of Non-European Man.* Trans. Elizabeth Wenholt. Middletown, CT: Wesleyan University Press, 1988.

Baum, Tom, "The Fascination of Islands: A Tourist Perspective." In *Island Tourism.* Ed. D. G. Lockhardt and D. Drakus-Smith. London: Pinter, 1997, pp. 20–35.

Bauman, Zygmunt. *Globalization: The Human Consequences.* New York: Columbia University Press, 1998.

Beer, Gillian. "The Island and the Aeroplane: The Case of Virginia Woolf." In *Nation and Nationalism.* Ed. Homi Bhabha. London: Routledge, 1990. pp. 267–90.

Benchley, Peter. *The Island.* Garden City, N.Y.: Doubleday, 1979.

Berger, John. *And Our Faces, My Heart, Brief as Photos.* London: Writers & Readers Press, 1985.

Berlanger, Pamela J. *Inventing Acadia: Artists and Tourists at Mount Desert.* Rockland: Farnsworth Museum, 1999.

Berlin, Ira. "From Creole to African: Atlantic Creoles and the Origins of African-American Identity." *William and Mary Quarterly* 52, no 2 (April 1996): pp. 251–88.

Bernbaum, Edwin. *Sacred Mountains of the World.* New edition. Berkeley: University of California Press, 1997.

Biggs, Michael. "Putting the State on the Map." *Comparative Studies in Society and History* 41 no. 2 (1999): 374–405.

Blanchard, Fessenden S. *Ghost Towns of New England.* New York: Dodd, Mead, 1960.

Bloch, Ernest. *The Principle of Hope.* Vol. 2. Cambridge: MIT Press, 1986.

Boorstin, Daniel. *The Discoverers.* New York: Random House, 1983.

Bourgeault, Cynthia. "Living There." *Island Journal* 14 (1997): 8–18.

Bowen, E.G. *Britain and the Western Seaways* (London: Thames and Hudson, 1972).

———. *Saints, Seaways, and Settlements in the Celtic Lands.* Cardiff: University of Wales Press, 1969.

Boxer, C.R. *The Dutch Seaborne Empire, 1600–1800.* London: Penguin, 1973.

Braudel, Fernand. *The Mediterranean and the Mediterranean World in the Age of Philip II,* Vol. 1. New York: Harper & Row, 1972.

———. *The Mediterranean in the Ancient World.* Trans. Sian Reynolds. London: Allen Lane, 2001.

Brennan, Denise. "Selling Sex for Visas: Sex Tourism as a Stepping-stone to International Migration." In *Global Woman: Nannies, Maids, and Sex Workers in the New Economy.* Ed. Barbara Ehrenreich and Arlie Russell Hochschild. New York: Metropolitan, 2002, pp. 154–68.

Brotton, John. "Terrestrial Globalism: Mapping the Globe in Early Modern Europe," In *Mappings,* ed. Denis Cosgrove. London: Reaktion Books, 1999, pp. 71–89.

Brower, David. "Forward." In *Galapagos: The Flow of Wilderness,* Vol. 1, ed. Kenneth Brower. San Francisco: Sierra Club, 1968, pp. 18–20.

Brown, Dona. *Inventing New England: Regional Tourism in the Nineteenth Century.* Washington, D.C.: Smithsonian Institution Press, 1995.

Browne, Janet. *Charles Darwin: Voyaging: A Biography.* Princeton, N.J.: Princeton University Press, 1996.

Butel, Paul. *The Atlantic.* New York: Routledge, 1999.

Cahill, Thomas. *How the Irish Saved Civilization.* New York: Doubleday, 1995.

Campbell, Mary B. "'The Object of One's Gaze': Landscape, Writing, and Early Medieval Pilgrimage." In *Discovering New Worlds: Essays in Medieval Exploration and Imagination.* New York: Garland, 1991, pp. 1–13.

Carpenter, Rhys. *Beyond the Pillars of Heracles: The Classical World Seen Through the Eyes of Its Explorers.* New York: Delacourte, 1966.

Carrington, Richard. *A Biography of the Sea.* New York: Basic Books, 1960.

Carson, Rachel. "Lost Worlds: The Challenge of Islands." In *Lost Woods: The Discovered Writings of Rachel Carson.* Ed. Linda Lear. Boston: Beacon, 1998, pp. 63–75.

———. *The Sea around Us.* New York: Oxford University Press, 1951.

Carter, Paul. *The Road to Botany Bay: An Exploration of Landscape and History.* New York: Knopf, 1988.

Cassidy, Vincent H. *The Sea around Them: The Atlantic Ocean, A.D. 1200.* Baton Rouge: Louisiana State University Press, 1968.

———. "The Voyage of an Island." *Speculum* 38 (October 1963): 595–602.

Chaoy, Francoise. "Utopia and the Philosophical Status of Constructed Space." In *Utopia.* Ed. R. Schaer, G. Claeys, and L. T. Sargeant. New York: Oxford University Press, 2000, pp. 346–52.

Chatwin, Bruce. *The Songlines.* London: Jonathan Cape, 1987.

Childe, V. Gordon. *The Dawn of European Civilization.* New York: Knopf, 1958,

Clarke, Thurston. *Searching for Crusoe: A Journey among the Last Real Islands.* New York: Ballantine, 2001.

Coates, Peter. *Nature: Western Attitudes since Ancient Times.* Berkeley: University of California Press, 1998.

Cohen, Anthony P. *Whalsay: Symbol, Segment, and Boundary in a Shetland Island Community.* Manchester: Manchester University Press, 1987.

Coleman, Simon, and Jack Elsner. *Pilgrimage Past and Present: Sacred Travel and Sacred Space in World Religions.* London: British Museum Press, 1995.

Conley, Tom. *The Self-Made Map: Cartographic Writing in Early Modern France.* Minneapolis: University of Minnesota Press, 1996.

Conlon, Michael, and Tom Baum, Introduction to *Island Tourism: Management Principles and Practices.* Ed. M. Conlon and T. Baum. New York: John Wiley, 1995, pp. 5–18.

Connell, John. "'My Island Home': The Politics and Poetics of the Torres Strait." In *Small Worlds, Global Lives: Islands and Migration.* Ed. R. King and J. Connell. London: Pinter, 1999, pp. 195–212.

Connell, John, and Russell King. "Island Migration in a Changing World." In *Small World, Global Lives: Islands and Migration.* Ed. J. Connell and R. King. London: Pinter, 1999, pp. 1–26.

Conrad, Joseph. *The Mirror of the Sea.* Garden City, N.Y.: Doubleday, 1924.

Corbin, Alain. *The Lure of the Sea: The Discovery of the Seaside in the Western World, 1750–1840.* Trans. Jocelyn Phelps. Berkeley: University of California Press, 1994.

Cosgrove, Denis. *Apollo's Eye: A Cartographic Genealogy of the Earth in the Western Imagination.* Baltimore: Johns Hopkins University Press, 2001.

———. *Social Formation and Symbolic Landscape.* London: Croom Helm, 1984.

Crosby, Alfred. *Ecological Imperialism.* Cambridge: Cambridge University Press, 1986.

Cross, Amy Willard. *The Summer House: A Tradition of Leisure.* Toronto: HarperCollins, 1992.

Cunliffe, Barry. *The Extraordinary Voyage of Pytheas the Greek.* New York: Penguin, 2003.

———. *Facing the Ocean: The Atlantic and Its Peoples, 8000 B.C.-A.D.1500* New York: Oxford University Press, 2001.

Darian-Smith, Eve. *Bridging Divides: The Channel Tunnel and English Legal Identity in the New Europe.* Berkeley: University of California Press, 2001.

Davies, Gordon J. *The Earth in Decay: A History of British Geomorphology, 1578–1878.* New York: Elsevier, 1969.

Davies, K. G. *The North Atlantic World in the Seventeenth Century.* Minneapolis: University of Minnesota Press, 1974.

de Camp, Sprague L. *Lost Continents: The Atlantis Theme in History, Science, and Literature.* New York: Gnome, 1954.

Delumeau, Jean. *History of Paradise: The Garden of Eden in Myth and Tradition.* Trans. M. O'-Connell. New York: Continuum, 1995.

Dictionary of Imaginary Places. Ed. Alberto Manguel and Gianni Gaudalupi. New York: Harcourt Brace, 1980.

Dolman, Anthony. "Paradise Lost? The Past Performance and Future Prospect of Small Island Developing Countries." In *States, Microstates, and Islands.* Ed. Edward Commena and Philippe Hern. London: Croom Helm, 1985, pp. 44–62.

Drayton, Richard. *Nature's Government: Science, Imperial Britain, and the "Improvement" of the World.* New Haven, CT: Yale University Press, 2000.

Duncan, T. Bentley. *Atlantic Islands: Madeira, the Azores, and the Cape Verdes in Seventeenth-Century Commerce and Navigation.* Chicago: University of Chicago Press, 1972.

Durrell, Lawrence. *Reflections on a Marine Venus: A Companion to the Landscape of Rhodes.* London: Faber & Faber, 1953.

Edmond, Rod, and Vanessa Smith, eds. *Islands in History and Representation.* London: Routledge, 2003.

Edney, Matthew. "Reconsidering Enlightenment Geography and Map Making: Reconnaissance, Mapping, and Archive." In *Geography and Enlightenment,* ed. David N. Livingston and Charles W. J. Withers. Chicago: University of Chicago Press, 1999, pp. 165–98.

Ehrlich, Gretel. *Islands, the Universe, Home.* New York: Viking Press, 1991.

Einarsson, Magnus. "The Wandering Semioticians: Tourism and the Image of Modern Iceland." In *Images of Contemporary Iceland: Everyday Lives and Global Contexts.* Ed. Gisli Palsson and E. Paul Durrenberger. Iowa City: University of Iowa Press, 1996, pp. 215–34.

Eliade, Mircea. *Patterns in Contemporary Religion.* New York: New American Library, 1964.

———. *The Sacred and the Profane: The Nature of Religion.* Trans. William Trask. New York: Harcourt Brace & Company, 1959.

Eliade, Mircea, and Lawrence Sullivan. "Center of the World." In *The Encyclopedia of Religion.* Vol. 33. New York: Macmillan, 1987, pp. 166–70.

Eliot, T. S. *Four Quartets.* New York: Harcourt, Brace and Company, 1943.

Elliott, J. H. *The Old World and the New, 1492–1650.* Cambridge: Cambridge University Press, 1970.

Ellis, Markham. "'The Cane-land Isles': Commerce and Empire in the Late Eighteenth-Century Georgic and Pastoral Poetry." In *Islands in History and Representation.* Ed. Rod Edmond and Vanessa Smith. London: Routledge, 2003, pp. 43–62.

Ellis, Richard. *Imagining Atlantis.* New York: Knopf, 1998.

Ennow, Judith. *The Western Isles Today.* Cambridge: Cambridge University Press, 1980.

Eriksen, Thomas Hylland. "In Which Sense Do Cultural Islands Matter?" *Social Anthropology,* no. 1 (1993), pp. 133–74.

Febvre, Lucien. *A Geographical Introduction to History.* New York: Alfred J. Knopf, 1925.

Fernandez-Armesto, Felipe. *Before Columbus: Exploration and Colonization from the Mediterranean to the Atlantic, 1229–1492.* London: Macmillan, 1987.

———. *Civilizations: Culture, Ambition, and the Transformation of Nature.* New York: Free Press, 2001.

Fitzhugh, William W., Elizabeth I. Ward. *Vikings: The North Atlantic Saga.* Washington, D.C.: Smithsonian Institution Press, 2000.

Flint, Valerie. *The Imaginative Landscape of Christopher Columbus.* Princeton, N.J.: Princeton University Press, 1992.

Flower, Robin. *The Western Island or the Great Blasket.* Oxford: Oxford University Press, 1996.

Foster, John Wilson. "Certain Set Apart: The Western Island in the Irish Renaissance," *Studies: An Irish Quarterly Review* no. 246 (winter 1977), pp. 261–74.

Foucault, Michel. *The Order of Things: An Archeology of the Human Sciences.* New York: Pantheon, 1980.

Fowles, John. *Islands.* Boston: Little, Brown, 1978.

Fox, Robin. "Tory Island." *The Problem of Smaller Territories.* Ed. Burton Benedict London: Althone, 1963, pp. 113–33.

———*The Tory Islanders: A People of the Celtic Fringe.* Cambridge: Cambridge University Press, 1978.

Fredericks, S. Casey. "Plato's Atlantis: A Mythologist Looks at Myth. "In *Atlantis: Fact or Fiction?,* ed. Edwin Ramage. Bloomington: Indiana University Press, 1961, pp. 81–91.

Frith, Raymond. *The Tikopia: A Sociological Study of Kinship in Primitive Polynesia.* 2nd ed. Stanford, CA: Stanford University Press, 1983.

Fritzsche, Peter. "Spectors of History: On Nostalgia, Exile, and Modernity." *American Historical Review* 106, no. 5 (December 2001): 1587–1619.

Frye, Northrup. "Varieties of Literary Utopia." In *Utopias and Utopian Thought,* ed. F. Manuel. Boston: Houghton Mifflin, 1965, pp. 25–49.

Fuson, Robert H. *Legendary Islands of the Ocean Sea.* Sarasota: Pineapple, 1995.

Garber, Marjorie. *Sex and Real Estate: Why We Love Houses.* New York: Pantheon, 2000.

Garfield, Robert. *A History of São Tomé Island, 1470–1655.* San Francisco: Mellen Research University Press, 1992.

Gibson, Sally. *More Than an Island: A History of Toronto Island.* Toronto: Irwin, 1984.

Giddens, Anthony. *The Consequences of Modernity.* Stanford, CA: Stanford University Press, 1990.

Gifford, Donald. *The Farthest Shore: A Natural History of Perception.* New York: Vintage, 1991.

Gillis, Christina Marsden. "Island Mysteries." *House Beautiful,* May 1997, pp. 25–30.

Gillis, John R. "Places Remote and Islanded." *Michigan Quarterly Review* 40, no. 2 (winter 2001), pp. 39–58.

———. "Taking History Offshore: Atlantic Islands in European Minds, 1400–1800." In *Islands in History and Representation,* ed. Rod Edmond and Vanessa Smith. London: Routledge, 2003, pp. 19–31.

———. *A World of Their Own Making: Myth, Ritual, and the Quest for Family Values.* New York: Basic Books, 1995.

Giot, Pierre-Roland. "The Attractions for Coasts and Islands from later Prehistory to the Dark Ages." In *Atlantic Visions,* ed. John de Couray Ireland and David C. Sheely. Dublin: Boole Press, 1989.

Golding, William. *Lord of the Flies, a Novel.* New York: Coward-MCann, 1954.

Goodenough, Elizabeth. "Introduction to Special Issue on the Secret Spaces of Childhood." *Michigan Quarterly Review,* 29, no. 2 (spring 2000): 179–93.

Gottmann, Jean. *The Significance of Territory.* Charlottesville: University of Virginia Press, 1973.

Grant, Peter, ed. *Evolution on Islands.* New York: Oxford University Press, 1998.

Greene, Jack. "Changing Identity in the British Caribbean: Barbados as a Case Study." In *Colonial Identity in the Atlantic World, 1500 to 1800,* ed. N. Canny and A. Pagden. Princeton, N.J.: Princeton University Press, 1987, pp. 213–66.

Greene, Roland. "Island Logic." In *'The Tempest" and Its Travels,* ed. Peter Hulme and William H. Sherman. Philadelphia: University of Pennsylvania Press, 2000, pp. 138–45.

Grove, Richard. *Green Imperialism: Colonial Expansion, Tropical Island Edens, and the Origins of Environmentalism.* Cambridge: Cambridge University Press, 1995.

Gupta, Akhil, and James Ferguson. "Beyond 'Culture': Space, Identity, and the Politics of Difference." *Cultural Anthropology* 7, no. 1 (February 1992): 6–23.

Gurevich, Aaron J. *Categories of Medieval Culture.* Trans. G. L. Campbell. London: Routledge, 1985.

Hamilton-Paterson, James. *The Great Deep: The Sea and Its Thresholds.* New York: Random House, 1992.

Hansen, Gunnar. *Islands at the Edge of Time: A Journey to America's Barrier Islands.* Washington, D.C.: Island Press, 1993.

Harbison, Peter. *Pilgrimage in Ireland: The Monuments and the People.* London: Barrie & Jenkins, 1991.

Harvey, David. *Spaces of Hope.* Edinburgh: Edinburgh University Press, 2000.

Hastrup, Kirsten. "Nature as Historical Space." *Folk* 31 (1989): 5–20.

———. *A Place Apart: An Anthropological Study of the Icelandic World.* Oxford: Clarendon Press, 1998.

Hastrup, Kirsten, and Karl Fog Olwig. Introduction to *Siting Culture: The Shifting Anthropological Object.* London: Routledge, 1997, pp. 1–16.

Hau'ofa, Epile. "Our Sea of Islands." *The Contemporary Pacific: A Journal of Island Affairs* 6, no. 1 (spring 1994): 148–58

Hay, Denis. *Europe: The Emergence of an Idea.* Rev. Ed. Edinburgh: University of Edinburgh Press, 1968.

Helms, Mary W. *Ulysses' Sail: An Ethnographic Odyssey of Power, Knowledge, and Geographical Distance.* Princeton, N.J.: Princeton University Press, 1988.

Higonnet, Anne. *Pictures of Innocence: The History and Crisis of the Ideal Childhood.* London: Thames & Hudson, 1998.

Hirsch, Eric. Introduction to *The Anthropology of Landscape,* ed. E. Hirsch and M. O'Hanlon. Oxford: Clarendon, 1995, 1–30.

Hobsbawm, Eric. "Exile: A Keynote Address." *Social Research* 58, no. 1 (1991): 65–68.

Hobson, Will. "Trawling for Facts." *Granta 61* (spring 1998): 186.

Holm, Bill. *Eccentric Islands: Islands Real and Imaginary.* Minneapolis: Milkwood, 2000.

Homer. *The Odyssey.* Trans. Robert Fagles. New York: Penguin, 1996.

Horden, Peregrine, and Nicholas Purcell. *The Corrupting Sea: A Study in Mediterranean History.* Oxford: Blackwell, 2000.

Hughes, J. Donald. *Pan's Travail: Environmental Problems of the Ancient Greeks and Romans.* Baltimore: Johns Hopkins University Press, 1994.

Hughes, Kathleen. "The Changing Theory and Practice of Irish Pilgrimage." *Journal of Ecclesiastical History* 11, no. 2 (October 1960): 143–51.

Hughes, Miranda. "Tall Tales or True Stories? Baudin, Peron, and the Tasmanians." In *Nature in its Greatest Extent: Western Science in the Pacific,* ed. Roy MacLeod and Philip Rehbock. Honolulu: University of Hawaii Press, 1988, pp. 65–86.

Islands in America. Washington, D.C.: Bureau of Outdoor Recreation, Department of Interior, 1970.

Jackson, John Brinckerhoff. *The Necessity for Ruins and Other Topics.* Amherst: University of Massachusetts Press, 1980.

Jewett, Sarah Orne. *The Country of the Pointed Firs and Other Fiction.* New York: Oxford University Press, 1996.

Johnson, Donald S. *Phantom Islands of the Atlantic: The Legends of Seven Lands That Never Were.* New York: Walker, 1994.

Jourdin du Mollat, Michel. *Europe and the Sea.* Oxford: Blackwell, 1993.

Kelly, Joseph T, Alice R. Kelly, and Orrin H. Pilkey. *Living on the Coast of Maine.* Durham, N.C.: Duke University Press, 1989.

Kemble, John H. "Maritime History in the Age of Albion." In *The Atlantic World of Robert G. Albion,* ed. Benjamin W. Labaree. Middletown, CT: Wesleyan University Press, 1975, pp. 3–17.

Kenway, Rita Johnson. *Gotts Island Maine: Its People 1880–1992.* Privately printed, 1993.

Kilgannon, Corey. "Just a Speck of an Island, With a Power of Its Own" *New York Times,* August 17, 2003, p. 21.

Kincaid, Jamaica. *A Small Place.* New York: Penguin, 1988.

King, Russell. "The Geographical Fascination of Islands." In *The Development Process of Small Island States,* ed. Douglass Lockhart, David Drakakis-Smith, and John Shenlori. London: Routledge, 1995, pp. 14–35.

Klein, Barbro. "Folk Art in the Backyards and Frontyards of the Industrial World." In *Swedish Folk Art: All Tradition Is Change,* ed. B. Klein and W. Widden. New York: Abrams, 1994, pp. 165–73.

Klein, Bernhard. *Maps and the Writing of Space in Early Modern England and Ireland.* New York: Palgrave, 2001.

Knapp, Jeffery. *An Empire Nowhere: England, America, and the Literature from Utopia to the Tempest.* Berkeley: University of California Press, 1992.

Knox, Bernard. Introduction and notes to *The Odyssey,* by Homer. Trans. Robert Fagles. New York: Penguin, 1996.

Kolodny, Annette. *The Lay of the Land: Metaphor as Experience and History in American Life and Letters.* Chapel Hill, N.C.: University of North Carolina Press, 1975

Konstan, David. "Ocean." In *The Encyclopedia of Religion* Vol. 11. New York: Macmillan, 1987, pp. 53–56.

Koslofsky, Craig. "From Presence to Remembrance: The Transformation of Memory in the German Reformation." In *The Work of Memory: New Directions in the Study of German Society and Culture,* ed. A. Confino and P. Fritzsche. Champlain/Urbana: University of Illinois Press, 2002, pp. 25–38.

Kunzig, Robert. *The Restless Sea: Exploring the World beneath the Sea.* New York: W.W. Norton, 1999.

Kupperman, Karen Ordahl. "International at the Creation: Early Modern American History." In *Rethinking American History in the Global Age,* ed. Thomas Bender. Berkeley: University of California Press, 2002, pp. 103–22.

Labaree, Benjamin. "The Atlantic Paradox." In *The Atlantic World of Robert G. Albion,* ed. B. Labaree. Middletown, CT: Wesleyan University Press, pp. 195–217.

———, ed. *America and the Sea: A Maritime History.* Mystic, CT: Mystic Seaport Museum, 1998.

Lange, Caitlin. "Dead on Revival: The Blasket Islands of West Kerry." Senior history honors thesis with highest distinction, Rutgers University, 2004.

Larson, Edward J. *Evolution's Workshop: God and Science on the Galapagos Islands.* New York: Basic Books, 2001.

Lavelle, Des. *Skellig: Island Outpost of Europe.* Montreal: McGill & Queens University Press, 1976.

Lawrence, D. H. "The Man Who Loved Islands." In *Selected Short Stories.* London: Penguin, 1982, pp. 458–80.

Lazardidis, Gabriella, Joanna Poyano-Thetoky, and Russell King. "Islands as Havens for Retirement Migration: Finding a Place in Sunny Corfu." In *Small Worlds, Globalized: Islands and Migration,* ed. R. King and J. Connell. London: Pinter, 1999, pp. 297–320.

Lears, T. J. Jackson. *Fables of Abundance: A Cultural History of Advertising in America.* New York: Basic, 1994.

Leed, Eric. *The Mind of the Traveler: From Gilgamesh to Global Tourism.* New York: Basic Books, 1991.

LeGoff, Jacques. "The Wilderness in the Medieval West." In *The Medieval Imagination,* trans. A. Goldhammer. Chicago: University of Chicago Press, 1988, pp. 47–58.

Le Guin, Ursula K. *Searoad: Chronicles of Klatsand.* New York: HarperCollins, 1991.

Leming, David. "Quests." *The Encyclopedias of Religion.* Vol. 12. New York: Macmillan, 1987, pp. 146–52.

Lestringant, Frank. "Iles." In *Geographie du Monde au Moyen Age et la Renaissance,* ed. Monique Pelletier. Paris: Editions du C.T.H.S, 1989, pp. 165–67.

———. *Mapping the Renaissance World: The Geographical Imagination in the Age of Discovery.* Cambridge: Polity, 1994.

Lewis, Martin W., and Karen E. Wigen. *The Myth of Continents: A Critique of Metageography.* Berkeley: University of California Press, 1997.

Lippard, Lucy. *The Lure of the Local: Senses of Place in a Multicentered Society.* New York: New Press, 1997.

Little, Carl. *Art of Maine Islands.* Camden: Down East, 1997.

Löfgren, Orvar. "Landscapes and Mindscapes." *Folk* 31 (1989):183–208.

———. "Learning to Be a Tourist." *Ethnologia Scandinavica* 24 (1994), pp. 102–25.

————. *On Holiday: A History of Vacationing.* Berkeley: University of California Press, 1992.

Lopez, Robert. Epilogue to *First Images of America: The Impact of the New World on the Old,* Vol. 2. Ed. Fredi Chiapelli. Berkeley: University of California Press, 1976, pp. 887–91.

Lowe, Donald. *The History of Bourgeois Perception.* Chicago: University of Chicago Press, 1982.

Lowenthal, David. *The Past Is a Foreign Country.* Cambridge: Cambridge University Press, 1985.

————. "Small Tropical Islands: A General Overview." In *The Political Economy of Small Tropical Islands: The Importance of Being Small,* ed. Helen M. Hintjens and Marlyn D. D. Newitt. Exeter: University of Exeter Press, 1992, pp. 18–29.

————. "Tragic Traces on the Rhodian Shore." *Historic Environment* 17, no. 1 (2003): pp. 3–6.

Loxley, Diana. *Problematic Shores: The Literature of Islands.* New York: St. Martin's, 1990.

Luce, J. V. "Ancient Explorers." *The Quest for America.* London: Pall Mall, 1971, pp. 86–96.

Lydon, James. *The Making of Ireland.* London: Routledge, 1998.

MacArthur, Mairi E. *Iona: The Living Memory of a Crofting Community, 1750–1914.* Edinburgh: Edinburgh University Press, 1990.

MacArthur, Robert H., and Edward O. Wilson. *The Theory of Island Biogeography.* Princeton: Princeton, N.J.: University Press, 1967.

MacKinder, Halford J. *The Scope and Methods of Geography and the Geographical Pivot of History.* London: Royal Geographical Society, 1951.

MacKinlay, J. M. "'In Oceano Desertum'—Celtic Anchorites and Their Island Retreats." *Proceedings of the Society of Antiquaries of Scotland* 33 (1889–99): 129–33.

MacLean, Charles. *Island on the Edge of the World: The Story of St. Kilda.* New York: Taplinger, 1980.

MacMahon, Elizabeth. "The Gilded Cage: From Utopia to Monad in Australia's Island Imaginary." In *Islands in History and Representation,* ed. Rod Edmond and Vanessa Smith. London: Routledge, 2003, pp. 190–202.

Maier, Charles. "Consigning the Twentieth Century to History: Alternative Narratives for the Modern Era," *American Historical Review* 115, no. 3 (June 2000): 807–831.

Mancke, Elizabeth. "Early Modern Expansion and the Politicization of Oceanic Space," *Geographical Review* 89, no. 2 (April 1999): 225–36.

Mandeville, John. *The Travels of Sir John Mandeville.* London: Penguin, 1983.

Manley, Sean, and Robert Monley. *Islands: The Lives, Legends, and Lore.* Philadelphia: Chilton, 1970.

Manuel, Frank E. "Toward a Psychological History of Utopia." In *Utopias and Utopian Thought,* ed. F. Manuel. Boston: Houghton Mifflin, 1965, pp. 69–98.

Manuel, Franke E., and Fritzie F. Manuel. *Utopian Thought in the Modern World.* Cambridge: Harvard University Press, 1979.

Marin, Louis. "The Frontiers of Utopia." In *Utopias and the Millennium,* ed. Krishan Kumar and Stephen Bann. London: Reaktion, 1993, pp. 6–16.

Martin, Martin. *A Description of the Western Islands of Scotland, circa 1695.* Ed. Donald MacLeod. Stirling, Scotland: MacKay, 1934.

Marx, Leo. *The Machine in the Garden: Technology and the Pastoral Ideal in America.* New York: Oxford University Press, 1961.

Mathewson, Kent. "St. Brendan: Mythical Isle and Topographical Drift: From Iceland to Ecuador." In *Atlantic Visions,* ed. J. de Courcy Ireland and David C. Sheehy. Dublin: Books Press, 1989, pp. 51–60.

McLellan, Robert. *The Isle of Arran.* New York: Praeger, 1970.

McNeill, J. R. "The End of the Old Atlantic World: America, Africa, Europe, 1770–1888." In *Atlantic American Societies: From Columbus through Abolition, 1492–1888,* ed. A. Karras and J. R. McNeill. London: Routledge, 1992, pp. 249–66.

McNeill, John Thomas. *The Celtic Penitentials and Their Influence on Continental Christianity.* Paris: Librarie Ancienne Homme, 1923.

McNeill, William H. "World History and the Rise and Fall of the West." *Journal of World History* 9, no. 2 (fall 1989), pp. 215–36.

McPhee, John. *The Crofter and the Laird.* New York: Noonday, 1969.

Melville, Herman. *Moby Dick.* New York: Oxford University Press, 1988.

Menard, H. W. *Islands.* New York: Scientific American Library, 1986.

Messenger, John C. *Inis Beag: Isle of Ireland.* New York; Holt, Rinehart, & Winston, 1969.

———. *Inis Beag Revisited: An Anthropologist as Observant Participant.* Salem, WI: Sheffield, 1983.

Montrose, Louis. "The Work of Gender in the Discourse of Discovery." *Representations* 33 (winter 1991): 1–41.

Moore, Ruth. *The Weir.* New York: W. Morrow, 1943.

Moreton, Cole. *Hungry for Home: Leaving the Blaskets: A Journey to America from the Edge of Ireland.* New York: Penguin, 2001.

Morison, Samuel Eliot. *The European Discovery of America: The Northern Voyages, A.D. 500–1600.* Vol. 2. New York: Oxford University Press, 1992.

———. *The Maritime History of Massachusetts, 1783–1860.* Boston: Houghton Mifflin, 1921.

———. *Portuguese Voyages to America in the Fifteenth Century.* Cambridge: Harvard University Press, 1940.

Muldoon, James. *The Expansion of Europe: The First Phase.* Philadelphia: University of Pennsylvania Press, 1971.

Mumford, Lewis. *The Story of Utopias.* Gloucester: Peter Smith, 1954.

Nicolson, Adam. *Sea Room: An Island Life in the Hebrides.* New York: Northpont, 2002.

Nicolson, Nigel. *Lord of the Isles: Lord Leverhulme and the Hebrides.* London: Weidenfeld and Nicolson, 1960.

Nisbett, Richard E. *The Geography of Thought: How Asians and Westerners Think Differently and Why.* New York: Free Press, 2003.

Nobles, Gregory. "Straight Lines and Stability: Mapping the Political Order of the Anglo-American Frontier." *Journal of American History* 80, no. 1 (June 1993): 9–25.

Nolan, Mary Lee, and Sidney Nolan. *Christian Pilgrimage in Modern Western Europe.* Chapel Hill: University of North Carolina Press, 1989.

O'Crohan, Sean. *A Day in Our Life.* Trans. Tim Enright. New York: Oxford University Press, 1992.

O'Crohan, Tomas. *The Islandman.* Trans. Robin Flower. London: Chatto & Windus, 1934.

O'Gorman, Edmundo. *The Invention of America: An Inquiry into the Historical Nature of the New World and the Meaning of Its History.* Bloomington: Indiana University Press, 1961.

Olschki, Leonardo. *Storia Litteraria della Scoperte Geograpfie.* Florence: Leo S. Olschki, 1937.

———. "What Columbus Saw on Landing in the West Indies." *Proceedings of the American Philosophical Society* 84, no. 5 (July 1948): 633–59.

Olwig, Karen Fog. "Cultural Sites: Sustaining a Home in a Deterritorialized World." In *Siting Culture: The Shifting Anthropological Object,* ed. K. F. Olwig and K. Hastrup. London: Routledge, 1997, pp. 17–38.

O'Meara, John J. Introduction to *The Voyage of Saint Brendan.* Trans. John J. O'Meara. Gerrard Cross, England: Colin Smythe, 1991.

O'Sullivan, Maurice. *Twenty Years A-Growing.* New York: Viking, 1933.

Outram, Dorinda. "On Being Perseses: New Knowledge, Dislocation, and Enlightenment Exploration." In *Geography and Enlightenment,* ed. David N. Livingston and Charles W. J. Withers. Chicago: University of Chicago Press, 1999, pp. 281–94.

Pagden, Anthony. *The Fall of Natural Man: The American Indian and the Origins of Contemporary Ethnology.* Cambridge: Cambridge University Press, 1982.

———. *Peoples and Empires: Europeans and the Rest of the World from Antiquity to the Present.* London: Weidenfeld & Nicolson, 2001.

Pagden, Anthony, and Nicolas Canny. "Afterward: From Identity to Independence." In *Colonial Identity in the Atlantic World, 1500–1800.* Ed. A. Pagden and N. Canny (Princeton, N.J.: Princeton University Press, 1987, pp. 267–78.

Panek, Richard. *Seeing and Believing: How the Telescope Opened Our Eyes and Minds to the Heavens.* New York: Viking, 1998.

Parman, Susan. *Scottish Crofters: A Historical Ethnography of a Celtic Village.* Fort Worth: Holt, Rinehart & Winston, 1990.

Parry, J. H. *The Discovery of the Sea.* New York: Dial, 1974.

———. *The Discovery of South America.* London: Paul Elek, 1979.

Partin, Harry B. "Paradise." In *Encyclopedia of Religion.* Vol 11. New York: Macmillan, 1987, pp. 185–89.

Phillips, J. S. R. *The Medieval Expansion of Europe.* Oxford: Oxford University Press, 1988).

Phillips, Seymour "The Outer World of the European Middle Ages." In *Implicit Understandings,* ed. Stuart Schwartz. Cambridge: Cambridge University Press, 1994, pp. 23–63.

Phillips, William D. *Medieval Origins of European Expansion.* Minneapolis: University of Minnesota Press, 1996.

Piel, Tiina. *Islescapes: Estonian Small Islands and Islanders through Three Centuries.* Stockholm: Almquist & Wiksell, 1999.

Pitt, David. "Sociology, Islands, and Boundaries," *World Development* 7, no. 3 (December 1980): 1051–59.

Pocock, J.G.A. "The Atlantic Archipelago and the War of the Three Kingdoms," In *The British Problem, 1524–1707,* ed. Brendan Bradshaw and John Morrill. New York: St. Martin's Press, 1970, pp. 171–90.

———. "Nature and History, Self and Other: European Perception of World History in the Age of Encounter." In *Voyagers and Beaches: Pacific Encounters, 1769–1840,* ed. Alex Calder, Jonathan Lamb, and Bridget Orr. Honolulu: University of Hawaii Press, 1999, pp. 26–44.

Polk, Dora Beale. *The Island of California: A History of the Myth.* Spokane, WA: Arthur H. Clarke, 1991.

Pomeranz, Kenneth, and Steven Topik. *The World That Trade Created: Society, Culture, and World Economy, 1400-present.* Armonk, N.Y.: M.E. Sharpe, 1999.

Porter, Eliot. *Summer Island.* San Francisco: Sierra Club Books, 1966.

Porter, Philip W., and Fred E. Luckerman. "The Geography of Utopia." In *Geographies of the Mind: Essays in Historical Geosophy,* ed. David Lowenthal and Marilyn Bowden. New York: Oxford University Press, 1976, pp. 197–223.

Porter, Roy. "Afterword." *Geography and Enlightenment,* ed. David N. Livingston and Charles W. J. Withers. Chicago: University of Chicago Press, 1999, pp. 415–31.

———. *The Making of Geology: Earth Science in Britain, 1600–1815.* Cambridge: Cambridge University Press, 1977.

Prest, John. "Garden." In *The Encyclopedia of Religion.* Vol. 5. New York: Macmillan, 1987, pp. 487–88.

———. *The Garden of Eden: The Botanic Garden and the Re-creation of Paradise.* New Haven, CT: Yale University Press, 1981.

Pyne, Stephen J. *How the Canyon Became Grand.* New York: Viking, 1998.

Quammen, David. *The Song of the Dodo: Island Biogeography in an Age of Extinction.* New York: Scribner, 1996.

Quinn, David Beers. "New Geographical Horizons: Literature." In *First Images of America: The Impact of the New World on the Old,* ed. Fredi Chiapelli. Vol. 2. Berkeley: University of California Press, 1976, pp. 635–58.

———. *North America from Earliest Discovery to First Settlement.* New York, Harper & Row, 1975.

Raban, Jonathan. *Coasting.* London: William Collins, 1986.

———. *The Oxford Book of the Sea.* New York: Oxford University Press, 1992.

Ramage, Edwin S. "Perspectives Ancient and Modern." In *Atlantis: Fact or Fiction.* Bloomington: Indiana University Press, 1978, pp. 3–45.

Ramsay, Raymond R. *No Longer on the Map: Discovering Places That Never Were.* New York: Viking Press, 1972.

Rapport, Nigel, and Andrew Dawson. "Home and Movement: A Polemic." In *Migrants of Identity: Perception of Home in a World of Movement,* ed. Nigel Rapport and Andrew Dawson. New York: Berg, 1998, pp. 3–38.

———. "The Topic and the Book." In *Perception of Home in a World of Movement,* ed. Nigel Rapport and Andrew Dawson. New York: Berg, 1998, pp. 3–16.

———. *Migrants of Identity: Perspectives of Home in a World of Movement.* Oxford: Berg, 1998.

Rediker, Marcus, and Peter Linebaugh. *The Many-Headed Hydra: Sailors, Slaves, Commoners and the Hidden History of the Revolutionary Atlantic.* Boston: Beacon, 2000.

Rees, Ronald. "Landscape in Art." In *Dimension of Human Geography,* ed. Karl Butzer. Chicago: University of Chicago Department of Geography Research Paper 186, 1978, pp. 49–61.

Reynolds, Robert L. "The Mediterranean Frontiers, 1000–1300." In *The Frontier in Perspective,* ed. W. D. Wyman and C. Kroeber. Madison: University of Wisconsin Press, 1957, pp. 21–34.

Riesenberg, Felix. *Vignettes of the Sea.* New York: Harcourt, Brace, 1926.

Rifkin, Jeremy. *Age of Access: The New Culture of Hypercapitalism, Where All of Life Is a Paid-for Experience.* New York: Putnam, 2000.

Ringrose, David. *Expansion and Global Interaction, 1200–1700.* New York: Longman, 2001.

Robbins, K. G. *Insular Outsider? "British History" and European Integration.* Reading: Stenton Lectures, 1989.

Robson, Catherine. *Men in Wonderland: The Lost Childhood of the Victorian Gentleman.* Princeton, N.J.: Princeton University Press, 2001.

Romm, James S. *The Edges of the Earth in Ancient Thought, Geography, Exploration, and Fiction.* Princeton, N.J.: Princeton University Press, 1992.

Roy, James Charles. *Islands of the Storm.* Chester Springs, PA: Dufour Editions, 1991.

Royle, Stephen. "From the Periphery at the Periphery: Historical, Cultural, and Literary Perspectives on Emigrants from the Minor Islands of Ireland." In *Small Worlds, Global Lives: Ireland and Migration,* ed. R. King and J. Connell. London: Pinter, 1999, pp. 27–54.

———. *A Geography of Islands: Small Island Insularity.* New York: Routledge, 2001.

Ryan, Chris. "Islands, Beaches, and Life Stage Marketing." *Island Tourism: Management Principles and Practice,* ed. M. V. Colin and T. Baum. New York: John Wiley, 1995, pp. 79–93.

Sanford, Charles L. *The Quest for Paradise: Europe and the American Moral Imagination.* Urbana: University of Illinois Press, 1961.

Saramago, Jose. *The Tale of the Unknown Island.* New York: Harcourt, Brace, 1988.

Sauer, Carl. "Seashore—Primitive Home of Man." In *Land and Life: A Selection of the Writings of Carl Ortin Sauer.* Berkeley: University of California Press, 1963, pp. 300–12.

Sayers, Peig. *Peig: The Autobiography of Peig Sayers of Great Blasket Island.* Trans. Bryan MacMahon. Syracuse: Syracuse University Press, 1974.

Scafi, Alessandro. "Mapping Eden: Cartographies of Earthly Paradise." In *Mappings,* ed. Denis Cosgrove. London: Reaktion, 1999, pp. 50–70.

Schama, Simon. *Landscape and Memory.* New York: Vintage, 1996.

Schor, Juliet. *Overworked Americans: The Unexpected Decline of Leisure.* New York: Basic Books, 1991.

Schultz, Max F. *Paradise Preserved: Recreations of Eden in Eighteenth- and Nineteenth-Century England.* Cambridge: Cambridge University Press, 1985.

Seed, Patricia. *Ceremonies of Possession in Europe's Conquest of the New World.* Cambridge: Cambridge University Press, 1999.

Semple, Ellen Churchill. *Influences of Geographic Environment on the Basis of Ratzel's System of Anthropo-geography.* New York: Henry Holt and Company, 1911.

Severin, Tim. *In Search of Robinson Crusoe.* New York: Basic Books, 2002.

Shepard, Paul. *Man in the Landscape: A Historic View of the Esthetic of Nature.* New York: Alfred J. Knopf, 1967.

———. *Nature and Madness.* San Francisco: Sierra Club, 1982.

Simmel, Georg. "Bridge and Door." *Theory, Culture, & Society* 11 (1994): 5–10.

Skinner, Jonathan. "Managing Island Life: Social, Economic, and Political Dimensions of Formality and Informality in 'Island' Communities." *Social Identities* 8, no. 2 (2002): 205–15.

Smail, Daniel Lord. *Imagining Cartographies: Possession and Identity in Late Medieval Marseille.* Ithaca. N.Y.: Cornell University Press, 1999.

Smyth, Alfred P. *Warlords and Holy Men.* London: Edward Arnold, 1984.

Sobel, Dava. *Longitude: The True Story of a Lone Genius Who Solved the Greatest Scientific Problem of the Time.* New York: Walker, 1995.

Sondergaard, Lief. "At the Edge of the World: Early Medieval Ideas of the Nordic Countries." *Medieval Spirituality in Scandinavia and Europe,* ed. Lars Bisgaard. Odense: Odense Press, 2001, pp. 53–56.

Stagl, Justin. *A History of Curiosity: The Theory of Travel.* Chur, Switzerland: Harwood, 1995.

Steel, Tom. *The Life and Death of St. Kilda.* Glasgow: Fontana, 1972.

Steele, Ian K. *The English Atlantic, 1675–1740: An Exploration of Communications and Community.* New York: Oxford University Press, 1986.

Steinberg, Philip E. *The Social Construction of the Oceans.* Cambridge: Cambridge University Press, 2001.

Stewart, Susan. *On Longing: Narratives of the Miniature, the Gigantic, the Souvenir, and Collection.* Baltimore: Johns Hopkins University Press, 1984.

Stilgoe, John. *Alongshore.* New Haven: Yale University Press, 1994.

———. *Common Landscape of America, 1580–1845.* New Haven: Yale University Press, 1982.

Stoddard, David. *On Geography and History.* Oxford: Blackwell, 1986.

Strommel, Henry. *Lost Islands: The Story of Islands That Have Vanished from the Nautical Charts.* Vancouver: University of British Columbia Press, 1984.

Symcox, Geoffrey W. "The Battle of the Atlantic, 1500–1700." In *First Images of America: Impact of the New World on the Old,* ed. Fredi Chiapelli. Vol. 1. Berkeley: University of California Press, 1976, pp. 265–77.

Synge, John Millington. *Aran Islands.* Boston: J. W. Luce, 1911.

Tall, Deborah. *The Island of the White Cow: Memories of an Irish Island.* New York: Atheneum, 1986.

Taylor, Charles. *Sources of the Self: The Making of Modern Identity.* Cambridge: Harvard University Press, 1989.

Taylor, E. G. R. *Late Tudor and Early Stuart Geography, 1583–1650.* London: Methuen, 1934.

Thompson, William P. L. *History of Orkney.* Edinburgh: Mercot, 1987.

Townsend, Richard. "Geography." In *The Encyclopedia of Religion.* Vol. 5. New York: Macmillan, 1987, pp. 509–12.

Trachtenberg, Alan. *Brooklyn Bridge: Fact and Symbol.* 2nd ed. Chicago: University of Chicago Press, 1979.

Trompf, Gary. *Islands and Enclaves: Nationalism and Separatist Pressures in Island and Littoral Contexts.* New Delhi: Sterling, 1999.

———. "Utopia." *The Encyclopedia of Religions.* Vol. 15. New York: Macmillan, 1987, pp. 159–60.

Tuan, Yi-Fu. "Rootedness versus Sense of Place," *Landscape* 24, no. 1 (1980)

———. "Sacred Space: Exploration of an Idea." In *Dimensions of Human Geography,* ed. Karl Butzer. Chicago: University of Chicago Department of Geography, Research Paper 186, 1978, pp. 84–99.

————. *Segmented Worlds and Self: Group Life and Individual Consciousness.* Minneapolis: University of Minnesota Press, 1982.

————. *Space and Place: The Perspective of Experience.* Minneapolis: University of Minnesota Press, 1977.

————. *Topophilia: A Study of Environmental Perception, Attitudes, and Values.* Englewood Cliffs, N.J: Prentice Hall, 1974.

Turner, Victor. "The Center Out There: The Pilgrim's Goal." *History of Religions* 12, no. 3 (February 1973): 191–230.

Van Gennep, Arnold. *The Rites of Passage.* Chicago: University of Chicago Press, 1960.

Verlinden, Charles. "The Transfer of Colonial Techniques from the Mediterranean to the Atlantic." In *The European Opportunity,* ed. Felipe. Fernandez-Armesto. Aldershot: Variorum, 1995, pp. 225–48.

The Vinland Sagas: The Norse Discovery of America. London: Penguin, 1965.

Wallace, Alfred Russel. *Island Life or the Phenomena and Causes of Insular Fauna and Flora.* 2nd ed. London: Macmillan, 1892.

Washburn, Wilcolm. "The Form of Islands in Fifteenth, Sixteenth and Seventeenth-Century Cartography." In *Geographie du Monde au Moyen Age et la Renaissance,* ed. Monique Pelletier. Paris: Editions du C.T.H.S., 1989, pp. 201–206.

————. "The Meaning of 'Discovery' in the Fifteenth and Sixteenth Centuries." *American Historical Review* 67, no. 1 (October 1962: pp. 1–21

Watson, Ian. "The Challenge of Maintaining Parity for Offshore Islands." *Middle States Geographer* 31 (1998): 132–37.

Watts, Pauline Moffatt. "Prophecy and Discovery: On the Spiritual Origins of Christopher Columbus's Enterprise of the Indies." *American Historical Review* 90, no. 1 (February 1985): 73–102.

Wells, H. G. *The Island of Doctor Moreau.* London: Heinemann, 1896.

Wesley-Smith, Terrence. "Rethinking Pacific Island Studies." *Pacific Studies* Vol 18, no. 2 (June 1995): 115–37.

Westbrook, Perry. *The Biography of an Island.* New York: Thomas Yoseloff, 1958.

Westropp, T. J. "Brasil and the Legendary Islands of the North Atlantic." *Proceedings of the Royal Irish Academy,* 3rd ser., 30 (1912): 223–60.

Wigen, Kärin E., and Martin W. Lewis. *The Myth of Continents: A Critique of Metageography.* Berkeley: University of California Press, 1997.

Wilde, Oscar. *The Soul of Man Under Socialism.* Boston: John W. Luce, 1910.

Williams, George. *Wilderness and Paradise in Christian Thought.* New York: Harper & Row, 1962.

Williams, Michael Ann. *Homeplace: The Social Use and Meaning of the Folk Dwellings in Southwestern North Carolina.* Athens: University of Georgia Press, 1991.

Williams, Raymond. *Keywords: A Vocabulary of Culture and Society.* New York: Oxford University Press, 1976.

Withers, Charles. "Geography, Enlightenment, and the Paradise Question." *Geography and Enlightenment,* ed. David N. Livingston and Charles W. J. Withers. Chicago: University of Chicago Press, 1999, pp. 68–92.

Wolf, Eric. *Europe and the People without History.* Berkeley: University of California Press, 1982.

Wolfe, Roy. "About Cottages and Cottagers." *Landscape* 15, no.1 (Autumn 1965): 6–9.

Woodward, David. "Reality, Symbolism, Time, and Space in Medieval World Maps." *Annals of the Association of American Geographers* 75 (1985): 510–21.

Woodward, David, and J. E. Harley, eds. *The History of Cartography.* Vol. 1–4. Chicago: University of Chicago Press, 1987–1998.

Wright, John Kirtland. "Terrae Incognitae: The Place of Imagination in Geography." In *Human Nature in Geography.* Cambridge: Harvard University Press, 1966, pp. 68–88.

Wylie, Jonathan, and David Margolin. *The Ring of Dancers: Images of Faroese Culture.* Philadelphia: University of Pennsylvania Press, 1981.

Zaleski, Carol. *Otherworld Journeys: Accounts of Near-Death Experiences in Medieval and Modern Times.* New York: Oxford University Press, 1987.

Zerubavel, Eviatar. *The Fine Line: Making Distinctions in Everyday Life.* Chicago: University of Chicago Press, 1993.

———. *Terra Incognita: The Mental Discovery of America.* New Brunswick, N.J.: Rutgers University Press, 1992.

———. *Time Maps: Collective Memory and the Social Shape of the Past.* Chicago: University of Chicago Press, 2003.

Zuckerman, Michael. "Identity in British America: Unease in Eden." In *Colonial Identity in the Atlantic World, 1500–1800,* ed. N. Canny and A. Pagden. Princeton, N.J.: Princeton University Press, 1987, pp. 115–51.

INDEX

Breinigsville, PA USA
15 July 2010
241849BV00003B/31/P